Deanne Tafuri, May, 1986

THE THIRD MUSIC

by Ann Ree Colton

ARC PUBLISHING COMPANY
Post Office Box 1138
Glendale, California 91209

Dedicated
to
The
New-Era Dharma

For, lo, the Christ cometh.

Copyright © 1982 Ann Ree Colton

All rights reserved, including the right to
reproduce this book or portions thereof in any form.

First Edition

For information regarding the teachings
and writings of Ann Ree Colton, write:

Ann Ree Colton Foundation
336 West Colorado Street
Post Office Box 2057
Glendale, California 91209

Printed in the United States of America

CONTENTS

Book One: The Esse and the Undersoul

Chapter 1	*Prelude:* The Dance of the Cosmos....	3
Chapter 2	The Undersoul.....................	20
Chapter 3	Cleansing of the Undersoul...........	38
Chapter 4	The Sacred Articles of the Esse or the Passing Power..............	64
Chapter 5	Movement and Meditation..........	81
Chapter 6	Esse in Action....................	105
Chapter 7	The Nature of the Mind and the Ego..	123

Book Two: Hierarchy-Nature Healing

Chapter 8	The Coinciding Principle	149
Chapter 9	Healing With the Hierarchy Nature ...	182
Chapter 10	The Continuum Sacrament	208
Chapter 11	Holy Conscience....................	232

Book Three: Exercises and Practices

Descriptions of Transcendental Centers 271
Chapter 12 The Mind and the Hierarchy Nature .. 273
Chapter 13 Healing Through the Constant 303
Chapter 14 Contacting the Third Music.......... 332
Chapter 15 Mastery Through the Mandala 357
Chapter 16 The Third Music 387

Book One
The Esse and the Undersoul

CHAPTER 1

PRELUDE: THE DANCE OF THE COSMOS

*The Dance of the Cosmos is within the soul
of each person of the earth.*

In the universal whole, there are no statics—all is movement. To move is to live. All things having movement have some degree of consciousness.

Universal movement as rhythm provides individual movement as cycles. A cycle is a fulfillment of energy. A cycle is not just a statistic; it is a gift, an inheritance. One must decide what he will do with the energy-fulfillment in a cycle.

The unison mastery *within* the molecule provides the rhythm of the Cosmos. The unity in the molecular system is supported by cycles. The cycles give the variation within the molecular system, maintaining the universal flexibilities of the eternals existing in the atomic system.

Every one contains the dance of the Cosmos in his nature. His movement as freedom keeps him free, makes him whole. One must learn the intricacies existing between rhythmic movement and cyclic movement in his own nature. Rhythmic movement seeks to make the life processes flow toward or return to the Cosmos. Cyclic movement seeks to draw one's nature downward to the Earth. These two pull against each other, that man may find his center and step into the whole to be equipoled or godly.

The cyclic is saying: "I will return you to death." The rhythmic is saying, "I will return you to God." The cyclic and the rhythmic must be poised and maintained in a holy equilibrium controlled by the Eternal, which is Spirit.

Gravity determines the cycles. Universality determines the rhythmic.

In the ballet, the dancer with the left foot balanced upon the large toe raises and rotates his right leg to whirl it in circular motion, at the same time keeping centered within the Constant of movement. This represents how man maintains his gravity poise and moves within Universal Spirit, thus assuring himself of unison in both gravity and Cosmos.

The dancer is the Eternal Self controlling both gravity and Cosmos through the will as the Will of God in his own nature; he is poised and centered, tapping out his own unison-measures of Creation with the play of the dance.

Time and Space are twin functions of Cosmos and Cosmic. Death and birth both offer experience into Space dimensions. In birth, one is given Time-measurement limited by Space. In death, one is given Space-limitless measured by Time. All must beat out their measure, whether in birth to the gravity world or whether by death to the world of Space.

It is the work of man in earth to balance Time and Space. This can be done only by a leap of joy as a creator through movement with God. Joy is the leap. Movement is the freedom.

Once one has made union with the movement of his hierarchy nature, he is Space-centered and Time-mastered. He can no longer think in singularities. He must include the Universal in his Space-realization and all of the humanities in his Time-mastery. When the inner movement is free, such persons become giants alongside of one who thinks only in the limited terrains of short-term energy-processes of the lesser self.

In the present era of man's development, his closest access to movement—if he has yet to unite with the Cosmos—is the inner music. The raucous music and movement of this time and era have been produced as a recoil against man's misuse of mind-creation. These raucous, harsh and dissonant sounds from the lower astral world are outpictured into man, causing spiritual tone-deafness, playing upon sensual sensibilities.

Insensitive exaggeration accompanying raucous astral music; the use of drugs; sexual experimentation producing perversions—all are influenced subjectively by the dissonant sound currents in the lower astral world which has for ages reflected a form of condensed or collective repression in man's desire nature. His nongiving; his lack of interest in learning and knowing; his greed at the expense of others—these have accumulated as energy tensions in the lower astral world and are now playing upon the Undersoul of man. This condensed sound in the lower astral planes is producing a theme of music obscenely heard upon the suggestible sexual nature of man.

At the present time, the great Warring Angels, the Guardians of cleansing for man, hover closely over mankind. These Angels are warring with counter-sound to clear the emotional energy fields in the Undersoul of man. They provide a new trumpet or resurrection sound upon the conscience of mankind as a whole.

Following this era of the obnoxious overflow of sound and movement, ear-heard musics will come, rising upon the horizon of man's higher soul-nature, that he may step out of the grave-clothes of his own self-made purgatorial descent.

Movement and Sound are one in the Universal. When man translates these into acts of perversion, the result causes painful self-obliteration. In this present era, one must sweep clean his darkness to prepare for the Age of Light seeking to come to birth through the soul-powers of man.

Movement and Sound seek to find in man an instrument to play the Cosmos tones which accompany at all times the birth to Great Eras. In these periods, God reveals Himself to show man what he truly is.

All must move. All is moving. Death comes to the physical body when movement is no longer the incentive for individuality.

To think is to act. Consciousness before movement goes before man, creating his actions.

Action must follow thought. When one fails to act out the result of his thinking, this is a form of death to his mind. His life then is taken over by predetermined correcting laws, which are offended by the failure to act. If one continues to think negatively without creative action, the result is destruction to some portion of his nature, his physical body, the appearance of his body.

Thinking without acting produces abnormality and deformity. Thinking with creative movement produces godly vision, illumination and beauty.

The Divine Harmonics flow, blessing all when the movement of the harmonics is free. A beautiful hand, a beautiful body, grace in movement, a relaxed poise—all come from Cosmos oneness with perfection as grace from a creative mind. And within creation, one flows within the Divine Harmonics to make every portion of his life graceful, beautiful, harmonious.

There is not one person in the world who does not reveal the movement-processes of his mind. A fearful, furtive face; a bloated, distended body—all speak plainly of wrong use of movement in mind-creation. Expressive use of the hands testifies to the Divine-Harmonic measures of the creative flow existing between the self and Creation.

The dance of Shiva relates to the use of the mind-movement energies of Creation. Sooner or later, all must unite with this dance of life, of love, and of the Universal-Eternal in one's nature.

The first step of freedom in movement is the complete dropping of the rigidities within the resisting side of the mind. Thus, renunciation and accepting are the first step of the dance movement of spirituality. This dance of movement of oneness with God is the only reality.

The counterpart of the physical body, which is called the etheric body, is the first actor for the drama of the Shiva dance. The etheric body provides the energy for the dance. The emotional body of man, or the feeling body of the astral nature, provides the feeling and sensitivity through which one taps out the rhythm of his own Time-units of measure or *the count* in his dance.

At birth, the first inhaling breath draws one into gravity. In this, he unites with the cycles of his timing and the units of measure of his Time-limits in the earth. With the first exhaling breath at birth, one brings down the Cosmos into gravity; this enables him to master the cycles of Time and limitation.

One cannot be separated from gravity after birth to the Earth until his Time-limit of cycles has been fulfilled, for that which is Cosmos in the exhaling is the determiner of God in him. One dies because he has need of greater space through which he may supervise his reincarnation return to his next experience in gravity.

Every time one exhales, he brings more Cosmos into his nature. One must listen to this exhaling side of God as Breath in him. *For God is in the breath, and breath is God.* To realize the Cosmos side of breath is to hear the music and know the dance.

The Three Musics

When the crescent moon lies on her back in the sky and is seen by the eye, the OM sound sits as a pearl shining its luster, perfectly centered in the medulla oblongata at the base of the skull. United with the pineal gland, the Third Eye is free to reveal. The heartbeat of the soul's pulsation secures the breath into the Third-Music exaltation; the soul as power becomes the Face of God and the Spirit manifested. The OM sounding at this time supernaturally perfects the Image, and man becomes Godlike.

There is Movement of the atom; Movement of the energy-fields; Movement of the mind; Movement of the body; Movement of the primordial; Movement of the soul—all expressing the Movement of God.

The Third Music is Movement of the primordial. Movement of the primordial is freedom from disease, from anxiety, from negativity, from ignorance.

The First Music is experienced as sound through the hearing. The Second Music is the atomic, the vibrational, electrifying and magnifying. This is the Sound Current received on and from the existent waves of birth, life and death.

The Third Music is Spirit of God as Holy Spirit acting upon the primordial involuntary systems indented into the etheric nature. From these man expresses himself through rhythmic and cyclic compulsions, through realization and healing.

The Third Music incorporates the Archetonal Sound Current or the *Word*, the Vibrational Sound through which God is present as Omnipresence. When the Third Music sounds in the mind, one is in the Eternal Omnipotent, the Eternal Omniscient, and he becomes Omnipresence for God.

Collective Omnipresence functions as the Higher Unconscious. The Third Music, resounding without ceasing in the soul, seeks to make itself at home in the higher minds of all persons where God is realized. When this occurs, the Esse or Holy Spirit takes command of the atomic energies, the life renewal and creative forces, the visualization and manifestation powers of the soul.

The left side of the brain functions as a geometrical imager and mover. The right side of the brain functions as a Third Music. Music in the right side of the brain contains the rhythmic flow of the higher unconscious whereby man receives the vibrational wellsprings of the soul and Spirit.

THE ESSE

The Esse, the Esse,
is uniting me with the Cosmos.

God, as Consciousness, is moving
me forward into the movement
of Knowing, Learning and Being.

There lives in the thinking of everyone a desire to unite with the Intelligible or the First Cause in command of the Universe; and more, an intense desire to come under a Guiding Principle within the Law of Providence watching over worlds and over the human-condition states of all in this earth and in all worlds. It is clearly seen by those who are experiencing more of God than can be taught in institutions and formats supporting morality, ethic and rationality, that man as an existing particle of God is presently undergoing a birth to the inner life—a birth to a degree of consciousness never before expressed in this world.

From age to age, men of rare quality and sensitivity as individuals have known and responded to the Guiding Principle in their human and spiritual affairs. Never before, however, has there been such mass accumulative levels of response to this inward search—so fragile, so exposed to dimensions neglected and unknown.

In this time of death to a total format for survival, men are approaching the unveiling of worlds unseen and of little-known thresholds of Consciousness.

The tumult and psychic states prevalent among many materialistic persons are incomprehensible to some. In the present art forms and in certain life styles, one sees the flagrant display of distortion in style of dress; the desire for environments expressing in the eye of the beholder extreme and antagonistic effects upon the senses; the use of dissonant sounds in music playing upon the psychic side of sexual habits; the disruption of the flow within the life-chain of giving birth through the use of abortion and genetic experimentation; the abnormal life-styles imposed upon the aged; and irreverence concerning the dying. All of these in our times—the cynical, the atheistic, the agnostic, the experimental—are *signs* to be read, seen and understood in only one sense or interpretation: *Birth* is at hand to a new theme; a new birth in soul, in mind and in body. The spiritual worlds, the spiritual planes, the spiritual atmospheres are now impregnated with birth—a birth long pressing upon the souls of men. Men formerly seeing in part in the many aeons past are now beginning to *see clearly* and thus prepare to be whole within the One.

A psychic state of sub-sensible chaos invariably precedes mind and soul birth. This state of mind birth provides liberation. The leap forward in consciousness is producing a duality race or marathon so strained that man as a whole will be embattled in his duality nature that he may see with clarity all that he has pursued and all that has pursued him throughout the ages.

A non-polarized mind believes that the other in his own nature is outside of himself. He is to learn that *in his own nature* is his battle. He has failed to accept this reality as being the terms on which he has lived and functioned in this Maya-fated, physical, atomic-energy system called Earth.

Mankind, overlong too gross and dependent only upon its materialistic existence, is now being flooded with astral phenomena incited by astral forces and fantasies. When this has played out its force, and the last laggard souls are finally moved into this world or earth existence upon the conveyor belts of reincarnation, the stage will be set for a religiosity return to God through worshipful processes of beauty, culture and creation.

Men must take hold of themselves. Through the inward life, they must grow and observe the growing. Through the inward involvement, they must shape and hew out their own archetypal and prototypal themes. God has so willed it that man must conjoin the personalized forces of self and consciousness within his own true existing self with the Power and Omnipresence of God, that he may fulfill that which is destiny for him and this earth—this eternity system of solar light, moon light, planetary light and soul light.

The search for truth begins with self. Soul is ever waiting for the awakening of this hunger, this desire.

The soul is ignited with energy-vibrating joy when one surrenders to God. When man surrenders to God, holy music is resounded in Heaven or that world where dwells the Divine. The seed of soul presses into earth existence to break open the soil of materiality and to thrust one up to the Light to become Light-Realized, God-Realized.

Where are the signs to be read; how is the message of the Divine to be seen? To the mortal witness, everywhere there is suffering, separation, distortion, manipulation.

The Seers, the Saints, the Angels, and the Great Immortals are very present in this Shiva dance of increasing energy. As Divine companions, they are incalculably close in dimensions nigh unto the soul cry of the desolate, of the repentant and of those hungry to know and to be.

Slowly, death to unknowing or nescience will become resurrection through the Christ. Fiery astrolocity will be cooled and stilled, made pure in this birth of the becoming. All men are to be lifted, for He who is the Light, the Christ, and all of His agents and regents are at work to initiate men within this era and time.

Birth to transcendent mind and soul powers must fulfill the supreme law of birth. To live in the physical world, men are given sense to experience, to function in all planes and in all worlds suitable for God as Omnipresence.

The inner life is the only true and everlasting life. This is the first basic truth; it is the mantra thought-key to spiritual knowledge by which one explores the inward life and its eternality. This is the faith-bulwark by which man climbs to the door of knowledge, whereby he enters into the sweet and pure luminous dimensions of extended consciousness.

All in Heaven and earth presently are receiving voltages of the holy electricities causing increasing movement in the vibratory supports of the sheaths and the bodies, giving increasing receptivity to the extended powers of mind and soul. Life in earth is a mind and soul sojourn to produce a degree of superconsciousness suitable to the Plan of God in Creation.

In this time, the majority of men in earth are dependent upon the primal in their unrealistic interpretations of God. Seeing Him as a material extension of their own self-wills, they put Him into their personalized situations: as a warden over their imprisonment in the earth; as a revenge figure or father overlord; or as a wish-provider for any and all cravings to further their own concept of paradise on earth.

God is seen as Reality by advanced souls who have made union with Him through the Cosmos union. God is rarely understood by one seeing through the eye of Maya gullibility and shadowed light. The Lord Christ came to change the vibratory status of the earth's axis, that man might be lifted from darkness to the Light.

The soul of man is a velocified vehicle of superconscious *movement;* this movement knows not separation from God, from His Creation, from His Universe. The instrumentality through which man maintains this universality or oneness with God is through the vehicle of his Soul, his Higher Self and his Higher Mind. These vehicles divine are in a constant state of increasing *movement* equal to the Eternal-Spirit velocities as Mind or Purusha in God.

The energized vibratory God-Essence overflowing into man in the life of form and life as consciousness is transmitted to man by the aspect of God called *Holy Spirit, Holy Ghost* or *Spirit of Truth.* This movement *Essence* feeding the soul and all soul-life functions of and in the earth is called *Esse.*

As OM is the Power mantra name for the Omnipotent Power of God, *Esse* is the mantra name for Holy Spirit. Esse is the Life-Spirit or Holy-Spirit mantra name for holy powers providing vision, revelation, guidance, cleansing, purification, healing. All life-sustaining energies are under the Holy-Spirit power passed on by the soul to man as the Holy Esse, or Essence of life eternal, life immortal, life functional.

The Esse makes man a witness for God, an articulate creator for God, and eventually a son of God. Through initiatory processes destined for man in the uncovering and bringing to birth soul-powers, movement as creation within the Eternal is to be understood; and the pace of each soul, mind, body and emotion is to be researched in the temple, in the church, and in the life-motivation for man.

The future scientist will concern himself in relation to human behaviour with the use and utilization of Time and timing. He will study, define and rely upon timing, rhythms and cycles: hetra-cycles, neo-cycles and repetitive cycles governing growth, evolvement and the development of man as a conscious and aware creating being.

The higher mind of man is the Witnessing mind. In true Self-Realization, one reveals beyond earth-mind speculations. The Witnessing mind draws the diagrams by which the Archetype is stepped down into the prototypal mind-action of self-discovery and of eventual higher Self-Realization.

All Esse functionings of the Holy Spirit are expressed by the Witnessing and affirming of the Witnessing mind. All such revelatory experiences are life-shaping, life-understanding and life-fulfilling. The intricate movement and velocity of the Witnessing mind desire to work directly with man, that he may become Niscient or Knowing: Knowing of the Omnipresence or God Presence as Reality.

The prolonged agony of the nescient play or the unknowing state is now coming into the Niscience rhythmic flow of eternality. The fatalistic cycles of the personal will are to conjoin with the destiny rhythms of God. Man as an open soul with out-of-the-body knowledge of the Reality of God enters now as a true recipient of Holy Niscience or Knowledge.

The Esse upward vibrational flows in Kundalini and the chakras are quickening the Third Eye working directly with the Witnessing mind to produce Cosmos phenomenal results on the level of science, religion and psychology. The holy gas of Esse as a Holy Wind is the Prana divine, furnishing the energy viewing screens through which God is to be seen and known. All things presently repelling and repugnant to those more spiritually inclined are to be transenergized through the Esse Holy Wind stirring and stimulating all life and consciousness processes in the earth.

The Spirit of Truth working through the downpouring of the Holy Esse seeks to return man to his state of pure Image. It seeks to remove him from the suggestible state of sin; the belief that he is destined to sin; or that he is by nature on the human plane *born in sin and fated to sin.* The Esse flow is to reveal that all sin is nescience or unknowing with the exception of that which man does in malice and love for the doing of evil. The Christ Light has come to this earth to relieve men of the false in doctrinal beliefs, and to return men to the dignity of their souls' intent.

The spiritually-oriented souls in this time of the ending of the Kali-Yuga chaos are looking with compassion on those who are unwitting victims of false beliefs, of hedonistic concepts fertilizing the life of moral irresponsibility. In their Niscience or Spiritual Knowing, they understand the astral ploy and play as energized by those who have the partial chakra opening. These spiritual ones have been touched by the lightning blast of the higher energies of the Esse; they are saturated with the audible hum of the thunder of enlightenment, whereby they are marshaling their forces so as to serve where God would send or place them in their serving.

A BODHISATTVA PROMISE

It is said unto the Householder or the Earth Honey-Soul: O Domashi, the faithful, in Paradise there are the Faithful who dwell there to feed and nourish the faithful of the earth. For the Faithful in any world—Earths or Heavens— are fed on the honey-elixirs of the Holy Esse.

The physicians of the Holy-Spirit Esse are the Esse healers with souls of elixir gold. The Teachers of the Holy-Spirit Esse are the enlighteners within the thrice-wisdoms of Will, Life and Light. God as Love is the Sponsor of those who carry the cargo of the Esse.

As the Earth is a moving, rounded domicile for the Earth-Honey Souls of the Esse, so is the movement of the Esse upon the Undersoul the key and the Way that the Son of Man may have His say in the Truth and the Life.

The Faith nourishments from the Faithful are unceasing, working as the Holy Wind to cleanse out the resisting particles in the untrained will. The Faith elixirs of the Esse pour into the inertias or the life-fungus of the tamas hates and separations.

The Faith Esse pours the salves of Truth through the light of enlightenment. In the Esse, Truth is known upon the ear as a moving vehicle for happiness and bliss-joy.

To pray in the Esse is to move with the world beyond the world into the energized processes of the Universal Esse which is the Omnipresence of God: God, the Absolute, the One.

Only the Esse can dissolve the vanities of the ego registered in the Undersoul. Only Esse as grace can reach that core of the non-self to disperse and evaporate it. No outer object, person or condition can remove the Maya coverings of the Undersoul velocities. Only the Esse can make revolution in the Undersoul, whereby the government of Holy Spirit may reign.

The whole Esse state is oneness with God. Oneness with God is God-Realization. Esse is the vital air or Holy-Spirit energy sustaining oneness within God.

Esse, meaning God or Spirit Essence in all, is the Intelligible divinity-energy assuring perfection to all, created of and through God.

God is Creation. His first substance through and by which He Creates is the Esse.

Esse is Presence of God as the Intelligible Creation. In the midst of the Creative, *Esse* is present. In the midst of Preservation, Esse is present. In the midst of destruction, Esse is there.

Esse cannot be expounded by intellect. Esse can only be fully received and manifested through complete faith and submission to the Will of God. According to one's faith in God as the Omnipresence, can Esse manifest as a perfect life and a perfect peace.

An Esse blessing is an Eternal-grace manifestation.

The Esse is the Holy-Spirit Energy sent down from the Most-High Eternal-Soul essences into the Undersoul.

The Esse, when active, is a grace-vehicle functioning to prevent disaster, sorrow and separations.

The Esse is the Essence of God overcoming absence from God.

The Esse is the volatile quickener for the Holy Spirit.

The Esse as movement is the peace-soother.

The Esse as white fire is the cleanser.

The Esse is the downpouring of holiness into the center or midst of the unholiest.

The Esse assures that the works of good shall surface and be salvaged beyond gross ignorance or evil.

The Esse gives assurance of bliss.

The Esse sifts, purifies and spiritualizes.

The Esse pervades all climates of consciousness and unconsciousness.

The Esse is freed by movement and sound in conjunction with visualization, meditation, contemplation, mantras, prayer, and by unclaiming or ego-less service for God.

The Esse is as a gas — or holy intelligible Will-of-God vapor acting as the Will of God through the Holy Spirit.

Esse acts beyond Maya-measurable karma.

Esse is beyond ego willing or mental trades and bartering.

Esse is beyond fantasy, beyond chimera.

Esse is at all times in its rightful place.

Esse accompanies every prayerful breath, every hopeful sigh.

Esse moves one beyond the gaps of measurable apana and prana. The measures of quality, quantity and activity in Esse are determined by the faith and belief in the Holy-Spirit Power within the Soul.

Esse Movement within the Will of God sends the holy vapors and energies of Esse into the task of dissolution, of preservation, of creation.

Esse is an intelligible energy acting with the Coinciding Principle.

Esse goes where cleansing, purging and casting out are needed.

Esse wipes the soil from the mind-mirrors and the mirage from the fantasized emotional atmospheres.

Esse provides a cool peace in the midst of the heated ego-passions.

Esse keeps the purity of Truth inviolate within the rationale principle.

Esse flows to the point where the dissension is: to heal and to reconcile; to clarify or to make clear the unclear.

Esse works as the *white silence* beyond the tumults in vocabulary.

Esse through the Most High Soul works with the *Word* and the Holy-Spirit movement of the Soul to cast out the demonic-residue in the darkest side of the Undersoul.

Esse erases and neutralizes the negative habit energy-drives in the lower emotional and etheric bodies.

Esse is activated and expressed on the outward conscious plane by movement, by mantra and mantram sound, by music, by meditation, by mandala, by prayer, by worship, by contemplation, by work-service for God.

Service to God as Agape keeps alive the Esse.

Through God-Essences or Esse, one extracts the Essence of Good from all conditions and situations.

God-Essence goes directly to the purity seemingly latent in old situations.

The Esse discerns and extracts the Eternal Positive within the mortal substance.

The Esse is the overflow of the Eternal in the Soul, assuring man that he is to rise.

Man is an irrational creature until he unites with the Esse.

In the movement kingdom, everything is touching. The illusion of separation ends with the practice of the Esse.

Through touching, one lives, and identifies himself as living. Maya awareness while touching is consciousness through sense. Awareness as touching while practicing the Esse is God as Life.

Through the Esse, Omnipresence is *Passed,* giving life, health and healing.

2

THE UNDERSOUL

When one acts within the spirit of rightness, the Esse comes forth. The soul ignites the mysterious force called Holy—and one stands in the power of Spirit.

Eternal Life is in the soul of man. This provides him with eternal powers, bringing peace, bliss and joy into his life. By grace one opens himself to the Light of God. Uniting with his tone of life and soul, he merges with the vibration of the Word or God. He attunes his consciousness through the curative and healing sounds coming to him on the wavelengths of the Love and Mercy of God. The power of Eternal Life within his soul carries the light, the tone, the vibration and the sound to heal any organ in his body out of harmony with the prototypal and archetypal plan supporting his body. The spiritual providence of God has provided man with the Way he can remake and shape his body with hierarchy powers.

To discover one's own tone, one meditates with total reliance upon God; he abandons himself to God's guiding and directing principle. In meditation, every sense supporting one's survival instincts and intellect is extended. Stillness of the lower mind and of the experimenting senses unites him with their opposite—the holy sound or tone of God in one's own being.

God as the *vibrating Word* in all life resides in the soul of each one in the earth. This vibration in man is experienced in and through *movement*. Man opens himself to the other side of stillness in his meditation through movement of the body, movement which generates etheric, emotional and mental flow outwardly into the world as energy. Such movement in life as energy is a means by which God makes Himself known, seen and heard.

God uses the energy of movement in man and the energy of stillness in soul-moments of meditative rapport with God as the way in which man experiences his own God-nature and hierarchy powers, which are the birthright of his soul. Thus, meditation must be accompanied by movement. Movement may be work, walking, rhythmic or ritualistic formats of movement, music, breath, speech, embracing, touching, thoughts, feeling, thinking, acting. All things having movement are energized processes through which the Face of God is seen, and the original face of one's own True Self is made manifest.

Every molecule, every atom, every cell and every portion of life in which man is involved is in constant states of vibrational movement and motion. There are no vacuums or vacuities in life and consciousness. All is movement.

When movement is used sacredly as service for God, one is in a transcendental and spiritualized state. The most chief agent to inspire the highest use of movement as an intelligible vehicle of service to God is the Holy Spirit. The Holy Spirit works through what is called in the Heaven Worlds *The Esse*. The Esse, as a Holy Wind or Gas, accompanies all spiritualized and service-to-God movements.

All great seers and sages have known that meditation

without distribution of the after-effects of the energy-processes brought forth in meditation produces irritation, disorientation and astrolocity-thinking and feeling. Therefore, it is the first prerogative of all sages, seers, gurus and teachers to *Pass* on to their disciples the necessity to put into action in a sacramental fashion the energies produced by meditation, prayer and contemplation.

The inner life is a vibrating, dilating life. The inner bodies may be compared to the lens of a watch or to the lens of the eye, which, when dilated, centers itself upon some holy intent toward perfection or betterment in earth. When one meditates, he puts into motion the dilating processes of the inner bodies. These lens-like functions are intelligible, working directly with the soul to enable him to bring forth from God His Plan and His Will.

The inner nature of man, when polarized, is a forward, outgoing nature toward the needs in the world. Through the Esse or the Holy-Spirit movement, the inner life presses forth and out into the world.

All persons having failed to use the movement processes flowing out from the inner life through the urging of the Esse have collected a sedimentized energy-envelope around the astral, the etheric and mental bodies. This energy oval sphere and envelope is surrounded by an egotistical shell. Within this envelope is a cloud-like mass of floating thought forms, frustrated emotions and mass-energized nuclei of guilt or sin produced by lack of conscience, by deviation, by lack of faith in God, by complete dependence upon sense and sensuality.

This mass sedimentized energy-field of deviation is called the *Undersoul*. In the present era of Kali-Yuga, the Undersoul has become a burdensome, weighted vehicle.

The Undersoul is connected with the Most High Soul by the *Upa-Soul* or Antakarana. The Antakarana or Upa-Soul is a bridge which one must cross over through meditation and in dreams to unite with the Most High Soul. If the Antakarana or Upa-Soul is blocked and clogged due to mental darkness, lack of faith in God, and dependence upon sense as the materialistic and sole way of life, one enters into the darkened tunnels of initiation through the Undersoul pressures.

If there be grace, the downpouring of the Holy Spirit as the Esse Gas is free to move one over the Bridge of the Antakarana or Upa-Soul, that it may begin its purifying work. During this period of time, the egotistical shell, similar to the outer encasement of an egg, begins to shatter. The Esse penetrates the Undersoul as a Holy Gas; cleansing comes, and the desire to know and relate to God increases. This occurs when one enters into a more advanced way of understanding God through the channel of meditation. Meditation inevitably slows down the outer life and speeds up the inner life.

The true Holy Spirit cannot be functional as the Esse in man until his desire is total and wholly to know God, to give himself to God, and to live as a godly reflection in the world.

All spiritual initiations stir and quicken the Undersoul. The Esse vibrational quickening of the Undersoul produces more movement as action in the outer life; more knowledge and wisdom in the inner life.

In the present era, there is appearing in the world certain phenomena relating to spiritual progress and advancement. Many schools on the searching levels for truth or Satsanga expression are encountering the need to open themselves to the movement processes stemming from little-known soul-hungers. This is a natural process and phenomenon existing in the present era of spiritual advancement.

In religions making the deepest impressionable mark upon man, there has always been an accompanying process of rhythm, ritual and movement. This has been a natural and holy phenomenon accompanying the Omnipresent power of the Holy Spirit or Esse, as spiritual ecstasy must be accompanied, and is always accompanied, by some form of movement.

The body of man is an action vehicle. When body movement is used in conjunction with meditation, the Holy Spirit is activated when the movement is expressed through a sacramental and devotional emotion, for the Esse or the Holy Spirit cannot function without its companion: Holy Emotion.

The doing of good, the use of the Agape or the *holy concern,* the giving-channeling for the love of God—all are manifestors of the Holy Spirit outwardly experienced by man and through man in the world.

When the heart in its systolic action (contracts), the subconscious, working through the nervous systems, inscribes into the Undersoul any feeling of suffering, anger, hostility or unhappiness. The slowing down in the stillness of the blood-flow through the help of the subconscious sedimentizes or cements the imaging power of the subconscious. Guilts are sedimentized and photographed upon a heavier ether in the blood and in the Undersoul, where these images move and float as a collective mass of unresolved mental and emotional energy.

The Esse or Holy Spirit works in the life of the body upon the cell. A healthy cell in the body fulfilling its function in the blood indicates a healthy Undersoul functioning.

If the diastolic function of the heart is out of balance, this produces heated or feverish situations in the physical body, the emotions and the mind. A rightful flow of Esse or Holy Spirit in the blood stream of man works directly with the yin dilation and yang contraction processes of the

Undersoul. When these alternating processes are out of rhythm, the Undersoul speaks loudly and clearly, leading one to identify with the combating forces within the Undersoul.

During the contracting of the heartbeat—if there be any guilt—the guilt is transposed and passed on by the photographing-ether in the blood to the Undersoul; this is a picturing Passing. In the dilation time of the heartbeat, if one fails to act out or to externalize his guilt into repentance or desire for restitution, this is recorded in the Undersoul.

The Undersoul has its own rhythm. The subconscious furnishes this rhythm.

The Upa-Soul has the rhythm beat of 1, 2, 3. The Undersoul has the rhythm beat of 1, 2, 3, 4. When one responds by moving to these rhythms, he is actively freeing the Undersoul from the debris flowing from the subconscious into the Undersoul.

The subconscious works with the dilation process in conjunction with the heart, and the Undersoul works with the heart's contraction.

The heart is the first organ of conscience. The human heart works directly as a vehicle for the conscience. The subconscious is an activator for the conscience. The Undersoul contracts and draws to itself the record or picture of one's shame, guilt, inertias, faults and sins.

The world at present is undergoing a combined scourging from the mass Undersoul action within the collective subconscious of mankind. In this Kali-Yuga time, or dark aeonic day termination, this scourging is flowing into mankind as friction and initiation, which is producing the Self-Genesis Age of individualization, or man taking command of his own conscience and consciousness principle through mind, emotions and body.

All piteous suffering men undergo is due to unknowing. Each one of the earth is enlisted as a soul in a school of cosmos universality.

The feeling nature of man and the desire to depend upon feeling rather than thinking have developed a powerful collective desire nature. This desire nature when nescient or unknowing is the adversary in the learning life of man.

Spiritual scientists understand that these fantasized desires reside in the subconscious and in the collective Undersoul mirrored reflections. In applying movement through the Esse or Holy Spirit, one enters into a realistic confrontation with the powers of his own soul, conscience, subconscious and Undersoul. In certain illuminative and realized states of consciousness, in dreams, in post-meditation energized reflections, one can literally enter into and explore the territory or domain of the Undersoul.

All of the processes of energy man is presently using are organized to act and react in a sphere-like fashion. As the aura is oval-like, the action of the Undersoul is sphere-like.

The Undersoul is an existing verity; it is tangible. It is made up of energized, electrified memory-particles of astral substance called *gross akash*. One visually entering the terrain of the Undersoul sometimes feels that he is in a mist-like atmosphere having many variations of contesting currents or movements.

The atmosphere of the Undersoul has a similarity to one's being transposed to the Milky Way with the macrocosmic power to enlarge himself to universal capacity. In this, he may comprehend and understand the relatings between starry bodies where tremendous sounds, musics, explosions, and thrusts of interplay and creation are at work between interterrestrial forces.

The spherical inner condensed point or void of the Undersoul acts to duplicate or reveal pictures of the colliding forces of energy life-functions. If one is directly aware of

Undersoul functioning, this reality assists him in the use of hierarchy visualizing powers. The masses of unmanifested energy in the Undersoul or unrealized creations involve the seer with the *Making process,* placing him as an individual creator in mental proximity and ideation with Hierarchy and Hierarchy powers.

Through Undersoul awareness, man has the power to *remake* himself, to extend himself, and to work with creation as the overlord of his own nature and his own potential as a son of God. The Undersoul, when balanced, acts as a center for cosmic forces, using energy as a gift from God.

Sages die, but prophets submerge. Sages prepare men to receive the prophets. Prophets live in the subconscious side of the conscience of a race, a people, a religion, a nation. Such prophets stir people to overthrow the villainy in experimentation.

Scientific experimentation without the heart fixed on God is human-less. This era is the victim of scientific tinkering with the forces of Nature and with the forces of the mind while neglecting the forces of the soul. The prophets of old who have kept the inward vigil with Truth and Morality will now reincarnate and surface that the efforts of good men will not be totally destroyed.

The precincts of the soul of mankind are in danger. Science has now penetrated the soul's terrain. Trickster and exploiting minds seem to think themselves in this time to be in possession of the forming, growing and developing life.

God is calling forth His prophets, that men may be assured of the continuity memory cells in their forming developments structured throughout the ages. These prophets will be born in scientific and academic surroundings.

The awesome face of Nature even now gathers her thunder, for lightning has pierced the heart and homeplace of corruption. God through Nature and through soul will not let His little ones, His Abels and His Jesus, come to naught in this world.

The Guardian Angels of the Greater Thresholds stand at the gates of the Eternal Fiats: So far and no farther. When the battlefield has become a smoking plain desolate with death, there will arise the true birth to the New Age and New Era. Men shall mark well the year of 1996: there will no longer be a vision of power for power's sake. There will be a new century envisioned for the Elysian fields of productivity and grace.

From diseases of the mind and the body, man will learn there are diseases incurable brought to this world through greed, envy, hate and separateness.

If men of the earth are to be saved from the infections of mind incompetence centered on the ego-self as the real, they must go inward and maintain the tryst for the inward way.

> *God help those who have chosen for their beloved their little self. God bless those who have chosen their true beloved who sees with clear and pure sight the animosities and would claim them not.*

The Law and the Undersoul

> *There is a door to the Path where stands the Lord, but he who is fantasized in the thickets of ignorance knows not this passage-way neither can he find it. His intoxication of self and self-desiring extends his time, or units of measure, and as a wastrel he wanders, seeing not the Path or the Door or the Way.*

As surely as man is born as human to the world, it is inevitable that he will come under the Law when he offends the Law. A certain function of the Undersoul is asking for punishment. This sets up subjective responses to overburdened guilt-aspects in human nature—thus, one's wrongdoing inevitably invokes retaliation from the Law.

A fantasized person is terrified by the Law. A truth-teller stands alone among the fantasized and the spiritually illiterate. A truth-telling prophet speaks for a tomorrow when men will have come to the end of their agonies caused by their infamy.

He who tells the truth must be prepared for loneliness, for society does not want to hear the truth. When Jesus began His truth-telling, they said He was beside himself.

Fantasy also is a path of aloneness, and the greatest fantasy of all is that one knows not that he is alone in his fantasized dream. A truth-teller knows that he is alone. And in his aloneness, he is in grace and in peace-joy through the Law, a pilgrim walking the earth, a voice in the wilderness. However, he knows the way out of the wilderness, while he who is fantasized is in the thicket which bears the marks of the thorns yet to become the crown of his illumination.

To know truth and to be a fool for God—asserting and acclaiming God—is the Divine Way, the Omnipresent Way. The two-edged sword of truth provides the way through which a pathway is made for the walk of light. Truth must be the beginning or there is no Path.

Heritage

Sin-pollution is a contagion which is communicable to those who have weakened grace-immunities in their natures.

The Undersoul is carrying the greatest ancestral-gene karmic burden it has ever carried in history. This is the cause of man's upheaval and the distortion of his conscience. The pressure of the gene ancestral record comes that men may be cleansed in preparation for the Self-Genesis Age.

When one is born to the Maya scene in the physical world, his Undersoul inheritance covers him as a cloak, sealing him into gene-memory of good and evil. His own ego-memories of good and evil set the scene for the drama of the years facing him in the world.

As all infants swim in the womb and all men in the earth breathe the same air, so does one encounter his Undersoul karmic debts at birth which he must assume in the promise of a new look on life.

Every man enters this world burdened by Undersoul contamination which he has written into his account of life in earth. The record in the Undersoul inevitably calls for payment of karmic debts incurred by one's ancestors and ego in former times. One must battle the memory flowing from the attitudes and prejudices of ancestors.

Every act of virtue one would seek to attain is sifted through the screening process of past-life grace and past-life karma. If there is more grace than karma, one enters the world unburdened, free. If there is more karma than grace, one assumes his ego-karma and the karma of his ancestors at birth; and, throughout life, he must weigh the works of this life and works of other lives against the scales of grace. If one has energized his grace in a past life and has built a reservoir of grace, he operates and functions in a new life without the compounded chemistries and biased outlooks of his ancestors and ego of the past.

To be grace-born is to be destined to fulfill an aperture in the Maya chain as a grace-blessing to all.

In every ancestral inheritance, one is fortified to some degree by some strong virtue existing in the ancestral gene memory. If there is ego-strength, one brings into the world an ancestral strength; this is birthright-grace, enabling the one entering the world to fulfill the higher ideals which have been manifested in previous lives.

Many egos born with weak life-force resolution, having good ancestral or gene memory, fail to activate the strength of their ancestors. However, such egos, having progeny, can pass on to their grandchildren character-strength which they have failed to use. Grace invariably marries strength of soul, mind and body to one another; in this, a grace-destined ego is born in unusual environments with unusual opportunities.

In animal breeding, specie-strengths are cultivated by man. In breeding or reproduction of man, the complexities in grace and karma being unidentified in the present consciousness of man—and reincarnation being little known in the Western world—men will continue to be deceived in the understanding of inheritance and of gene succession as given to the human soul.

The knowledge of the Law of Reincarnation, the understanding of grace and karma, will enable men to use to the fullest their inherited propensities. Those who truly understand reincarnation understand also that an ego consists of many loaned and borrowed attitudes in the mind and in the emotions. And in true understanding of reincarnation, the soul is clearly known and utilized from birth to birth.

Niscience-Knowing

Niscience is God-Realization within all planes, spheres and kingdoms. Niscience, when born through victory over *nescience,* is the Light of the world, or Christ in consciousness. Niscience Initiation through the downpouring of Esse Holy Spirit brings freedom to act spiritually and live spiritually.

Undersoul darkness in this Self-Genesis era is thick, heavy, brackish, dark. The down-flow from Most High Esse is a Niscience Holy Spirit vehicle of white Light, that the sediments of evil in the Undersoul may be cleansed and washed out.

Only one letter in nescience (unknowing) when changed to the i as in Niscience (Knowing) makes the difference between dark and light or the pure and the impure: E as in ego, nescience; I as in the Divine or Niscience in God.

The Undersoul is a fabricated, energized subconscious structure built by the ego or the Maya exploration in countless lives. Mechanically, Undersoul functions best when in a state of pride in ego as being all-sufficient.

When the Undersoul becomes overweighted with ignorance and neglects of God, nescience becomes a strongly resisting vehicle in the Undersoul. Birth to Niscience during Undersoul darkness is a dry-birth experience causing suffering. On the Path, each birthpang produces Niscient revelations pertaining to the inadequacy of the ego or nescient self.

Fantasy feeling and emotions feed the Undersoul. The *craving mind* works with *time,* saying "Hurry, hurry, hurry." The fantasy mind works with *space,* saying "Me, me, me." These two have their dwelling in the Undersoul.

The Undersoul is first washed or baptized by the Esse Holy Spirit; secondly, it is set afire, heated and boiled by electrified emotional and mental tensions. The soiled portions are then thrown off or ejected as a meteor falling away from a planet. The Undersoul soiled-darkness is cast out that it may become a cleansed and pure companion for the Most High Soul which contains the original seed or pure Image of God. The Most High Soul is a superconscious energy-vehicle of movement.

The Undersoul is as old as man's sentient beginning. Through the aeons, it has been developed into a sensitized and entitized companion soul-vehicle for earth experience. Its commander is the ego.

The ego is the *lesser "I"* or the experiencing vehicle for the earth survival mind. The ego is deluded as to its adequacy. The ego is limited and hypnotized by Maya grossity as to the extent of its power. The ego is a projected gravity-vehicle extended by the greater I or the True Self.

The True Self is the Imaged Self as envisioned by our Father in Heaven assisted by the Elohim gods or Hierarchy. The ego is an externalized vehicle mentally feeding upon the intellectual exploring aspect of the senses. In the ego there are many lesser selves created by earth experience.

There are many states and existences in the afterlife as well as in the physical world. However, if one does not have Reincarnation Memory-Grace, he will continue to have rebirth to Undersoul disciplines of existence in each coming life. Very little progress is made through Undersoul Initiation unless one utilizes the knowledge of Reincarnation.

The reincarnating soul is the connecting vehicle between the True Self and the ego's work upon and with the Undersoul. Therefore, True Self, the Most High Soul, ego, and the Undersoul are soul-extended necessary vehicles for man in all states of consciousness as related to the Earth-developing planet.

The True Self is the Real, Deathless, Eternal, Everlasting Self Imaged of God. The ego takes on a different personality in each reincarnated existence. With each life there is something of other lives sedimented into the feelings, acting and thinking. Niscience or Knowing through the Esse as movement in conjunction with meditation and other spiritual practices produces the awareness that the lesser self or ego is a composite accumulation of many life experiences — and beyond and over-directing this is the *True Self* centered in God, the One.

Esse as realization phases out or dies if obstructed by a non-agape spirit. The desire to heal and to serve cleanses the Undersoul. Through Esse-awareness of the movement impulses within the Esse flow harnessed to action as service for God, the Esse Holy Spirit is kept alive, useful and functional in a state of the Intelligible Grace.

Esse movement flows first downward into the Undersoul. Grace reaction in the Undersoul frees the Esse into upward surges of living joy whereby God is realized as the One, the All.

There exists in all persons an inborn sense of an endless Agape or a knowledge that every man's hunger is the hunger to be fed by the Love of God. This is the freeing-grace of the Esse in action. Sincerity in hospitality offered in a genuine sense of love for all persons lightens the load of the Undersoul.

The world subconscious or collective Undersoul begins its work first through tumults, then by grace. Peace comes for all.

THE TRUE SELF AS A GUIDING PRINCIPLE

In the True Self there is but *One* Real which acts as the overdweller of the ego. This True Self is not the direct participant in the ego's actions. The True Self projects the ego as an ambassador. The True Self records and watches rather than acts. The nature of the True Self is to be the Guiding Principle. The ego's main goal is to ultimately fulfill the true Image of the True Self.

It is the nature of Maya or earth existence to energize substance through form. True Self having spirit rather than physical form relies upon ego as the form-functional vehicle. The Most-High-Esse cleansing comes when one sees the need and goes forth in the Agape Spirit to heal, to teach, to free, to feed, to comfort.

In this era of Kali-Yuga, the collective Undersoul has reached the state of an astrolocity-heated gel. Only the Holy Spirit movement as Esse can cool, free, transenergize and give a fluidic flow of purity to the astrolocity pollutions on world-scale dimensions. Manifold incarnated births of lawless egos are occurring that they may be offered or given the opportunity to experience and make lawful on the physical plane their lawless rituals of life. Apathetic egos unable to function due to psychic densities in the collective Undersoul add to the Maya deliriums. Everywhere may be seen and heard the clamor as a statement for nescience rather than Niscience. These atmospheres are nescient, ignorant, violating life as God or Niscient.

To know God as the Will is to invite the guiding downflow of the Esse. To know God as the Life is to live in the Holy movement of the Esse. To know God as the Light is to be in a constant state of revelation, vision, inspiration and realization. To know God as Love is to be a vehicle of Agape, of Peace, of Truth, of movement through works supreme.

THE UPA-SOUL AS THE WINNER

Upa-Soul* is the bridge between Soul and Undersoul. Upa-Soul is the spiritual name for the mediating aspects of the soul. The Upa-Soul term is used to identify the soul's relationship to the Undersoul. When the soul moves toward gravity, the Undersoul acts as the understudy or actor in the dense and unmanifesting phases of consciousness. The Upa-Soul is a free bridge to the Most High Soul.

*See Chart on Page 124.

Undersoul is a vehicle built through countless ego-experimentations in the earth. Most High Soul and Upa-Soul are vehicles of the Eternal, the Imperishable.

Through the freeing Esse, the *Passing Power* is received and the Opening Power follows according to grace.

Esse as vibration and movement of the Holy Spirit acts as an Intelligible Vehicle going directly to the Cause, cleaning out the Undersoul, which consists of the lower subconscious and the egotistical shell. The egotistical-shell substance is crystallized prana built by the sentient energies of gravity-ego thinking and emotion.

The dark samskara seeds in the subconscious, or karmic *tendencies* of negativity, and the egotistical collectivity of pride and vanity are swept clean through meditation, prayer, movement, sound, work, service and creation.

The True Self is the eternal *winner* through the mediation of the Upa-Soul. When the ego is intent upon winning, one is functioning on the level of the Undersoul. The Upa-Soul bridge and the soul are the winners by their eternal hierarchy nature: they cannot lose. The ego and the Undersoul are subjected to the duality of winning and losing. In life, the more heated the ego is to win, the more the ego loses. In the game of life, one must be selfless and he must care less whether he wins or not. God is the only Winner. Soul, as a vehicle of God, cannot fail. This is one of the meanings of "selling all."

The Upa-Soul as mediator makes it possible for one to receive the Esse Holy-Spirit Passing flowing from the Most High Soul.

The Undersoul desires to push the ego forward, and thus obscures the True Self. The True Self remains a patient Watcher over the ego; but when the time is ripe for the True Self to reveal the shining face of its truth and reality, the ego-self consciousness must be consumed in the fires of the Undersoul.

The Undersoul

Conscious functioning in the Undersoul is all fire and energy. The Upa-Soul is the Pathway to superconscious energy and mediating transcendence within the Most High Soul.

Every man who has exalted himself through pride or intellect or talent falls inevitably when the True Self comes forth in timing to the birth of greater or transcendent states of consciousness. In the search for truth through Undersoul awareness, one should not look upon defeat and demotion as failure of the Self. One should rejoice that he has come to the holy threshold of humility and purity as a soul under God.

As long as one dwells upon his failures, and his lack of winning or recognition, he is still in the ego state. But when the bright day of illumination comes, and one knows himself to be free of self-ambition and ego-exaltation, he has come to the *true* face of the True Self. The true face of his spirit reality will then reign over the limited ego.

3

CLEANSING OF THE UNDERSOUL

The Never-Nevers

Pettiness never purchased a spiritual mantle.
Retaliation never won a divine-companion guidance.
Hatred never bought peace or happiness.
Rigidity never attracted a Teacher or Master.
Self for self never provided happiness in old age.
Indulgence never won the blessing of a Saint.
Vice never invited the most pure Angels.
Prejudice never produced charity.
Criticism never protected one from being judged.
Penury never provided prospering.
Sloth never built an industry.
Haziness never made a right decision.
Foolishness never slept in peace.
Misery never found its right medicine.
Stuffiness never appeared with brilliance.
Haste never produced coordination.
Pressure never gained any thing in time.
Untruth never built a virtue.
Revenge never found a true justice.
Self-lying never attracted honest praise.
Conceit never found sincerity.
Pride never kept company with the humble.

Slander never used a clear mirror.
Envy never overcame malice.
Covetousness never owned a perfect thing.
Boasting never escaped reduction.
Carelessness never mastered a hurricane.
Lust never ceased to burn and be burned.
Suspicion never put a fire out.
Stubbornness never found kindness.

Love and Hate

Hostile persons develop allergies to people. The only cure for such allergies and hostilities is love of people. Should one be hostile to people, he should throw himself into the human race as a server and an apprentice of love. The greater servers are those who have a sense of concern without a sense of meddling.

When the love-body is absent, there cannot be healing. Healing thrives in a love-atmosphere. Consciousness energy begins in the heart. Souls who are on the forefront of the Archetypal Day express loving hearts.

The two great emotions are hate and love. Hate has six derivatives. Love has infinite dimensions.

Hate is an obsessing vehicle where all is seen through the vision of distortion. Hate involves man in a world of fantasy and untruth.

Hate has a venom, dispensing poisons. Hate has a violence, contributing to death and murder. The ultimate of hate is torture and suffering. Man who takes upon himself a life of hatred is a killer and a keeper of the guillotine.

Jealousy, anaspect of hate, is a death sentence to the self.

Everything is creative. Every mental aspect is creation. Jealousy creates terminal diseases.

Hatred is the heaviest energy in the earth. Jealousy, its

chief attribute, is first manifested outwardly; but with a boomerang action, it inevitably turns back upon the person who is jealous, causing black electricity, immobility.

Love is the element uniting the flexibilities of existence. Hate acts as a solder or hardened psychic mineral holding together the negatives within the Undersoul.

Love has an essence. Love is the flame floating upon the ocean of truth. Love is greater than hate. Love is light. Love is the healer. Love is the exorcisor. Love embraces all. The embrace of love provides justice, mercy, peace, happiness, joy.

To love is sacred. To hate is to curse. Love mixed with hatred is evil, and begets evil. Love unsullied by hatred is the power of God in the human heart, producing grace-works of holiness. *Pray to be love, total love. He who shuns evil has obtained love. Be not tempted to hate. Be prepared to love. Keep a love vigil with love consciousness, which is God in you.*

VOLITION AND VOLTAGE

The majority of persons are slowed-down automated energy masses of emotions and thoughts. The warming breath of versatility must be breathed into the frozen states of the Undersoul so that the Universal Versatility may possess the soul and be Passed on as the Esse.

Man will never be a hierarch or act as a god until he becomes first a *son* of God. A son of God must be an apprentice of the will within the Will of God before he becomes a hierarch under God.

Men are always seeking enough voltage to reach Heaven. Through Volition the Voltage of Heaven opens one to God.

He who revolts against God and His Laws and Commandments is absent from the Greater Voltage, which is God, or Spirit Eternal. He who is self-willed has made himself a god out of timing. Sooner or later the Greater Voltage of God will catch up with one who thinks himself to be a god.

To identify oneself with the self-aggressive electricities is death to the conscience. Unrealistic wills seek to crucify the pure and to exploit the good. One should beware of the unrealistic will, which severs him from the Greater Voltage.

The Great Voltage is regulated by the Laws and Commandments. To seek to be exempt from the Laws and Commandments is to be deluded. All evil is fantasized by a hardened heart and an unrealistic will and mind.

The Great Voltage is God. In the energy processes, God is Movement and Voltage.

Spiritual Volition is automatically responsive to the Will of God. Volition puts one into a God-situation where he can serve God; it is a spontaneity fully-clothed in Godly incentive and attributes.

Esse works in conjunction with the Grand Psyche, which is the conscience. When the Undersoul is fallen into the tamas inertia, conscience must first work that Esse, the volatile side of Spirit Eternal, may quicken the tamasic inertias of the samskara tendencies into the states of purification or sattvic.

The rajasic with conscience becomes sattvic through the work of Esse.

In tamasic, the Esse is stifled and smothered. In rajasic, the Esse is fanned to extinction. In sattvic, the Esse is luminous, irradiating as the transcendent luminosity.

The three force-functions or gunas are permeated by Esse only through total reliance upon the Holy Spirit and the Will of God. All activities where Esse is functioning occur only when absolute faith in Absolute God is present.

Absolute faith acts as Esse, bringing the inertias in the physical into right works. Absolute faith stills the overzealousness of the rajasic, bringing right resolution to the etheric. Absolute faith brings the sattvic into the pure emotional and pure desire, thereby producing a perfect Bhakti love so that God's Voltage can manifest in the soul, the Buddhi-mind and the heart.

Nescience and Niscience

When the will of the people is under domination, the incentive dies—and the Esse cannot speak through the people.

In the dark time of the collective Undersoul as in the present, the forces of nescience seek to prey upon the helpless, or those who have ignored God throughout many states of consciousness in the past and present. Such egos are penalized for their apathies, their neglects. The price is lethargy in works, in vision, in enlightenment, plus the restriction upon freedom to act.

He who lives in and for self-pleasure lives in blind astral fantasy. Truth is clean, pure; pleasure from truth obstructs not Reality, as it is of God. It is the Father's Pleasure the soul is seeking. This pleasure comes from order, perfection, peace. Pleasure for ego-self lives in a fantasy-shadowed world producing inevitable pain.

The higher mind and the lower mind have the power of clinging, cleaving and enclosing. The best of these is to cleave to God; all growth then will be of the Light and in the Light.

Memories of the past and of the old assist in the cleaving, clinging and enclosing powers of the lower mind. In Undersoul encounters, one must die literally to memories containing hostility, hate, fear, cowardice, double-mindedness, anger.

For spiritual experience, the first vehicle of the soul is the higher mind. The ego functions through the lower mind

CLEANSING OF THE UNDERSOUL

where the remains of hate and hostility dwell. If faith is weak, the soul-grace can be negated through the darkness of the lower mind continually clinging to the false, the untrue.

In the lower-mind function within the Undersoul, angry memories are as stalking beasts never ceasing to prey upon the weakness of the spiritually ignorant. When Undersoul is cleansed, the Most High Soul, through the power within the Esse, can bring remembrance of the *true past*. The true past, by nature of Eternal Love, can recall the memories of one's true and divine nature as related to God and His World of Reality.

To seek to mentally will or force the lesser mind to empty itself of hate awakens the fiery side of the Undersoul processes. An overload upon the psychic rajasic nature overheats the Undersoul, which causes suffering and defeat.

The lower mind can empty itself only in one manner: by total and complete submission to God through the downpouring of the Esse. By acceptance of grace as ever-present through faith in God, the lesser mind empties out its foulness; the Undersoul is cleansed to become a viable vehicle for the Most High Soul.

The Undersoul clings by nature to sensuality. Until the desire for union with God penetrates and transposes the contents in the lower mind to the higher mind, the Undersoul is fixed or glamorized in rigidity both painful and repetitive.

At the ending of an Archetypal Day or Kali-Yuga time as in the present, mass Undersoul rigidities must be cleansed. God sends those with grace-gift powers to assist in the birth to the new mind velocities for the total human race. Only those who have endured for many Archetypal times have these powers.

To receive and behold the grace-gift powers, one must

have the realization of the need for them. To be assisted by the grace-gift powers, one must have mastered his own holy war against the forces of the dark dwelling in the Undersoul.

During a Kali-Yuga darkness time, spiritual death is the threat for the masses. Oblivion becomes a downward chute toward the painful dark.

By remembrance of one's own blundering, one discovers his lower-self weaknesses. His ignorance comes to light when, with honesty, he flushes out the evil propensities of the lower-mind desires residing in the Undersoul.

The soul and the True Self, in the days of Eternal Creation, sent forth the Undersoul and the ego as many-faceted pilgrims to go forth into the earth carrying life's eternal message of the True Self. The ego is sent forth to obtain earth experience, thereby creating a consciousness dimensionally unique for this earth or eternity system. The Undersoul presently seeks to build another brain-vehicle which will become the center for the higher mind when once it is perfected.

Undersoul debris produces automated suffering. An overburdened Undersoul creates combustion, then fire, then pain. Undersoul burdens accumulate when one fails to think and act within the inward laws sealed into the inward parts or chakras.

Faith in God sets fire to the accumulated debris in the Undersoul. Such fire produces purification. The false must be consumed by the Esse explosions and combustions in the Undersoul. *Pure is the Esse Gas of the Holy Spirit.*

To be out of timing is nescient. To be in timing is Niscient. Prayer, when resounded with mantra, selflessly lifts the veils of Time. The prayer and the future are co-creators; mantra explodes the present so that the response to prayer be experienced *as* the future.

Cleansing of the Undersoul

The OM sound is both prayer and mantra. OM erases the negative past, explodes the present negatives, creates the future as perfect, as joy.

The Undersoul is nescient as to true Selfhood. The Undersoul can become Niscient through the Esse cleansing white fire of the Holy Spirit Esse.

Esse, the Holy Gas of God, is the sweeper of all evil, the eradicator of all vice, the emancipator for the Self. The Self functions in the Clear Light through the Esse. Esse as power is grace in action.

He who has mastered competitiveness has no enemies. He who is free from the evil without cannot be tempted by Satan within. Christ, being free of evil, was not tempted to betray Himself, His mission, or God.

Ego-temptations beset all who take the dust from the feet of Jesus. Temptations abound in the world of man and in the lower astral world. Pleasure-principle obsession leads one to the temptation trials.

The ego acts as many faces or projections for the True Self. The lower mind with its egotistical tendencies is deluded to think the ego is the original face of True Self. The higher mind knows *That Self* to be the *True Self*.

What is good about the Undersoul?

1. As a vehicle for earth experience it is a purposeful energizer for the use of an earth perfecting consciousness.

2. The main organisms for its functioning are: the ego, the senses, the lower emotions, obsessed desiring, the lower mind, the instincts, the lesser will, and the conscience.

3. Its tan-matra powers are: ingesting, absorption, retention, destroying, reproduction and production, stimulation, fixation, divisions, assimilation, dissolution, repetition, transposing stagnation, stigmatization, lunar cycling and timing, transposing of habit retention, and resurrecting of death impulses.

4. As a vehicle for the astral and lower emotional nature, it is a feeling magnifier; an energy-motivated vehicle for the ego, for self-survival, self-pleasurable glamorization, self-pity, self-pride, ego-assertiveness, ego-aggression, ego-claiming, fantasy; a karmic recorder and reproducer of ancestral weaknesses and former-life states of ignorance-omissions and violations against Nature and Nature's laws through sex as disloyalty, adultery, or the offense against the Ten Commandments. As a lower-mind vehicle, the Undersoul compulsions and fantasies seal away entry to the higher mind, the higher emotions, the soul and the Higher Self.

When the Undersoul becomes a cleansed vehicle, which is only possible through spiritual rebirth to the Holy Spirit of the Esse, its functions are magnetic, holy, pure, sensitive, peaceful, happy, bliss-giving, higher devachan revealing, healing, optimism, joyousness. With faithful transmission powers, the cleansed Undersoul can manifest as miraculous occurrences in the physical world to be seen and received by the world of man as the Holy Witness of the Power of God through His Spirit.

The Undersoul must be cleansed as a vehicle for its true manifested realization or else one gives off the gross psychic of the seeing darkly or in part.

The harmonized Undersoul is a vehicle of whole and total desire to serve God and only God, using the aspects of the mind with a total and complete mind as an unsullied sapphire jewel containing the fire and light of revelation through the Son, the Christ. With the birth to and through the Esse, one attains all of those things of godly desire in the soul.

It is not asked that the Undersoul die, only that the sedimentized vileness of sin of the past and the present die, and thus be transposed and transenergized that the appearance of God in the physical world be made manifest. From the death of each sin a soul power or gift is made manifest.

Happy is the song of the Undersoul when lifted beyond the gross, fiery vibration of sin. A free Undersoul sings in conjunction with the Universal tones centered in all planes, all worlds freed from the sense of sin or sinning.

The True Self has a holy desiring nature. As the Nature of God desires His perfection to be made plain, the True Self awaits the Eternal timing to take possession of the Undersoul that it, as the True Self, may function as the Face of God in the affairs of the physical world. As God incarnates through His Avatars, the True Self seeks to take possession and utilize the Undersoul.

All of the struggle for earth, the mastery of gravity through mind, is designed that in some future time of earth evolvement the Undersoul will become the total centering, polarizing point for the Most High Soul and for the Higher and True Self.

The Undersoul throughout the ages has come to the one-half point of its perfection as a vehicle for the Most High Soul and the True Self. Since Jesus, men are seeking, searching, and moving toward the goal of Oneness for self and for God. All of the lesser selves developed by the expressing ego in the earth are portions of the potential perfection to be gained in life mastery over earth energies and processes of earth experiencing.

The Undersoul is nescient rather than Niscient. Nescience as power in the Undersoul acts as the primal instinctual will, the conscience primal, the sentient survival. Thus, the intelligence of the Undersoul is powerful in many and varied ways: to preserve, to tear down, to retain, and to record to time as in birth and in death, to reject as in suffering.

The most negative aspect of the Undersoul is when it falls into deviation due to a misdirected will and the ignoring of conscience. Repetition is the major attribute of the Undersoul. Repetition is harmful when one is tamas, or disobedient to the Will of God.

Everything of the Real is centered in the Esse *Flowing*. To resolve the negatives of the past, one must move into the *Esse Flow*. The Esse Flow automatically takes one into and beyond the vibration of tamasic heaviness and the rajasic hastes. To be sucked into vibrations of the Undersoul is to suffer. Sattvic Esse-Flow is peace and release from the Undersoul drag and tow.

The Undersoul sphere of tangibility manifests as an ambivalent field of forces of grace and of negativity. One having the seership powers of uniting with the primal survival-images of life and life survival can see and gauge his own evil and his own guilts.

Only through awareness and training can one utilize and make knowledgeable the Undersoul action. When the timing is right, the yang aspect or positive aspect of the subconscious is opened and activated by one's longing to know more, to be more and to become more. Encounter with the Undersoul is inevitable. In this era, in the Self-Genesis time of Kali-Yuga, the dark side of the Undersoul is seeking to pour out its ugliness, its distortion, which is the cause of blind mental suffering and agony.

The cyclic and regulated energies of the planets help to trigger Undersoul forces. The Undersoul acts as a replica or duplicate of a particular and creating black-hole galaxy sphere by which a soul is related to the familiar present and the past eternality existences.

The heart, in its beat of contraction and dilation, forms the energy relationships for the Undersoul. To the seer, this appears as a sphere-like energy cloud or a moving nimbus within the center of the aura of man.

The Undersoul acts as unceasing movement. These movements are negative and positive currents working with attracting and repelling powers in the desire nature, and also with the reflecting destroying archetypes limiting the lower mind.

Cleansing of the Undersoul 49

Undersoul works to ultimately become the clothing or garment for a fifth body which the soul and the Higher Self will wear as the natural soul and mind apparel in the earth.

The soul created first the four bodies of man: the mental body, the astral or emotional body, the etheric body, and the physical body. The soul is presently creating another soul-body which can function as soul-presence and God-presence in the world, and thus create the earth to be heavenly as well as earthly. The Undersoul is the matrix to become an additional body; this will be the soul-body of man, having tangibility, having transcendental, spiritual, extended extra-sense.

When the Undersoul has become a perfected vehicle, the soul will totally command this vehicle, and thus man will be more of himself and of God. This is the intent for man in his pursuit of consciousness in this eternity system, called Solar and Earth.

The Undersoul is presently a tenuous body of moving, chaotic and potential mind-forces containing the uncreated and also the record of that which man has created in part as of good and bad. In the present time, it is acting as a mirroring sin-body through which man must become more aware of his conscience.

The lower mind is an earth memory machine. The intellect is an earth sensory machine. Each works similar to a motorized belt returning to man the memory of his wrong-doing to use as an analytical conscience vehicle through which to weigh and to judge himself and his actions. In his search for good, this memory function must be experienced; it is experienced through the mental function of the Undersoul.

Presently, men are painfully relinquishing old methods and techniques which have before the yang state of Self-Genesis served as the means of earning and learning. That which formerly supported subjective yin-consciousness life or the primal survival existence is being transformed into the yang sentient.

On all levels, men are striving directly and indirectly to extend their mental dimensions and perceptions. The mechanics of living in the human condition under the quickened Christed Archetypal Light now prepare to move men beyond the subjective yin ritualistically-dependent, habit-bound processes into a more direct perception of life and its meaning as creative and creating.

The name of this mind-collective knowing is *Niscience*. Its synchronicity function will produce another kind of mind and emotion in man. The goal of this future man will be to become a polarized or equipoled being, both yin and yang: Androgynous.

At the present time, the chief function of the Undersoul is experienced at the yin subconscious levels. All men seek to be cleansed of racial, ancestral and primal samskara patterns seething in tamasic and rajasic states in the darkened yin turgid depths of the subconscious.

Each person in the world must encounter what he is, from whence he has come, and where he is going. The yang function of the subconscious now active is in a state of pressing forth great masses of debris into the Undersoul. These little-understood forces playing upon the will and the mind are frightening and terrifying to the immature, producing hysterias of mind and neuroses in the emotions. These dangerous states of mental and emotional transition moving into the human condition endanger the equilibrium of the soul-forces which the sentient subconscious yin nature has formerly provided.

Until this lesser Self-Genesis period of yang development, woman and man have instinctively leaned upon the protective strengths within the yin side of the instinctual nature. Now with the yang subconscient state, there is appearing a cold-hearted and insensitive condition. Men en masse as well as individually feel rejected and separated.

All are unknowingly reaching toward the higher polarized state of Self-Genesis. Through polarization of the yin and the yang into the androgynous or bipolarity, all seek to come to emotional and mental balance. In this post Kali-Yuga time, the necessity to go inward through the Clear Light is used by all advanced and synchronized initiates. These initiates see the present function of the collective world-subconscious and the agitation of the Undersoul of the world, and of the individual, as a God-compulsion through which the soul is at work.

Men of the earth are presently coming to birth to greater soul-powers, to higher mental capacities, and to more expressive emotions. To do this they must undergo the initiatory trials and master the yang rajasic heats residing in the Undersoul.

Yin and Yang Polarity between the Subconscious and the Undersoul

The Undersoul magnifies the cause and varied aspects of unrest in mind and in emotions. When the mental atoms and the emotional atoms are functioning in their most gross sense, their fiery energies fall into the Undersoul, causing traumatic discomfort, pain, unease and unrest.

The Undersoul is the expander and manifestor of what is sleeping in the subconscious. The residue in the subconscious is ignited and flows outward in periods and cycles to become the heated Undersoul turbulence.

The subconscious acts as the yin (expansion), and the Undersoul as its polarity yang-opposite (contraction). These function together as a normal ego-regulating process.

The subconscious records and collects the sense of sin, the

guilts, and all conscienceless acts. The Undersoul seeks to assimilate and project into ego or objective consciousness that which conscience is trying to say in the subconscious.

In spiritual life there are initiatory periods when one calls forth accumulative unresolved karmas or debts. There are also the after-periods of manifesting these karmas and soul-debts outwardly. These are experienced as frustrations, sickness, neurosis.

Should one be out of step with his conscience, Undersoul becomes congested, fiery, thrusting. The etheric sentient-atoms of the lower etheric body and the gross emotional and ego mental atoms of the lower will and mind become over-heated with Undersoul reactionary effects. Thus, the four bodies of man become alien to one another, causing nervous breakdowns, collapse of the cellular system, the nervous system and the glandular system.

When one meditates each day at sundown and reflects upon his motives and intent of the hours and day just past, he cools the subconscious yin and regulates the yang Undersoul flow.

Moods

All dark moods originate in the Undersoul. When one does not give circulation and movement to the Most High Soul, the result is negative moods surfacing from the Undersoul.

Every hurt and every pain and every human disappointment lies festering in the Undersoul. The Undersoul suffers more than the body suffers from frustration and disappointment.

Movement of the body is walking, work, pleasance and the Esse exercise called *Free Play*. In the energized emotional and mentalized nature of the Western Initiate, there must be movement to equal meditation.

Cleansing of the Undersoul

Water is a mood forming element. It is a submerging element and mingling element.

The moody ones are the Water Sign Prototypes. The Water Signs are more likely to reach oneness in meditation through moods and feelings.

Pisceans are more subjected to creative moods; Cancer, to brooding moods; Scorpions, to frustration moods.

The Scorpio is a regenerator, and he accuses himself when he does not have success in his endeavors. The Cancer person is moody because of ego resistance to sharing. The Pisces prototype is moody because of self-procrastination in creation.

An initiate or disciple should always be cheered by the fact that at the end of a mood-span or period there is an after-explosion of creation. He should also watch for this and take advantage of it. Such creation is pure energy undefiled surfacing from anguish and suffering.

In the ancient times, the sages respected mental and emotional depression, knowing that on the other side of a mood is the power of creation.

In India today, the insane are considered to be sacred by all guru schools, because these schools understand the pendulum action between insanity and lucidity.

It is inevitable that *whatever* one becomes the victim of, he must become the master of that thing. The Most High Soul is at all times giving birth to pure creation.

The Higher Self entitizes the ego. The ego entitizes the Undersoul. The Undersoul, when non-creative, creates suffering in body, in emotions and in mind.

Morning moods come out of the Night Ministry work or dream experience.

There are the lunar moods women experience before and during menstrual periods. These may be either excessively loving or excessively negative. A balanced woman watches these moods and controls them creatively.

In the male, Moon moods possess the sexual drives, programming the male for sexual fulfillment.

Some levels of mental depression are caused by immaturity in emotions.

Depression, as an indulgence, is a cardinal sin.

The Demonic Trials

That which was formerly a Satsanga or search for truth for self is now a World-Satsanga.

In the present time, one of the aspects of Undersoul research is that one must encounter the demonic or must re-live to some degree his former-life encounters with the demonic in which he has let down his guard against the evil. During certain planetary tides playing upon the lower astral or emotional nature, he is exposed to the demonic or to a confrontation with the intelligible forces of evil which stand as contesting forces competing with his desire for good. A demonic trial induced by penetrable or non-insulated chakra action can expose a person to abnormal states of mind, emotion and action.

One who has the grace to be insulated from the demonic is using freely the higher grace aspects of the subconscious. All soul-enlightened ones are healers and exorcisers against evil darkness.

The realities of subsentient evil forces are experienced in the most darkened side of one's Undersoul nature. Through the Esse as movement, one exorcises and throws off the pressures of the demonic. Through the Esse awareness or Holy Spirit movement, one tests all telepathic flows falling into his receiving sensitivities.

Three chakras are especially active in the present time of man's search into the chakra realities. These are the pelvic chakra, the solar-plexus chakra and the heart chakra. If one has failed to insulate himself in these chakras, he is open to the demonic flows of telepathy, which are profoundly impressionable and suggestible on levels of deception.

The telepathies from the demonic are hypnotic, sometimes causing those who are receptive to them to become obsessed in hatreds, in fears, in revenge attitudes against the good.

Drugs and the Undersoul

The path of drugs is not the Virtue Path; it is not the real; it is the path of the lower astral world.

Broken marriages, distortion of the mind, wrong choice in the use of discrimination, a lack of sense of direction—all of these result when one is dependent upon alcohol, or any form of drug having effect upon the muscular and nervous systems.

Drugs remove one from the time-clock of his grace, and center him in the lower aspects of retributive karmas. When one alters and immobilizes the respiratory flow in the medulla oblongata through the use of drugs, he is faced directly with accumulative karmas containing heartaches, separations and disillusionments.

A moment of drug-stimulated ecstasy is a disaster as compared to the spiritual life within the ecstasy-flow of grace and salvation.

All persons dependent upon a life of drug-stimulation eventually encounter the darkened influences of the Moon, and enter into a world of hallucination and fantasy. There is no reality-coherence or cognizance to be gained through the use of drug-taking dependency.

One who uses drugs to substitute for religious ethic and

morality exposes himself to the demonic—the dark and evil spirits whose sole ambition is to divert and detain the work of the soul in the physical world. The demonic contact the mind in the lower octaves of the Undersoul. The demonic world is directly under the command of the Satanic or Lucifer fallen archangel, Satan.

All drug-taking persons have a negative Neptunian aspect in their zodiacal charts. The Teacher healing one who takes drugs must possess the Sealing Powers against the demonic and the Exorcising Powers to overcome the Satanic. For the misshapen images and distortions in the emotions and mind of one using drugs, the Teacher must replace or redirect the imaging processes in the lower-mind functioning of the one who has been self-hypnotized through the taking of drugs.

Every person taking drugs subconsciously desires to return to the state of the womb or the state of irresponsible childhood; his basic attitude being that he wants someone to take care of him. The Teacher must never expose himself to an ego-relationship with a student who has had total dependency and sensual delight in the taking of drugs. The Teacher must stand in positive firmness as to the crippling effect and demotion of soul-powers in anyone who has fantasy ideas and conceptions relating to drug-taking.

Marijuana attacks the central nervous system. Marijuana is an attack on the moral character, on the integrity. Habit-forming drugs on any level are an outrage against Time.

When one goes the drug-route to gain psychic powers, he contacts the fantasy and grotesque worlds.

Men at large have developed a total exploitation of the energies of the mind through three abuses: smoking, drinking, and the taking of drugs. These spurious proclivities have developed a totally false mind relationship to reality existence.

Only centered persons in God can serve God. All forms of illusory addiction interfere with centering. A centered person draws to him those who are also centered. From this is the reinforcement whereby a perfected polarization becomes the vehicle for the God-Presence.

Smoking affects the etheric body. Alcohol of any nature affects the emotional body. Drugs affect the mental body.

He who has taken mind-altering drugs is open to the demonic; if he possesses grace from a past life, he is open to certain protective aspects of the angels. If there be spiritual-power essences retained from previous existences, he rises over the demonic fears, subtle-inferences. However, one must wrestle with the Satanic forces in certain climax periods of initiation, for drugs work with the etheric cyclic rhythms repeating and stimulating the reflex actions within desire.

He who does not dwell in the Holy Spirit will seek a false spirit — and the false spirit leads him to alcohol, drugs, soft living, sensuality-comforts. Invariably, softness turns to vulgarity, experimentation and perversion. A sensual, soft body produces a soft head; promiscuous experimenting attracts permissive companions and parasitical non-virtue living.

When a person succumbs to the seduction of drugs, and is a certain age, such as 15, 16, or 17, from this moment his emotional age becomes fixed — and he thereafter is as old emotionally and mentally as he was at the time of beginning the use of mind-altering drugs. In all persons with drug histories, one may gauge the emotional and mental maturity to be the age they were at the time the habit of drugs was formed. When a person steps away from drugs and "kicks the habit," he must retrieve and utilize the mental and emotional energies he set aside on taking drugs. Thus, a person, though he be 30 years of age, may be mentally or emotionally 16 or 17 years of age in his outlook upon life, in his sense of responsibility, and in his own self-relating as to self-understanding.

In the present life, one steps beyond Time to unite with Eternal Time. In the taking of drugs, one denies himself the processes of cyclic developments in mind and emotions. In turning toward the spiritual life, if one has by some form of misdirection been guided into the use of drugs, he must retrieve these years. Extreme tensions, ego-devaluation, and non-reality viewpoints must be replaced by realistic and pragmatic approaches to life.

The only way drug or narcotic damage can be repaired in the etheric body and transenergized in the emotional and mental ambivalent state is by coming under the direct guiding principles and disciplines accompanying spiritual enlightenment.

Pure love for God extends one beyond the vibrations of the lower psychic planes. Service for God gives mastery over the gross psychic forces. All methods directed to gain psychic power for the sake of self-power produce suffering. The psychic forces, when used for self, are unreliable forces.

In the use of drugs to gain psychic powers, the Mouth-of-God or the Master Bindu-center at the base of the skull is damaged. If there be grace, through meditation and prayer by others and by oneself, this can be slowly mended. However, if one has taken drugs over an extended period of time, there will remain, for more than one lifetime, damage to the etheric matrix protecting the Mouth-of-God Bindu, the medulla oblongata.

Drug-damage to the etheric matrix protecting the Bindu Center and the etheric matrix of the solar plexus is mended more quickly in the solar plexus. By right meditation, self-analysis and spiritual disciplines, one can restore some of the insulating properties to the etheric matrix of the solar plexus.

The Bindu or Mouth-of-God etheric matrix, when severely damaged, exposes one (1) to the demonic world and (2) to prolonged spells of mental depression.

If one has awakened the lower psychic powers through the use of drugs—and if there is severe karma involved—mental eccentricities and personality defects will appear, causing self-anguish, and, in some instances, disorganization in the total personality. If the Undersoul has become dependent upon drugs for psychic stimulation, a breakdown in all of the interconnected functions of the body, emotions and mind is inevitable.

When one damages the inhaling and exhaling pranic breath within the medulla oblongata by the use of drugs, he becomes subjected to tensions in cyclic periods of the Moon. If the damage has extended to the solar cyclic rhythms in the breath, the derangement is beyond repair—and one is then exposed to the demonic in cyclic intervals of both New and Full Moon.

Gravity, working with the Moon in the lunar cycle of the breath, fixes the generating aspect, causing a psychic toxism or unrealistic emotional and mental attitude. During these depressing lunar cycles, one becomes antagonistic to life. He is addicted to paranoia states of consciousness.

To free oneself from the automatic processes of deranged lunar cycles caused by the use of drugs, one should under meditation supervision by a Teacher set into motion the meditative processes accompanied by mantrams, marking and tracing, and definite self-disciplined service.

One should realize that on taking drugs he has distorted chains of memory which have supported him with reflexes protective and also intuitive. All persons who enter into the drug state should know that what is lost in the memory chain, or destroyed in the use of drugs, will never be recovered. One should seek to build new cycles and reflex-approaches to life through gaining higher sensitivities. He should be always on guard against subtle influences of the Satanic open circuit which he has unwittingly opened by venturing into a quick and temporary chimeric state of unreality. The purchase price is too high. Escape from life by deliberate choice is self-destruct on all levels—and by the route of drugs is the most deadly and damaging.

Spiritual Teachers understanding the Undersoul function and its supportive automation, when confronted with a student having drug damage, should guide and direct the student toward the reserves of protective grace. It is important that such Teachers give to a student of this nature reassurances of a world beyond excitation and self-gratification.

If basic traits of selfishness and manipulation are cemented into the Undersoul of a student, the work of the Teacher is to use his own powers of spiritual mediation to free the one caught into the snares of self-indulgence. A Teacher familiar with Esse movement moves his student beyond the dependency habit-patterns registered in the Undersoul. The vital issue of the situation is that the Teacher must return such students to a sense of purification and moral responsibility toward God and toward self.

Psychic experience occurring due to the use of drugs exposes one to obnoxious sounds and repelling colors, and in some cases the seeing of visions through the negative side of the *yantra* or geometric-symbology powers. The mental recording and interpreting principle being absent in these visions, one is unable to absorb and comprehend the visions; they have no lasting purpose in the mental cognitive flow of learning and experiencing. Such visions are out of touch with the powers of the soul and become addictive, psychically, with retaliative non-practical reactions more potently dangerous than the use of the drug itself. In other words, one who uses drugs to produce the play of psychic forces is *doubly* addicted. The altering of consciousness and the addiction to the psychic powers and forces become a fixture of dependency on the fantasy play of the Undersoul. To be free of addictive psychic expectancies through the use of drugs, one must undergo a reversing of the psychic forces through training, healing, mending. This can be done only through the calling forth of soul-powers extending beyond the psychic planes.

The Teacher assisting in this mending and healing works to heal, to exorcise and to close the subhuman doors which must be sealed from the darkened suggestibles of the demonic.

There are other worlds besides the physical world. Some of these are called *Kingdoms.* There is the Kingdom of the Angels, and there is the domain of man. It is of grace if one who seeks to walk the Path understands the Angel Kingdom. It is profoundly good and pure that one who understands this Kingdom can dwell within its precincts as well as within the domain of man.

The angels protect the pure and true in their dedication and service to God. If the Undersoul is lucid with good and pure motives, the Angel Kingdom sets up its throne in the Undersoul. As Jesus came down from Heaven, so do the angels come down from their Kingdoms to provide the protections and insulations against the demonic.

The Saints also set up their residence in proximity to the precincts of the Undersoul if purity in motive is the intent of that one seeking union with God.

The Undersoul and the Esse

Man is a walking purgatory in his Undersoul-consciousness. Through the use of Esse practices, one comes to know himself as he is; he comes free of the karmas imprinted and fixed upon the Undersoul.

Esse, meaning *Holy Spirit Essence,* is existing in everything as Life-Intelligible within Almighty God. The Esse acts as a Holy Gas or Intelligibility-Energy filling, animating and quickening every form of life. The Esse is the Holy Spirit transcendent substance of the Infinite—existing in the Infinite and the finite.

The Undersoul is projected from the Most High Soul as a supporting system for the ego. It is an entitized portion of the ego to keep the lesser self, the lower mind, the subconscious mind, the sense-filled desire, and the vital automatic reflexes of the physical body in a state of maintenance.

The Undersoul keeps alive the automated processes of habit in their state of repetition and reproduction. The solar, lunar and planetary cycles influencing the body control the automatic processes of the Undersoul. The Undersoul, as a vehicle for ego maintenance, is controlled also by the survival memory patterns of one's ancestors and by his own former-life survival tendencies or abilities.

On the physical plane one exists as an ego and as a personality automated by the repetitive processes in the Undersoul. In the spiritual planes, in the state of *Being,* one exists in soul-superconsciousness. The Most High Soul contains the Buddhi or Informing function of Supreme remembrances.

The Undersoul contains the memory of all past physical earth existences.

The memory in each cell within the blood is divided into three states of functioning: Ancestry, Ego and Soul. Man experiences these three functions of the cell and cell memory in the complex cycles of change within changelessness.

Esse frees the darker fixities of the Undersoul through *movement* in conjunction with meditation. Work as service for God is also a form of movement, and work is a direct collaborating action with the flow of the Esse.

Esse, through receptive movement with meditation while in unison with the Will of God, frees the primordial spiritual or virginal forces into the outer life. The Undersoul is thus quickened and becomes a finer and sensitized, accelerated vehicle whereby latent powers of the Most High Soul come forth. To be free within the Esse is to be at one with the Most High Pleasure-Principle and to be beyond the lower pleasure-principle existing in the habit-programmed Undersoul.

Jesus said: *"It is the Father's good pleasure to give you the Kingdom."* (St. Luke 12:32). As long as one is satisfied to be in the repetition of former habits based upon pleasure for self, he will be subjected to the alternate of pleasure and suffering. To live in Esse receptivity is to relax the tensions of habit which are out of timing to the need of the Most High Soul.

When one enters into bliss, he is in the Most High Pleasure-Principle. It is Esse's work to establish this High Pleasure as master over the lower-sense cultivation of pleasure for pleasure's sake.

The Self-Realized Initiate dissolves his *egotistical shell* so that he may transform his Undersoul. The Undersoul returns to the direct guidance of the Most High Soul and the Higher Self. Through the use and knowledge of Esse as Holy-Spirit White-Holy-Gas Essence, one comes to the true and only contentment, peace, joy and happiness.

4

THE SACRED ARTICLES OF THE ESSE OR THE PASSING POWER

God is not absent from that which He has given. From His only begotten Son, He cannot be absent.

Each one must become one who Passes the Holy-Spirit Esse from God. Each one must Pass that which he is, which is an aspect of God.

What one is, is what he Passes in the Name of God.

Doing all things in the Mighty Name of God, or His OM—which is the Name of God—all things are done according to His Spirit, of which the first aspect is His Mighty Will.

To be one who Passes, one uses his hierarchy nature, which is the Will of God, empowering him to will, to live, to know, and to love.

Question: What is the substance from which all life is formed?

Answer: God as Light and Life manifested as the Intelligible within Plasma or Ether, which science calls the molecular system.

Q. What aspect of God is used to activate it?
A. Holy Spirit as movement.
Q. What is the *moving aspect* of the Holy Spirit called?
A. Esse.
Q. What is meant by the Intelligible Plasma?
A. The Omniscience of God pervades and permeates the Intelligible Ether.
Q. How does one experience and know God as Omnipresence?
A. As being present in everyone and everything.
Q. How does one prove God?
A. By His effect as *Prescience* or as foreseeing insight into our need.
Q. When does one recognize the Power of God beyond one's own limited power?
A. By becoming a selfless channel to Pass on to others the Power of the Holy Spirit or Esse.
Q. What is this power called?
A. "The Passing."
Q. How was this power given?
A. First, before the earth system was formed, this power dwelt innately in the soul. Second, it was unsealed, increased and magnified through the Passion of Jesus. Third, it was established in its third and final aspect by the Resurrection and Ascension of Jesus.
A. Does the power of the Passing make anyone exceptional or more divine?
A. The power of the Passing makes one aware of God and of the Esse through the Higher Self. Having the power of the Passing makes one powerful yet humble. To receive

the Passing, one must first believe on the works for the works' sake. Second, one must seek to do the works as did Jesus through our Father in heaven. Third, he must become co-atom to Jesus. By this, one becomes divine.

Q. What is meant by being co-atom to Jesus?

A. To be equal in a wavelength of the soul to the divine wavelength in the soul of Jesus.

Q. What happens when one receives a "Passing?"

A. The recipient of the "Passing" will open the gifts of his soul. He will be transenergized, transformed, changed, healed, opened, blessed, and quickened according to the level of need or crisis. In the life of the recipient, he will receive one or all of these according to grace.

Q. How does one recognize a person having the power of the Esse Passing?

A. By the positive and miraculous grace-events which are set into motion, producing universal, supernal occurrences not personally instigated, contrived or planned. Such events stem from a grace-contact with a Living Teacher, who is a mediator acting as a channel or representative of God.

Q. How does one find the one having the power of the Passing?

A. When one is ripe or ready, the soul leads him to that one having the Passing powers.

Q. What is the Jesus Ethic in giving the "Passing"?

A. Esse is the Holy Wind. The Spirit quickeneth whom it will; or in works of grace, the Passing moves as Esse to the need, the burden, giving its revealment, revelation and realization.

Q. Of what essence is the vehicle for the Holy Spirit Esse?

A. When one becomes a vehicle for the Holy Spirit Grace of the Esse, he is that light acting as a candlestick in the midst of darkness.

Q. To what extent does one owe fidelity to the one channeling the "Passing" to him?

A. One looks upon the one "Passing" the Esse as the door to God. With respect, reverence and holy gratitude, one is divinely obligated thereafter to also become a channel even as the one Passing to him, and thus pass on *the Gift* with the increase of abundance of grace.

Q. Will any kinds or forms of movement produce the Esse? What kinds of movement are necessary to awaken or arouse Esse?

A. All common movement of mind, emotion, body is accompanied by ego or self-will to survive. Esse movement is opened by surrender of the self-will to the Will of God. From this, the Esse, as the most high aspect of grace, falls as the direct Will of God purifying and cleansing through movement. This movement is the Holy Spirit Essence or Esse which moves with the superconscious and primordial movement of the soul down into the lower electrical vibrational cavities of the Undersoul. Upa-Soul and Undersoul become one when the final merging and union occur. One is free to serve God as a selfless channel of pure love, pure motive, pure ethic.

Q. How often should Esse be called down?

A. The Esse may take many forms. First, Esse must be longed for and desired. Second, one should practice the Esse at least once a day. Third, Esse is experienced as lightness, freedom, clarity, openness, innocence, service to God, agape, healing, happiness, vision, insight and inner sight, truth, wisdom, humor, joy, acceptance, dreams, truth-telling, humility, unburdenness. This creates a sense of Godliness in being, and provides union in all relatings, all conditions. Thus, one draws upon the higher unconscious, giving to the Esse freedom that one may have realization of God and His oneness in all.

Q. Are there dangers in the Esse practices or the freeing of the Holy Spirit through movement?

A. There is no danger in the Esse practice when the Passing comes through a Teacher who has attained the complete or whole opening through union with God. If self-opening or desire for personal power is sought, one cannot cross over or pass over into the true Esse.

Q. Then for one to obtain the Esse, one must be opened by a Living Teacher having the power of the Passing?

A. Yes.

Q. In the exoteric form or movements, such as posture in yoga, dervishes, etc., is this also pure Esse?

A. Any form of movement which is directed by self-will or contains any form of desire for self-power, self-direction for personal power, opens the primal charismas in the Undersoul rather than the pure primordial Esse Holy-Spirit gifts and powers. Lower-self commands flow in the gross psychic lower-chakra heats of kundalini; this stirs the soil in the Undersoul rather than the Esse downpouring of the spiritual into the Undersoul. When all is grace in Esse movement, the primordial grace purifies. The primal heats electrify and produce magnified returns of karmas. The demonic powers are obtained when the Undersoul evils, as accumulated energies, are used for selfish and wicked manipulations.

Q. Is it necessary to surrender any or all of self-desire for the Upa-Soul to be a channel for the freeing of Esse in the Undersoul?

A. Yes.

Q. The Niscience practices stress or emphasize the power of the Angels in the spiritual life. What Angels are working with the Esse?

A. The Guardian Angel, the Recording Angel, the Angel of Pure Desire, the Angel of Luminosity, the Niscience Angel, and the Holy Spirit Angels. The Shining Spirits

(Devas) and the Archangels of the Planets, the Sun, Moon. The Archangels of the Greater Archetypes.

Q. What disciple of Jesus received the most pure aspect of Esse?

A. John the Beloved.

Q. Why?

A. He loved; he endured; he suffered; he obtained the victory in the Name of Jesus.

Q. When was the Passing experienced by the eleven disciples of Jesus?

A. The disciples were prepared to receive the Passing. Jesus initiated the disciples into the Holy Spirit at the Last Supper, the Sacrament, the breaking of the bread, the drinking of wine, the washing of the feet; at the Garden of Gethsemane; after His capture and scourging; the trial; after His Resurrection in the garden with Mary Magdalene; on the road to Emmaus; in the upper chamber; on the shore; and in His Ascension. The white fire of Esse or Holy Spirit was the last and final anointing; this anointing of the Esse was passed to the Apostles.

Q. Can the Esse be experienced in other forms of movement besides body movement?

A. Yes. By the inward etheric movement, acting from the level of the involuntary nervous system, sensed by the flow of ultrasense in postures, energy masses, flows, effects, colors. By clarity of the emotions. By a state of joy or happiness. By an awareness of freedom from negatives in the Undersoul. By throwing off the negatives, the guilts and the oppressions. By the use of the soul-gifts of seeing and hearing. By special sendings. By acts of visitation. By mind strengths and control. By illumined consciousness. By wisdom dimensional understanding. By union with one's own hierarchy nature. By Spirit, as the power to will, to act, to do.

Q. Is it necessary to use a mantra to open the Esse?

A. The best mantra sounds aiding in the Esse opening are *La, La, La; Ha, Ha, Ha; Ah, Ah, Ah; Hyee, Hyee, Hyee, Hyee.*

Q. Is it necessary to use the pranic breaths to open Esse?

A. To breathe quietly and contemplate quietly the downpouring of the Holy Spirit Esse as a glorious happening, to make oneself receptive to the Holy Spirit by a stilling within meditation, followed by the Esse receptivity or movement will produce an Esse opening to God, to His World, His Word, and His Way. With practice, the opening to God through the Esse becomes continuous, unceasing. It is possible that in time one will remain in the Esse freedom at *all* times. The Esse movement will take command of the negations in the Undersoul in body, etheric, emotion, mind, producing a right order and perspective in soul, mind and body. This is the ultimate goal of the practice of the Esse. To be at one with Omnipresence in or out of the body or in whatever state one is in, is to become Niscient or Knowing.

Q. Can one open the Esse by visualizing mentally the sounds of La, La, La, Ha, Ha, Ha, Ah, Ah, Ah, Hyee, Hyee, Hyee, Hyee?

A. Yes. However, the mental Esse provides a depth of realization with different after-effects. One can expect a changing of the mind and certain depth in thought on spiritual levels with a mental Esse.

Q. What is the most prominent aspect experienced by the body movement in Esse?

A. The purging out of guilt, or freedom from the overloaded burdens within the subconscious; with the resulting effects upon all levels of consciousness; with greater dimensions in the etheric, emotional, mental and soul freedoms.

Body movement produces freeing health and joy. Etheric movement produces freeing of energy and knowledge of forces. Emotional movement produces freeing of love and self-knowledge. Mental movement produces freeing of Illumination of consciousness. All aspects of Holy Spirit are simultaneously expressed when Esse is wholly free through both sound and movement.

Q. Can one practice the silent Esse and draw upon the inward omniscient grace, and thereby produce a form of freedom in Holy-Spirit wisdom consciousness?

A. Yes. There are infinite variables one discovers by the Esse guidance which mentally accompany the use of Esse in primordial movement.

Q. Can music be used to open the Esse?

A. The directed Esse with external music used by the one Passing can be used as a preparation for the third and final aspect of the Esse. In this, one is opened to the *Word* as the silent music beyond the outer hearing, functioning in the inner audibles. The inner music flowing through the mind and emotions opens the primordial movement (Esse) which frees that which moves of itself. This final stage of the Esse occurs as the Supreme gift of grace whereby the Upa-Soul and the Undersoul become one in the One.

Q. Can one instantly obtain the third aspect of Esse by stepping over the preparatory phases?

A. Rarely is this possible. Only in event of one having opened Esse in former lives. All forms of Yoga, T'ai Chi, Dervish, sacramental dancing, or Pleasance are degrees or forms of Esse. The true Esse is primordial movement by and through the Holy Spirit. Primal movement as sensuousness produces untimely karmas. Primordial movement as Esse produces union with grace and with God.

Q. Is the Undersoul necessary?

A. The Undersoul is developed by the ego and the subconscious to buffer the excruciating trials of effort and struggle in physical life. However, if the negatives in life are not assimilated and transenergized into right actions, they accumulate as inert psychic masses of energy and pain-causing energies in the Undersoul. These energies appear in the body as sickness and in the mind as derangements.

Conscience functions as a correlated vehicle with the Undersoul. This causes regrets, remorse, depression, suffering, and if there is heavy congestion, produces violence, especially when there is a heated subconscious seepage into the mind and emotions. The mind is trained by years of ego-experimentation to resist correction first, and to accept the remedy secondly. This negativity accumulates as a form of immovable adamance within the Undersoul.

Q. Why must the Undersoul be cleansed or emptied out through Esse movement?

A. Due to the tamasic inertia and resistances to Law, to Soul, and to God, the ego and the subconscious form an egotistical shell which acts as a web-like oval enclosure mechanized to compulsive repetition of offenses. Undersoul acts as a mind and emotional vessel of sedimentized omissions and faults until these are rectified by prayer, meditation, mantra and movement.

A heated Undersoul causes psychic and physical suffering. A burdened Undersoul causes wrong decisions.

When the Undersoul functions in unison with the Upa-Soul, the Most High Soul and the Higher Self, the Hum of Divinity is free; one becomes as a Sun, free, in command of all the affiliated processes as an eternity system functioning in Universal unison with God.

The Upa-Soul is the bridge or Higher Unconscious connecting the Undersoul with the Most High Soul. In Sanskrit, it is called the *Antakarana*. The *Buddhi* or the Informing Principle through which one relates to God-Realization is centered within the Antakarana or Higher Unconscious.

Q. Again, I would like to know what is meant by the Intelligible Plasma or Ether?

A. The Omniscience of God lives and dwells in every particle, every atom, every wavelength of Will, Life, Light and Love. Man in lesser nature is nescient; Niscient or Knowing is the higher or hierarchy nature. God is Omniscient. Eternal Spirit as Supreme Consciousness is latent in every state of Will, Life, Light and Love.

The stuff of life, Ether or Plasma, is Omnisciently permeated with the Eternal Spirit of God. Supreme Consciousness is the directing power, the pregnating power, the revealing power and the creating power; and finally, in man, the cognition awareness of Spirit as the One.

Q. In the Niscience studies, it is stated that science will break through into the Omniscient realms and states of consciousness in the latter part of this century and the earlier part of the coming century. How is this made evident now?

A. The diversified soul-acceleration of crossing thresholds has begun to merge. Western religion as men have known it since the Reformation is to undergo a shaking and cleansing in preparation for a second mystic birth to the Christ.

Q. Is there a collective Undersoul?

A. Yes. The collective subconscious and the Undersoul are presently heavily burdened with fiery karmas. In all walks of life, inclusive of the religious life, the collective Undersoul and individual Undersouls are in the state of a fiery spill-out and overflow. The lower astral world is in a state of cogurgitation or expelling out. This occurs especially at this time in the tamasic and rajasic persons or conditions. Men of tamasic nature are heavily dependent upon family, society and governments. Men of lower rajasic natures live in a state of incessant rage against life and against everyone. These are the egos most affected by the Kali-Yuga trials. Sattvic souls of Bodhisattva dedication must bear the brunt of those who resist God. To keep balance in this period of Kali-Yuga ending, one must hold to God as the almighty grace and let not go.

Q. Are there periods or times when one has a more fulfilled receiving of the Esse than at other times?

A. Yes. There exists in all persons periods of cosmos or unifying sensitivity. Esse then may be received without any special mantra or meditation preparation. One comes to recognize one's own degrees of sensitivity by the Constant of God in the Esse. When the opening to Holy Spirit has occurred, Esse continues in various ways and happenings, always as a blessing, proving Omnipresence and the Intelligible.

Q. How does one reach primordial Esse?

A. By meditation stillness or semi-contemplation, then by calling upon Eternal Spirit to pour down His grace as Esse.

In the Esse practices, one may be either sitting or standing. The Holy Esse movement takes possession of both the motor and involuntary systems of the body. A movement beyond the ego-willing takes place. One then moves as the body moves without willing. The total Esse is an experience of movement moving itself. To explain further, one may recall times in the past when walking or running or even in a state of work a second wind came into the legs or another energy took over the body; this is the *happening* of the Esse in its primordial state. All in the earth have this third energy which is Intelligible and tireless as well as freeing.

When the mantra is said, and the movement begins, the practice brings joy, peace, freedom from guilt and anxiety. By this, a vehicle of sattvic nature is formed so that Upa-Soul can function directly as a vehicle for God.

Q. Is the Esse Gas of the Holy Spirit the same as the Pranas?

A. The Esse is the Holy Spirit directing all Pranas, which are purified and made more vital by the Holy Wind refinements of the Esse. There are several degrees of Prana which act as a chameleon-like state when directed by the higher mind using the Esse.

Esse acts as the Intelligible of the Holy Spirit using the highest of Pranas which ego thought or mind cannot manipulate.

Prana on the level of mind and the senses can be used as a will-obedient vehicle by the human mind.

Esse goes to that place where it is needed and does its work with the Intelligible which is out of the range of man's ego-mind willing. Esse acts as God-willing. Prana on the level of man's thought is used by the mind of man through breath. Esse is sent of God as the Holy Spirit function of His Spirit. One receives Esse by surrender to Eternal Spirit or God. Prana through the life force of Kundalini is an energy reservoir to be used by the will and mind of man for breath, for energies within limited units of measure.

Esse is unlimited; one cannot will it through the ego. Esse must enter through the door of the True Self and the Soul. The knowledge and mastery of Prana prepare one for the Esse flow.

Q. What is the difference between Eternal Spirit and Holy Spirit?

A. Eternal Spirit is that One called God. Holy Spirit or Esse is an Intelligible attribute of Eternal Spirit or God acting as sound, movement, ecstasy, revelation, bliss, peace, power.

Q. Is there any process on the physical plane or the realm of the senses to define or describe what the Holy Spirit or Esse is like?

A. In the Undersoul, energy works as condensed or inert tamas and also its opposite, rajasic voltage. Esse as Holy

Spirit Gas is as a superconscious Wind sweeping out the assimilative pressures of unused energy condensed within the Undersoul. Every negative act forms a negative energized mass within the oval-like sphere of the Undersoul. When thoughts and feelings flow through these darkened energies of the Undersoul, as they must, they are automated and repetitious, causing inevitable suffering. The Upa-Soul becomes as a fixed sphere eclipsed by the darkened state of its protege, the Undersoul, which by divine law should react as a conductor of holiness rather than its opposite, darkness.

Q. What form of energy may be used besides the primordial movements of Esse to free the Undersoul, and thus make it a free vehicle for the sun of the soul to shine forth in all states of being?

A. Selfless work without thought of rewards. Work, with some sweat. Creation with intense, egoless attentiveness. Service to God as a Karma Yoga. Also, householder stewardship. When these are used reverently, all spiritual practices of Light will go directly to aid in the cleansing of the Undersoul.

A mantram used before sleep each night produces dreams which work as cleansers for the Undersoul, whereby one is given courses in the Hall of Learning in the use of transenergization powers for the day.

Walking mediatively, opening oneself to the Esse concealed in Nature. To lift the veil of Nature through the Esse sight is to learn of the Source of health and of the joy given through true health.

The Esse takes one to the Source of life. The Esse state was the natural Edenic state before man fell into gravity. Esse is called forth in man as a freeing vehicle which he has neglected until now due to his intensity to experience all things with the earthbound senses.

The overflow periods of the Undersoul call forth into mankind and the individual the neglected, radiating Esse, sealed away through selfishness and lesser self. Esse, by the Will of God, is ready to be re-activated in man. Presently, the Esse states are appearing in the world as the desire pressing forth to go beyond religious experience into the spiritual Paths. All of this is evidence that Esse is now stirring, moving. The Passion of the Christ is now entering into the Undersoul darkness. As Jesus went down into hell in His Passion, in His Crucifixion hours, so must Esse now Pass into these downward cesspools of the neglected birthright where is hidden man's True Self supremacy under and in the Will of God.

Q. What is the most obvious happening proving that one has spilled out the Undersoul?

A. One gains perspective into the real motives in his underlying sense of character. One makes a leap from self-fantasy to survey himself from many dimensions. The past moves into his consciousness tabulated and resuscitated by a pure and undefiled conscience.

Q. From what range of consciousness is Reality experienced?

A. From Buddhi, the true center of the higher mind.

Q. Will this unrelenting survey into the Undersoul enable the clutter and debris to evaporate or be erased?

A. In part. One must look into all of his post-Esse emotional states, his desires. Through the practice of Marking and Tracing with detachment, one can slow down the rajasic, heated thought-forms in his thinking. In the spilling-out, Undersoul casts its unrest upward into the screen of the emotion and the mind. By standing back from this with a cool detachment, one can clear the Undersoul with total awareness. From this come humility, flexibility and chastity.

Q. How does one look upon the overall effect of Esse in the daily happenings?

A. As a leading and a pointing. As a unique form of guidance, often containing humor with some wisdom beyond one's sense of ego. Also, experienced as rising waves of warmth and revelation of movement in the emotions and mind.

Q. Is bliss awareness of the ego or the mind?

A. Bliss-wisdoms are the Selfless Self's way of revealing that the True Self is beyond ego. All cunning, contriving, getting the best of the deal, is on the ego level.

Q. Will it ever be possible to be without the ego that seems so concerned with its own survival?

A. The ego is the donkey and the Self is the rider of the donkey. In the progress ahead, the ego will become the willing servant for the Self. Though darkness seems to have settled on the world, the Holy City or upper reaches of the Heavenly are closer to men of the earth than they realize. This permeation of Heavenly forces is entering into the earthbound gravity thoughts of man. Through desperation men will open their hearts to one another and thus subdue and redirect their senses to Upa-Soul powers now ready to be born.

As long as men live in earth bodies, they will have need of ego-functioning as a descended one-life vehicle. Having gained a certain proficiency in repetition through sense dependence in many lives, ego is deluded that it is the self, that death will end that self, and that it is an all-sufficient vehicle. Thus is the illusion of the Maya veils working directly with the subconscious and the Undersoul. The ego is necessary as an earth-face or mask representing soul and self. Beyond the masks of countless egos experienced in former lives is the True Self, the Real, the One in the One. The opening to Holy Spirit is the grace of God where one goes above and beyond the ego and sees the True Self motivating all.

As the shining light shone so brightly through Jesus when He was transfigured and through the horns of Moses, so will the Self shine through the ego when the soul experiences God as grace through the Holy Spirit. Then will the ego become the server for Heavenly forces.

Q. How does one stand back of his ego and experience the Self?

A. By going Inward through prayer and meditation, one observes the contrivances and manipulations of the ego. Also, in the spirit of total dedication as to service and in periods of creation inspired by God, one stands back or away from the ego. The ego seeks always the short-cut avoiding truth, excluding conscience. Thus is the Undersoul fashioned by the expediency of self-desire for the lesser self at the cost of others and also, indirectly, for the true and basic interest of the True Self.

In the post-Edenic states, or after man took on a coat of skin, Undersoul was a subjective vessel having union with the inward laws in the etheric body. As man progressed in earth and became more egotistical and self-willed, the primal instinct in his purer sense was submerged subconsciously as *samskara fire*. This fire then became the substance for the Undersoul. In all creation, Undersoul fire is intelligible fire with sentience or sense recording.

Undersoul is built by the primal instinctual will for survival regardless of soul or God. The primal will was once a vital and healthy vehicle for the sense and preservation of man. In the present day, man has developed other faculties which are no longer a vehicle for the lower mind and for the untrained desires. Tooth and claw existence has been transformed to mind or mental competitiveness.

The ego is built from the false conceptions of self as

excelling or superior. Esse uses the transition energies between force and form to keep the trembling equanimity balance between death and birth.

As feathers cover the bird, as skin the body, so is the self covered by the shell of the ego. Through movement, as in the Holy Spirit dance, Esse goes in; ignites the core of the Undersoul. Pain, heat—all work to remove the klosha veils. To stand free in Esse, is to be free in nakedness with truth. Esse. Esse. Esse.

5

MOVEMENT AND MEDITATION

Instant polarization is through Jesus. He is the Door through which I have dominion in this Maya world and a Kingdom in the Heavenly Kingdoms.

I seek not a kingdom to rule; I seek the Kingdom to set aright the unruly within me. I am the leper who would be cleansed through Jesus. I am the blind who would see, the deaf who would hear, the insane who would be exorcised, free. I am all of those who persecuted Him, flogged Him, denied Him, cursed Him; I am all of these. Free me, O Lord, from Undersoul corrupting, that I may walk in Thy Light and become like Thee. Amen.

SYMBOLS WITHIN THE UNDERSOUL

Morality and movement are the perfect Divine order.

The Omnipotent-God Presence is the Omnipresence in all worlds existing and nonexisting. God is total perfection and unceasing movement. All forms of life are in a state of seeking to find perfection through a constant state of movement. That which man moves in ego-will is yet to be perfect, but that which compels him to move is perfect.

The Esse is the movement of the Holy Spirit in the soul of man, which makes him divine in the midst of his own unknowing. This divinity now seeks to make its presence known and to demonstrate the Divine for the whole of mankind. Having a voice to express the soul is the greatest of gifts given from God.

The door of symbology through movement is the way to escape the oppressive limitations in the physical world. One can do no more in the physical world than his emotions and mind will allow. It is thus necessary that all movement in the physical body be cognizable to the emotions and mind through which the Intelligible may function as a coordinating vessel for the Holy Spirit.

If one has offended the outpouring of Holy Spirit in his etheric nature, he is subjected to fevers or infections in the physical body. If his movement rhythms are statically yoked to his ego exploiting, the movement of the physical body will become as a black fire in the Undersoul, causing chronic suffering to the skeletal structure of the body system, which must be cooled by the yearning and longing for union with a God-purpose of the Spirit in him.

As long as men live in fragmented symbology, they remain inarticulate and separate. When the Esse or Holy-Spirit articulation is open, one steps back from the darkened Undersoul compulsions, viewing them with detachment as erratic and presumptuous against that which is the true nature in self.

Symbiosis is the uniting of all symbols in one moment of understanding as a flow of mind-energy illumination. This takes place in a Maha-matra or coinciding incident. The Undersoul is then cleared of ambivalence; by this means, the Undersoul is cleansed. Movement ignites the symbiosis, catapulting the one experiencing the Esse movements into transcendental wisdom, knowing or Niscience.

All of the gifts which men inherit from other men have

MOVEMENT AND MEDITATION 83

been given by those who have mastered movement within the darkened corridors of the Undersoul.

The Undersoul is a cogurgitating vehicle. When all symbols come together and explode in one understanding, one clears the field of the subconscious and draws upon the primordial first-wisdoms of transcendental light.

When one undergoes perceptive instruction under a Teacher having symbiosity, the result is a parabolic functioning in knowing. Dream codes, visualized symbols, meditative symbols, the genre (commonplace) or basic biological symbols, the metaphysical self-knowing symbols, the apparitional symbols, and soul-symbols—all become as one, providing a holy linguistic function of the mind beyond alphabets, beyond hieroglyphics, beyond ordinary articulation.

In the physical life at the present time, music is the only open symbiotic experience. More than music, however, there is the Holy Intelligible in each man, which contains the memory of what he is and why he is, and the vision also of where and what he is to be. The symbiotic language acting within the Coinciding Principle is the one tongue of the Holy Spirit, providing meaning, wisdom, guidance.

The practice of visualization through symbols, of mental contemplation in meditation, of keeping a dream diary, of Esse movement allegories interpreting mantras through spiritual dramas—these techniques are available to the initiate or the forming initiate on the spiritual Path.

Mantras, mantrams, symbols and movement act as a rare oxygen upon the clogged hydrocarbon states in the Undersoul to become the blue flame of Transcendental Illumination.

Sedimentized accumulation in the Undersoul, while in the lowest state, is tamasically rigid; in its secondary state, as rajasic, it is heated; in its third state, as Sattvic, it is illuminative, revealing. Intelligible continuity of spiritual mental flow with movement as unison between mind and emotions produces Niscience-knowing, transcendental wisdom. From this illuminative flow, great paintings are produced; great musics flow into the vibrations of hearing; Scriptures are written by which men live and assess their moralities.

A Free Consciousness

The Undersoul has a warning system of perils to come, whereby the lower mind is filled with the prophetic psychic sense of dread and apprehension.

The Divine Laws sealed-in into the inner parts or chakras from the beginning of this eternity system abide in the Upa-Soul, where these mighty Laws function as conscience and act as a sense of guilt in the Undersoul.

More sensitively organized than the brain is the Undersoul's functioning use of the memory. One side of the subconscious provides the power to forget one's evils. At intervals, the subconscious activates or quickens into the Undersoul the sharp and painful reminders of one's wrongdoing in past lives and in the present. Undersoul then functions as a gross articulation vehicle, initiating one into the fine and sensitive Upa-Soul truths which seek to create an unburdened condition.

The power of forgetfulness passed onto the Undersoul by the subconscious is experienced by one's failing to remember that he is more than the ego.

Western man of the present calls himself modern. This is the delusion of all eras and times of the past and the fate for some in the future.

Unbiased man of the East and the West encounters Time as the Timeless, the present as the Reality, and the future as the Eternal in which Space is the servant to Creation. Unbiased man is poised in Space and Time through immortal daring. Through immortal daring, one uses and utilizes the inquiring insight of a spiritualized intellect within infinite Godly dimensions.

The human condition has been created by and through the exploding and discovery aspect part of the soul. The human condition when relying on the ego is all intellect minus spirituality, having neither hope, promise nor definition for a future.

Hope, joy, enthusiasm and interest in life and its processes produce incentive, vitality and satisfaction. To know with awareness that all one is doing is within the Plan and Will of the Creator, assures beauty, harmony, peace, creativity and contentment. Egoless creation provides one's ship of the soul, which is charted to fly to horizons beyond primal automation.

A free consciousness recognizes all human situations as self-created. With this knowledge, one moves beyond the karmic Maya chain of cause and effect. Free to activate the uncreate, free to channel the unmanifest, one stands in the Archetypal Light. To be in the free-consciousness state of his hierarchy nature, one stands in his own illuminative light, beholding creation as fluidic and unceasing.

THE THREE SPHERES

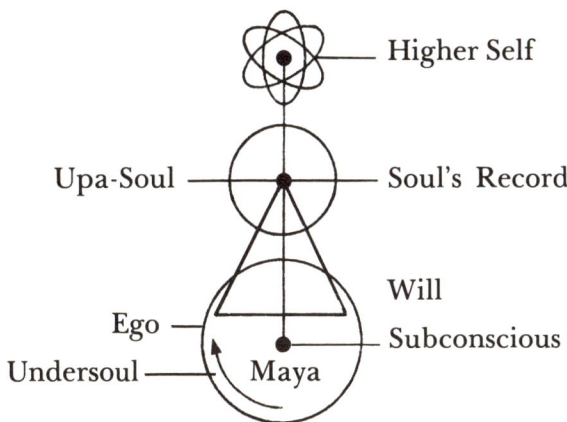

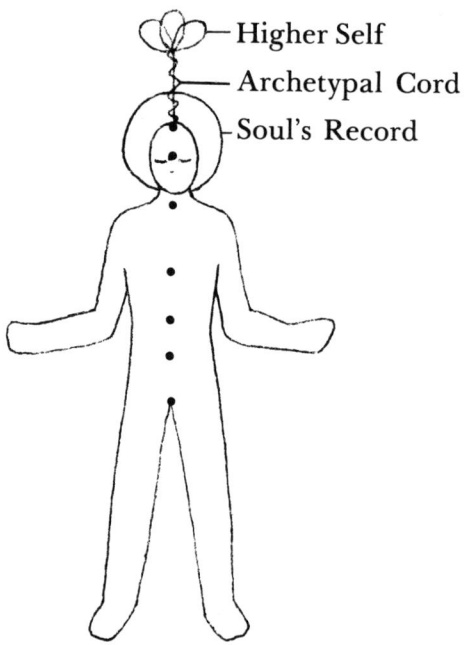

There are three energy spheres which relate to the developing birth and growth and fulfillment of man's spirituality as a unit of measure in the earth. The first sphere is the sphere of the Higher Self which contains the Eternal Sustaining Atom that makes man a deathless and immortal being. The second sphere is the sphere of the Upa-Soul which is the luminosity-nimbus of the soul's vibration around the head as related to the higher unconscious. The third sphere is the Undersoul sphere, the home of all ego reflections which contain all of the mechanical reactionary systems of former lives, ancestry and various personalities used by the ego.

The first sphere represents the Imaging Faculty of the Spirit, called Buddhi. The second sphere represents the Purusha or the Great Unconscious. The third sphere represents Maya, duality, or relativity cause-and-effect life between Spirit and soul, mind and soul, emotions and soul, body and soul. The three spheres, when working as one, produce happiness, bliss-joy and fulfillment.

The Undersoul is the *shadowed self.* The ego functions in the third or lowest sphere, wherein the Undersoul collects the debris of wrongdoing, non-doing, and fantasy astralocity. All omissions of mind, emotions and body are registered as samskara-seed karmic tendencies in the depth of the Undersoul where the subconscious reigns.

The outer consciousness mind, having as yet failed to form a perfect etheric vehicle for the mind, must suffer—through the ego—birth after birth until mind function can be totally free to use the two upper spheres freely and completely.

All evidence of things spiritual can come into the mind of man when he has cleared the Undersoul convulsions of karma registered and indented upon the labyrinth mirrors of the Undersoul. All of the unmanifested spirituality comes to birth by compulsion from the Higher Self and the soul pouring upon the collective subconscious sphere of the Undersoul.

Movement with dedication, devotion and selflessness enables one to make the Undersoul into a flawless vehicle whereby the function of the intellect becomes spiritualized; the ego becomes divine and one with soul and Eternal Spirit.

Units of Measure and Time

The number of Suns and Moons determines the mathematics of each eternity system.

If it were not for the soul's movement, mankind could not stand the rotation of the earth.

The less gravity in an eternity system, the less karma there is.

The light around the Higher Self is the inner galaxy

of the superconsciousness, where every atom is its own shining eternity system seeking to come to birth through earth-mastery.

The Holy Spirit works with the breath and with movement. Movement is freedom between Time and Space. Movement with meditation and the use of a mantra and the mandala rearranges the time-fixities within the Undersoul.

All Time is energy in units of measure. Every plane has its own system of timing and time measurement. There is an etheric scale of timing, the astral scale of timing, the mental scale of timing, and the spiritual scale of Timelessness. One must have coordinating and equal measures of Time in each of these planes before he can move beyond phenomena or relativity into Timelessness.

One earns the units of measure of Time in each plane through initiation in the physical world. The gravity clock of Time in the physical plane is the most difficult to master, as man wholly pursuing the physical life is sealed away from direct knowledge of the supernatural laws and eternal cyclic laws supporting the units of Time in Creation.

Man on the physical plane exists in the self-hypnosis of self-preservation and survival. Therefore, in his outer consciousness he has only conceptual knowledge of Time and the units of measure in life through his dependence upon his senses or sensory antennas. While living in the physical world, he is aware constantly of the danger of death, failing to understand the units of measure in the energy-processes of Time and Space. Knowing only his limited lesser self and its awkwardness, he restricts himself into centralized spheres of industry, thinking this to be the Real.

Men seek how to break the Time-barrier in the physical world so that they may master the Time-barrier in Space. Those who seek to thrust aside the Guardian *ring-pass-not* protectors of Time and Space court disaster, destruction.

Movement and Meditation

Presently, men are breaking the Time-barrier under the penalty of destruction, for they are ignorantly misusing Time-expenditure, or what is done with Time ethically. Those who are nescient are reacting to the limitless Time-barrier morality with barbaric attitudes and gross indulgence, thinking Time-barrier mastery to be rightful extension of their own sensual natures. Being unaware of the sacred use of Time and its responsibility, they face disaster, as they have intruded upon the elements and the cycled processes of Nature. The penalty for this intrusion is an insidious destruction faster than technology can meet or provide for.

Truth works with Time in this eternity system. No one can repress Truth when it comes to Time. The spiritual aspirant and disciple begins his spiritual life by observing the cycled Time-processes in his Soul and Undersoul.

There is a rajasic Time-scale, a tamasic Time-scale, and a sattvic Time-scale. To have the hierarchy-nature visualizing power is to move beyond Time. Fulfilling the duty of the moment is the healing of the past and the promise of a perfect future.

Anyone who experiences a minute sunbeam's tip of light into the interterrestrial is free. He becomes aware that he is in the Earth bringing a Hierarchy cargo. Knowing neither Space nor Time, he is free in God.

Meditation moves one beyond gravity timing. When one meditates upon the universals, he steps out of Time and Space into Universal Creation.

Prayer works with Time and timing. Meditation works with Timelessness. When one unites Time and Timelessness, he is a whole person in the body of God while living in this earth.

Prayer creates the future. Through prayer, man has in his hands the power to create the future.

Seeking to speed up one's perfection in meditation offends

timing. A passional nature puts too much fire into meditation; the result is friction and aggression challenges in the outer life. Meditation of the highest order is gentle, relaxed, delicate, soft, pure, revealing rather than tension expending. The approach to meditation is stillness, with total freedom from force, anxiety or ambition.

Post-meditation cleansing-results appear in the congested areas of the body, revealing congesting energies in a particular mind and emotion flow, such as lungs, heart, womb, head, feet, hands, back, shoulders.

Seeking to be ahead of Nature in the use of body energy creates death to the lower bodies while in the body. This results in withdrawal of supporting life-force energies in certain sections of the body: deafness, vision, limbs, hands, heart, lungs.

When one starts meditating, the two hemispheres of the brain come closer together until finally they interlink as a Great Dome. Then all mental attributes and spiritual faculties unite *equally,* making a person a whole being.

Every meditation is seeking to make this fusion between the two hemispheres of the brain a reality. When this happens, the Omniscient Cell within the brain functions; man becomes a greater dimensional being while living in the earth; his mind is as the Jesus Mind.

The crown of the head coincides with the apex point of the Galaxy Gate from which one is united with Cosmos. When the Yin and Yang hemispheres of the brain interlace, Buddhi, the Informing Principle in the higher mind, becomes active; one is no longer fixed to eternity-system or Time-relativities. He is Galaxy-related. Buddhi will then interpret to him what exists in his own Galaxy nature.

When one has rigidity in habits, he is in an enclosure of Time-limitation. The spiritual life begins with the change of habits. Transenergization of faulty habits propels one into the vital and vigorous Time-ranges of the Infinite; thus, he learns of the Cosmic.

Being on time; keeping a vow; making a sankalpa resolution and keeping it—are part of the initiatory process in the use of the units of Time. Punctuality leads one right to the Now of service to God.

Keeping a dream diary; using the counterclockwise introspection dusk-technique; fulfilling all physical duties creatively in the use of Time; eating one's meals when the true palate announces hunger—all of these processes are the ways and means through which one comes into Timelessness.

Keeping one's spiritual practices without fail; attending worship on time; prayer and holding in the Light to reverse the flow of sickness—are processes in the use of Time. Buying and purchasing on right days and in right hours; selling and planning through blueprints in right timing—also are part of the process of timing and use of the units of Time.

New Moon and Full Moon meditation; observances of the Equinoxes and the Solstices; using the full value of the Moon's influences in timing to one's own natal or rising sign; the giving of tithes on the Sabbath and on the New and Full Moon; the use of the meditative tides in the five periods of the day—these units-of-Time processes enable a person to be Timeless and to be ever aware of the eternal clock whose energy-governors for this eternity system are the Sun, the Moon and the planets.

Marking and Tracing as to the lunar cycles and the planetary energies affecting growth in consciousness are an infallible way to come into timing and the full use of the units of measure.

The negative use of the units of Time are: fearing death, fearing failure; wrong success-attitudes; egotism; feeling of superiority; failing to take advantage of human goodwill; miserly in the hoarding of money; imprudent in the stewardship of money; making of debts with little or no moral collateral; resenting others or blaming them for one's own failure; cursing; gossiping; slandering; misuse of property or possessions; desiring to inherit from those who have earned; living without earning; expecting society to support one; failing to keep contracts, marriage, business, professional; failing to listen; nonattentiveness; refusing training or teaching or instruction; disobedience; frittering away moments, hours and days in useless dreaming or dreams; fantasy astral-thinking; non-realistic self-esteem; under self-esteem; over self-importance; hypersensitivity; ingratitude; impatience; fearing change; non-acceptance of change; refusing to see another's view-point; failure to create in some manner each day.

Procrastination is a sin. People sense that a procrastinator will not keep his promises; therefore, they do not listen to him or keep their promises to him. A procrastinator must learn from his own deviation that he is contagious to others through his neglect, until finally he meets a greater procrastinator than himself and learns the major lesson of dutifulness to the Profound Law: Truth has no variation; the straight way is the way of Truth.

One has to pay Time back to those from whom he has taken Time illegitimately.

A person who has not found his creation is living in a state of semi-death. The spiritual, self-disciplined life keeps the vital flow of the etheric body alive.

The Destroying Archetypes are regulated to destroy through the Time-system in this eternity system. Man's Time-mechanism is presently being overstimulated by the Luciferic or Satanic Archangel, inspiring people to sit at the feet of the media, or TV, and to be held hypnotically into the dramas of violence. These dramas implant samskara-seeds of evil suggestions and motivations into the receptivity of the present or modern aspect of the subconscious of the individual and of the world.

The Ancient of Days, one of the Fathers, influences timing and Time. He works with each person's Recording Angel in allotting the soul-earned units of Time.

Under the Ancient of Days, the great Recording Angels, the personal Recording Angels, and the Cherubim, man is a unit of Spirit working with a soul. Eternally created within a Time eternity-system, he uses his soul-powers according to how many Suns or Moons govern the Earth system in which he dwells.

All Angels are knowers of the Time system; they work with Time, as man works with breath. The inward work of the Angels in turning their faces to God and their faces toward man is as the inhaling and exhaling breath of their life. Were it not for the Angel mediation, man could not sustain the point of union with God.

Angels are continually *inhaling* man's need within the Presence of God, and *exhaling* the answer of God back to the souls of men. The Name *God-Presence* is continually in the breath-flow of angelic inhalation and exhalation.

ENERGY PLAY OF ESSE AND THE UNDERSOUL

Almighty God, Omnipresence in all,
pour down upon me Thy Holy Esse. OM.

The Esse movement brings Release. Every time a person releases something — be it of the mind, the emotions or the body — Space with its Cosmos electricities becomes superior to Time, and the Angelic Seraphim Higher-Mind electricities can flow into the mind. The Seraphim electricities are of the higher cosmic order. These provide supreme and eternal cosmic and Archetypal ideas. Thus, when one meditates in a perfect quiet, the relaxed electricity within gravity-timing magnetisms permits the higher or timeless flow of Space to enter in. One is then in communion with the virginal unmanifested or uncreated Archetypal ideas—brilliant as diamonds, scintillating, pure, and crystal-like. This is Illumination as a reality, as a scientific confirming by factual observation and experience.

Meditation is relaxed mind electricity. With the single eye during meditation, one observes the gross and subtle energy play of the Undersoul. The single-eye contact fulfills the law of balance between meditation and movement.

Meditation is of the Holy Light; movement is of the Holy Fire. Fire in the Chakra Gate between the eyebrows is called *Agni* in Sanskrit. Agni without spirituality burns. With *pure desire* as love, one is spiritualized; Agni then can function as Esse or the Holy Spirit Gas.

To be free in Esse is to experience purity as Light, and freedom in soul movement and body. Esse is joy liberated into Consciousness. Esse produces God-awareness in the physical and in the transcendental states of consciousness.

An Esse person is God-Realized in each second of the day and the night. God-Realization exists in a state of cognizance and awareness of God as Omnipresence in all planes, kingdoms and dominions.

Through the Esse activities and practices, a dismal outlook on life is transformed into humor, purity in reasoning, honesty in self, and a practicality in proportion to the needs of life. Through movement conjoined with meditation, one comes into command of the Esse energy play affecting each body: the physical, the etheric, the astral or emotional, and the mental.

An open or uninhibited character expression is manifested by *Marking and Tracing*. Niscience is based upon the Marking and Tracing techniques that enable one to experience his frame of consciousness within the Greater Archetypes. One who works within the Greater Archetypes becomes a "Nisciene" beyond nescience or unknowing.

The first phase of movement experienced by man in the development of his consciousness is experienced in dreams. One should use the technique of Marking and Tracing that he might become fully aware of the third language — symbology — given to him by our Father in Heaven. To articulate his outer life happily, he should avail himself of the dream-symbology language.

To practice the Marking and Tracing techniques, one should:

1. Keep a Dream Diary. Research the Greater Archetypal and Moving-Archetypal myth-symbols.

2. Research the *code-rules* in dreams.

3. Each month's Dream Diary should be reviewed at the end of thirty days. Once a month, one should review the condensed dream-record — from the present, going backwards to the first of the month.

4. He should contemplate any dream-record emphasis correlating to past lives and to present ethic or motives.

5. He should seek to identify the model figures or ideas pertaining to the Saviour or religious aspects in dreams. He should review the antagonist-figures in dreams; promises in dreams.

6. He should keep records as to repetitive dream codes.

7. He should weigh his conscience against correction in dreams. He should record the Conscience teaching aspect in dreams. By this he will give freedom to the cleansing of the Undersoul through *natural grace* as provided by God; for that which is energized into outer-life resolution through dreams is called *"natural grace."*

In the dream-life exploration through the understanding of the Undersoul and the mighty cleansing and healing power of the Esse, one truly *sees*. *"Wherefore by their fruits ye shall know them."* (St. Matthew 7:20)

To *see* in the Esse is to be divine. To *know* in the Esse is to be found in the Kingdom—free in all worlds, all planes, within the Plan and Will of God.

Life is a dance attuned to the Universal sound of the Word. Listen with the heart. Hear what the music saith. Hear, and be free. Esse. Esse. Esse.

The Holy Liquids of the Bhakti

One draws the atomic energies from the etheric atoms which exist in the physical-body duplicate or sheath. One draws a certain kind of liquid from the astral atoms existing in the etheric body. These liquids are gel-like; they are controllable with power received through meditation, and come directly from the higher-will nature working with the emotions.

If there is full Bhakti love, this liquid is available to drown out the psychic-matter nature. In this state of liquid emotionality, one receives knowing beyond the intellect. He has the power to flow his blessings from the inward-heart Bhakti nature; the power to heal; and especially to encase his energy fields from psychic attack of alien minds or hate-telepathies. He thus becomes invulnerable to negative psychic voltage.

The emotional body atoms, when free to work with the will, enable a person to be at one with his creative hierarchy nature, whereby he builds through his ego without offense. The will of a Bhakti Initiate becomes a fluidic matrix for hierarchy nature to heal. The higher mind of a pure and true Bhakti Initiate functions through bliss-knowing.

As men move toward the ending of the present moving archetype, called by certain schools in India the Dwapara age, men will become more and more aware of the need to spiritualize their intellects.

In the present time and era, all that science has produced as technology has been produced through the intellect. The intellect is a limited vehicle. It is limited to a discovery side of the energy processes in the world and in the mind.

Science will never understand soul or spirit until the mass intellects in the world spiritualize individually their intellects. A spiritualized intellect provides the bridge whereby one moves beyond the 4th dimension into the 5th and thus becomes free to discover dimensions which presently do not register in the world of the senses and the intellect.

It is necessary for man to develop his Bhakti nature or love nature. By this he spiritualizes his intellect.

The first work of the seer is to explore and command his own nature. Space will never be conquered or utilized on the energy scale of the planets until one discovers his own units of measure, and thereby enters into the illimitable.

The liquid of the emotional or astral body correlates to the liquids in the physical body. If one is acid in his expression of love, he has in his emotional body hatreds and conflicts. His emotions being immature, it is impossible for him to even comprehend the enlargement of his own emotional and mental nature.

Religions that depend upon conceptual or theological knowledge fail to give instruction as to the soul. Such restrictions prevent one's individual encounter with his soul nature.

The emotional body is the body through which one enters the door in his seeking God. To depend on the instinct to interpret God, is to be disconnected from the language of the soul which is seeking to speak to the emotional nature.

Man's going through the door of liquid or baptism is his

first encounter with his soul nature. Baptism as purification is a natural process and necessary that one may know himself to be redeemable. However, there is a greater baptism which occurs through different intervals in the Bhakti or Love emotional nature. In this, one encounters the will initiations which control the elixir liquids in the emotional body.

Selfless will in the emotions prepares the way to open the will of the mind, whereby the hierarchy nature can will and create within the Will of God. When the fluidic matrix of the will is free within the emotions, one has unusual access to primordial water, sound and color.

The fluidic matrix of the will works as ecstatic vibration in the emotions. The astral or emotional body, when vibrating in its very high state of Bhakti or Love, is power. The Esse or Holy Spirit enters into the Bhakti nature when it has achieved the primordial water, color, sound; these vibrations give access to the soul need for those in the environment and for the true nature seeking to express God.

Movement in the highest vibrational state of the emotional body created as love produces movement for the mind to outpicture the true and archetypal design and Will of God.

When the Esse Holy-Spirit movement is used in the world, these holy-liquid vibrations go forth. The elixirs become the vapor for the Esse to function as a Holy Gas. Color becomes the intermingling, whereby all things are as one in feeling and in knowing.

The Esse Movement as action in the body during a period of realization in the Will of God produces vibrations into all areas of the world, increasing faith in God, faith in His Power, faith in His Will. Guidance directly in the Will of God comes when one is in the state of the Esse movement.

Movement and Meditation

It is the rule of creation that all things begin with the will followed by the life. It is the rule in man's spiritual development that the Will of God as life begins in the emotions, followed by guidance, by revelation in the mind.

In the power of Imaging through the hierarchy nature, one begins with the Esse through the emotions. The natural ensuing process is guidance and revelation in the mind.

To be a vehicle for the Esse, and to build the protective shield against the psychic-matter nature residing in the Undersoul, one feels through the love nature and the emotions, thereby using the holy liquids of the Bhakti.

In the movement of the Esse as movement awareness, one becomes a holy spectrum of colors far beyond the spectrum man knows with his physical eye. From this, the vibrations of color within the holy liquids are taken over by the Holy Esse. The mind functions as a will matrix for the higher mind. One becomes Niscient or Knowing. The Esse movement then becomes the true dance of the ecstasy the hierarchy nature envisions and knows.

In the Process of the functioning hierarchy nature through the movement of the Esse, one first overcomes the dark waters of the emotions; he purifies them through movement to the pure holy liquid of love and life. This next becomes the spectrum of holy colors beyond the range of human sight. From this comes the inner ecstatic movement; the will matrix for the mind is formed. Hierarchy nature begins its creation. Within the Absolute Will of God, hierarchy nature envisions *that which is going to happen.*

Mercy is the countenance for forgiving. Mercy flows from the Bhakti liquid. There can be neither mercy nor forgiving expressed unless one contains the Bhakti liquid manifesting as pure love in the heart.

From the Great Teachers, one is exposed to the true

Bhakti love. From Jesus, most of all, are men in the earth assured that they are loved. From the great Archangels, the Bhakti flow of God's Love is given as special grace.

As long as one retains antagonisms, hatred, separateness, he is feeling through the intellect. It is therefore necessary to spiritualize the intellect. The first aspect of this is non-judgment. To retain the analytical mind without judgment is to be in the state of the spiritualized intellect.

All Esse movement must be entered into in the spirit of surrender to the Will of God. By this, the holy liquids come forth and erase the condemning aspect of the intellect. The more Esse movement as a vehicle for God-directed guidance, the less critical mind, the less condemning and separation. The more surrender, the more love nature of the hierarchy nature in the Will of God is expressed.

If a religion does not carry the liquid Bhakti, its baptism cannot be true. The liquid Bhakti, producing mercy and forgiveness, gives to him who is immersed in the waters of the Holy Spirit true redemption.

The Passion of Jesus through which the Passing comes must return to the altars of religion. It is necessary in this era that men are confronted with their souls and understand their love natures.

The temple, the church, the synagogue and the sanctuary — these are but the cairn stones whereby the desire to worship is verbalized. But if there be worship of ecclesiastical formats, of dogmatically instituted rituals, the holy-elixir waters cannot flow there. The psychic-matter nature functions in all dogmatic, dualistic, creed-bound religions. The canals or conduits of the holy waters being cemented away by creedal pride, this builds the acid water, producing tamas stagnation and pollution.

The return of the Holy Esse as a correcting fire into the altars is now to create ecclesiastical differences, controversies and arguments. The "principalities and powers" overdirecting the creedal separateness will make a greater space between creeds. These creeds are being expanded out, that they might be contracted in, whereby the Holy Spirit may lift those who have chosen separateness into the enlargement of the holy vision of oneness.

Pride on the altar is of the satanic. Men in the world have reached the time where they come under the greater Will of God. Separateness is to become non-separateness.

Theological edicts founded upon dogmatic interpretation of the Holy Spirit are no longer responding to the great Soundless Sound or the Archetone of the Holy Spirit.

Those who speak with the tongue of the world from the altars of religion fail to unite with the sound of the Holy Bhakti uniting all. Men speaking of the Law from the altar and failing to understand the Law cannot interpret it to him who would live within the Law, nor can those who seek bread be fed by primroses or seasonal tidbits appeasing human frailties.

The true Bread which resounds the Music of God through the Spirit of the Holy Esse must be returned once again to the Holy Spirit within the Eucharist. And the true Wine which keeps alive the buds on the vine of worship and desire to be whole within the human spirit must be offered once again from the crucible of life eternal and everlasting.

The smokescreen of science which has obscured man from God must now bring forth the archetypal vision out of its substance. On the screen of space discoveries will be inscribed once more the Face of God. The avalanche of the Archetypal Plan of God will come out of season to man but in season to God and His Angels.

When the Spirit of God moves upon the face of the waters or upon the life substance or the nature of God, men are shaken, sifted, changed in the twinkling of an eye. The twinkling-of-the-eye mystery is revealed to him who sees God in every atom, in every molecule.

Light is the vehicle through which man sees; therefore, there must be more of Light. To him who would see God, he must have an eye filled with the likeness of God within the Light.

The Higher Self is the likeness of God. The Imaging Power of the hierarchy nature gives the use of the Light within the Likeness.

When one enters into a place of worship and sees the Light of God as the Omnipresence, he has moved beyond creed or dogma. He has dematerialized the walls and boundaries of the temple, church. He has entered into that point of Light where worship lives without end; worship of God as the Spirit of Truth; worship of God as the Will; worship of God as the Life; worship of God as the Light and the Love.

On going to worship the One and True God, one leaves his guilts and darkness outside of the Temple, and takes his good as the offering rather than his sins. He who takes the Holy Sacrament, offering his good as service to God within the knowing of God as Good, fills a church or place of worship with the Holy Light.

That which teaches on the altar when not filled with Light cannot give instruction. And that which speaks from the altar and gives not Life cannot heal. And that which speaks not Love on the altar cannot free.

A worldly partisan altar irritates the love nature of man in his place of worship. An unrealistic emotional fervor from the altar cannot send forth the sheep prepared to meet the wolves of this world.

It is said in the Scripture that he who serves the altar is set apart from other men. This being so, if faith is weak or wavering in that one serving the altar, he brings a message of harmfulness. He sows the seed of dissent, rather than the seeds of peace and union. He who is a wholly Bhakti vehicle for God, in full sincerity and the Spirit of Truth, carries with him the heavenly cements of the Holy Liquids of Love whereby anxiety and grief and weakness are healed.

If there is grace of the Holy Esse on the altar, the religiosity nature of those who worship will undergo spiritual experience with the sacred hour and time of worship. Such congregations are needed in this world.

The downpouring of the Holy Spirit in this present time of victory over the Kali-Yuga darkened materialistic mind will bring the return of the Holy Esse to the altars.

The Third Music will be heard by him who will be a tongue for the Holy Spirit. In the hushed, stilled quiet of prayer, contemplation and meditation, one will experience the Holy Wind of the Holy Ghost or the Esse.

In the present time, the Passion of Jesus is seeking to be the Passing of the Holy Spirit in worship places and in the hearts of men. *"He that hath an ear, let him hear what the Spirit saith unto the churches." (Revelation 2:11)*

The Maya liquid of the earth keeps alive the psychic-matter nature functioning in the Undersoul. The psychic-matter nature functions through tension. When one moves into spiritual practices, he moves into deeper degrees of vibration, which are extended beyond the psychic-matter nature.

The psychic-matter nature is stilled by the Bhakti water. Love is the power through which healing comes. The Bhakti water is the Love expression of the Love of God which healeth all.

The psychic-matter nature thrives on fear and apprehension. When self-survival is first, the psychic-matter nature uses fear as a form of prophetic apprehension. When the Bhakti love-nature liquids are free, psychic-matter nature is immediately placed into another gear shift in its functioning; psychic-matter nature becomes an energy used by the Bhakti nature of love. Thus, all spiritual persons seek to activate in their natures the Peace of the Bhakti, to still psychic matter and psychic nature existing within the karmic states of fate.

To take hold of one's psychic-matter nature with awareness, to see it as a volatile, useful energy, to create the earth for God rather than to build for self—is to be a true and holy servant of God.

All is moving. The hierarchy nature is at home with the movement of the Holy Esse. The hierarchy nature cannot be free or fulfilled in the movement in the psychic-matter nature. The hierarchy nature, when free, uses the psychic-matter nature as a servant, and thereby transposes that which is low into that which is high.

6

ESSE IN ACTION

Esse. Esse. Esse.
God Is. God Is.
God Is. God Is.

DIFFERENT KINDS OF ESSE

   Walking Esse
   The Single Esse
   Esse for Self-Healing
   Esse Movement for Prospering
   Esse to Unburden the Undersoul
   Sitting Esse
   Esse to Heal Another or to Bring World-Peace
   Apology Esse
   Scriptural Esse
   Group Esse

WALKING AS ESSE MOVEMENT

Man, being created of God, is an heir to this ball of Earth and its planetary systems and forces. There are periods, however, when he becomes an heir to more than Earth extension of consciousness. In these periods he returns to his God-nature and relates to God directly.

The system of Maya, called by the Hindus *illusion,* is in

reality a play of energy-forces through which the elements play upon the senses of man hypnotically, inducing him to feel that what his senses interpret is reality. In this period or era when the Greater Archetypes are being opened to man, he is beginning to stand back from these illusions so that he may directly see and know God as Omnipresence.

In the practice of Esse movements, one becomes free from the Undersoul compulsions which are primal, ancestral, and individualistically karmic. These compulsions rule the life of the average person in the world, controlling the outer-self nature, emotions and thoughts. Average man is totally unaware that he is a mechanized vehicle ruled by forces which he has as an ego-self set up through aeons in time in the developing consciousness.

Presently, the downpouring of the Greater Archetypes from the Great Unconscious, or the Purusha, is falling into earth-mind consciousness. Thus, man must encounter the compounded energies representing his ego and the Undersoul.

Through Undersoul awareness, one moves beyond the self that moves the furniture or events of life and sees it all as unlasting and limited. Within the *Essence* of God and through the *Esse* as Holy-Spirit knowing, observation and proving, one takes hold of his Undersoul energy-processes, making them into an energy-field of higher receptivity of learning, knowing and experiencing.

The key to the command of the Undersoul through the Esse movement occurs in various processes: Meditation, Mantram Speaking, Prayer, Movement, Creation, Music, Work as creation. These are perfect ways through which one moves beyond the frightening and repelling aspects of Undersoul assimilations.

By *meditation* one changes his auric energy-velocities into a stilled awareness of God as Spirit, as the One in All.

By *movement* through walking, T'ai Chi, Yoga, and the Esse movements of the Higher Unconscious in the etheric body, one transenergizes the Undersoul stuff into a lucid reflector of the true aura which emanates from the hierarchy nature within the Higher Self.

By the virtue of regulated *prayer* for others and their betterment, for prospering and health, one detaches the craving, clawing and clinging attachments to ego and to ego-claim, and becomes selfless.

By *right walking,* one overcomes the gravity downpulls of the atomic force-fields which cause the body to decay more rapidly and to respond to the death suggestibles. Through walking one unites with the Deva Kingdom or Shining Spirits, whereby he steps out of encasement laws beyond the time-limit's use of energy. Walking frees man from bondage to the Maya kingdom where he is pounded by the suction of the polarity alternates.

Walking is the key to polarizing the four bodies. Walking acts as a grounding vehicle for the four bodies, enabling these bodies to function as mind masters of gravity.

Walking is connected directly with the Intelligences within the Informing Principle which provides the solutions to healing, to the eating of food, to the solving of problems. A walker who walks mediatively unites with the All-Intelligence which is cradled in Nature.

A person running does not enter into mediation solutions; or a person walking just to get somewhere does not unite with solutions. Only one who walks mediatively with the love of walking—by repetition and hunger to walk as a mediative experience—receives the mediative solutions which are prevalent or provided by the wind, the sun, the air, the earth and the waters.

The restlessness of the mind is the product of the ego and the Undersoul. One should walk not aimlessly as going nowhere, but should walk with awareness of a companionship which is a part of his holy destiny.

The feet and the dirt are brothers; the feet and the asphalt are enemies. In walking, each time the heel hits the asphalt, there is electrical stricture in the bones. This is gross, unnatural friction, affecting the bony system. Every time the metatarsal arch beneath the toes touches the asphalt, this is an alien friction to the heart, the liver and the spleen.

Muscle built from running on asphalt may be likened to a suspended bridge with faulty undersupports. Sooner or later, muscles so energized will overdraw upon hormone reinforcements in the body, causing nervousness and mind tensions.

It is the ego that runs on the asphalt. It is the pure portion of the automation of the self that seeks living dirt of the earth to run upon. This is natural gravity motorized by healthy acquisition of Nature's good.

Playgrounds for children with asphalt or concrete base interfere with the natural etheric flow of growing. Posture problems and nervous irritation especially affect children who habitually run and play in asphalt areas.

Plant life and the grasses are a carpet provided by God for man. Nutrients taken from the earth in gravity-processes enter into the accelerated blood stream of those who run upon the earth. Breath sustaining, respiration and the circulatory system, all benefit by walking and running on earth, grass, sand.

When men become aware of the destructive side of walking and running on asphalt, there will be laws forbidding this practice. This will take two generations to occur.

Man must bring back his true life; he must return his earth to his life through right food, right posture, right work. In the use of the body, he will claim the etheric perfection seeking to come into his physical body in the Self-Genesis state.

ESSE IN ACTION

Everything man does in the West is colored by excess. When this is mentally and emotionally regulated, one returns to the inner-parts laws which govern his health and development.

In the world there are special polarized energy-fields. Eventually, every initiate will find his pole-point or energy-field whereby he will function effortlessly for God in realization of the processes of his own nature and of Nature.

Today in the world, city life offers little opportunity for units-of-measure walking. Pounding a sidewalk overshadowed by columns of man-made, obscuring monuments will only add to the Undersoul astral stereo sounds and voices of countless aches, groans, pains, and suffering stemming from the agonies of man's greed.

Everything experienced by man in the world is recorded. If his experience is spiritual, it is recorded in the heavenly archives of things immortal and eternal. Such spiritual records are deathless, leaving the hallmarks for self and others to come. There are hallmarks of the soul and there are priceless treasures of the soul.

The record of the ego's adventure in earth from reincarnation to reincarnation is recorded in two energy fields: one energy field is in the Undersoul and the other is in a vibratory hum around the head. In certain periods, these vibrational movements of negative recording become static, fixing mankind into a suffering. Mankind as a whole then suffers in the collective subconscious and conscience levels of the Undersoul. This is presently happening in the world. All the world is suffering in a conjoined agony so that it may come to birth and utilize what ego has done and, especially, be aware of the automatic processes of Undersoul suggestibility.

There are few persons in the world strong enough or brave enough to truly and honestly face their Undersoul realities. To those responding to such knowledge is given the responsibility and the techniques whereby they may prove that the suggestive deceptions of the Undersoul are unsatisfying to life expression. Through spiritual-movement exercises, one ceases to be victim to his own circulatory and periodicity forces in the Undersoul.

FREEDOM

The Western world is polarized to the Christ. Man experiencing God-Realization through the Christ is the heir to the Kingdom of Light. The spiritual polarities supporting the religions of the East presently are changing. The Western disciple and initiate is entering a period of time when he will produce new vitalities of the soul never before used by man.

In this chaotic time of crossing currents, men of the West who look toward spiritual realization are caught into the karmic mass enforcement of death to the traditional approaches to the Christ and birth to the Great Unconscious flowing from the Christ.

Movement in the ego's development is presently being restricted. The agricultural era, the industrial era having ended; and the energy between continent and continent, planet and galaxy opening—have been presented to man as a paradox. More and more, he is prevented from the use of space in his own environment due to crowding and over-population; being forced to step out of old freedoms as to limited expression, he is asked to do two things simultaneously: To make his life more profound personally in a smaller space and to provide his inner consciousness with the space he is oppressing outwardly. Thus, he must go inward for space, or move or take a leap outward. By this he will liberate his true nature, his true self, and relate himself to a spaceless and timeless mind structure.

The Esse movement given through the Great Unconscious by the Holy Spirit is a gift from Holy Spirit. To move within the Esse frees one from the tightened psychic tensions and atmospheres which are proving so devastating to body and to soul.

The Esse movement can be used singly for self. It can be used in company to suitable music. All music composed in this period, such as rock and country music, relate to the astral currents. Therefore, this music is not recommended to be used in conjunction with the Esse movement.

The Esse must never be taken or interpreted as exercise or as fun or as frenzy. It must be approached reverently with an awareness that the Great Unconscious will come forth when one through receptivity opens himself to the Third-Music movement of the soul.

While the Esse movements may be looked upon as therapy by those thinking through psychology, it is not a therapy. However, its results are always therapeutic, healing, opening, revealing.

The Esse movement is a spiritual practice which is provided by the Great Unconscious, which awaits to speak through all moving forms of life. If there is a problem in one's life creating emotional or mental fixity, through the Esse movement one relaxes; the solutions to problems come in the after-flow of the Esse movement. Friendships, hospitality, love expression beyond the erotic, come forth as the result of the Esse flow.

Meditation before an Esse, if possible, assures one that his meditative moments will be outpictured into actual circumstances in life.

The sweetness one produces from activating an Esse is an attracting sweetness which will bring to the one using this practice joyful correlationships through friends, through work, through creation.

The Single Esse

The single Esse is practiced by one person. One can do this Esse inside his home or in his garden and seek to make, while doing the movement in the Esse, a leap, freeing the emotions, building joy. If this is not possible due to some physical condition, one should move moderately in the Esse, with no form of exaggeration or of outdoing himself.

An Esse is not for excitation; it is for freedom, freedom of the Higher Unconscious which is seeking to speak and to cast out all of the restricting habits one has enclosed himself into by years of practice, of resistance, of fear.

If Esse is enacted in the home, be sure there is plenty of space and room for movement.

One should never overpractice an Esse. He should let his Unconscious flow with acceptance and receptivity. He will learn that its own volatile energies have their own Time-limit and spacing. He will know when he has had enough, unless he is using the Esse as a pressured, passionate, zeal function which is harmful and destructive.

It is always important to remember that an Esse is a quiet time of the soul designed to give freedom to the movement of the soul, which in turn teaches and heals.

Esse for Self-Healing

Posture: Stand. Stretch out arms. Feel the inner flow of the Unconscious. Start moving left to right in a circle. Let the movement take the body with complete reliance upon the Holy Spirit. Speak this Mantram as you begin the movement. Also speak it at intervals during the movement.

> *Healing in me*
> *Becomes the*
> *Healing free.*

Esse.
Esse.
Esse.
La La La, Ha Ha Ha, Ah Ah Ah,
Hyee Hyee Hyee Hyee.

When the movement has concluded, give thanks to the Father. Return to sitting position, retaining freeing joy of the experience.

If desired, meditate. If not, retain the reverence in actions of the day.

If possible, record in your diary or journal after-effects in the expansion of your consciousness. Behold new viewpoints, greater dimensions in realization.

ESSE MOVEMENT FOR PROSPERING

This Mantram can be used before a Self Esse Movement if one desires to prosper or to overcome lack or want.

I reaffirm my
soul-power of prospering.
In the abundance of God,
I am rich, full, well.

ESSE TO UNBURDEN THE UNDERSOUL

Use the same procedure as Esse for Self-Healing.

The darkened self functioning as the Undersoul is cleansed by the speaking of the mantram below.

While speaking the mantram, move and turn clockwise in spherical fashion, feeling freedom from guilt.

Move, and let the True Self come forth.

Exorcise your negations through realization of God as the Only Power. To erase your sins and errors, release them and give them to Him as an ignorance-offering to His Knowing.

Know that you are free in the Esse; that you are His true son; that you are no longer accepting immaturity or illiteracy. Keep repeating the mantram while moving. Feel you have been emptied out, that the Increase of God has cleansed you. Know it is going to happen! Be thankful!

> *Esse. Esse. Esse.*
> *In Esse, I am free.*
> *I am free within*
> *The Real, of the Esse.*
> *In my own divinity, I am free.*
> *Esse. Esse. Esse.*

Resolve in your mind to henceforth Mark and Trace what is said through your conscience.

To gain the greatest benefit from this Esse movement, one should watch his dreams and his post-meditation thoughts.

SITTING ESSE

If one is unable to walk or to stand, he can sit and do an Esse with very gratifying rewards. A change-over of breath renews and restores the vigors of the etheric body, where healing dwells.

If for any reason one cannot stand or move in the freedom of the Esse, he should move his arms or hands, or whatever part of the body is mobile. In time, outer movement will restore health and vigor in the lesser etheric body. This will appear outwardly as a love of life, regardless of restrictions upon the body.

Speak the following mantram while moving hands and arms during the Sitting Esse.

You may also use facial movements, eye movements, head movements — all within the flow of that which moves you.

> *I forgive those who have harmed
> me. I am free in the Esse.
> God in me is the Power.
> Esse. Esse. Esse.*

The Sitting Esse will reveal to you certain sensitive points of awakened energies in portions of your torso, the back, legs and feet. Each time a Sitting Esse is practiced, this energy will become more intelligible. You will become aware that you are the maker of your body. Be thankful. Be receptive. Be happy. Acquaint yourself with your true and inward nature.

MUSIC AND THE ESSE

If one feels inclined to use music during the Esse movement, he will learn in time that the theme of the music will interfere with his movement. He then will be inclined to discard the music background, and thus hear the true and Third Music accompanying the Esse movement.

The Third Music is the music of the Great Hum within the mighty Consciousness of God.

CALLING DOWN THE ESSE: ESSE TO HEAL
ANOTHER OR TO BRING WORLD-PEACE

> *Let the downpouring begin.
> Esse. Esse. Esse. Esse. Esse.
> Peace.*

The following Esse can be practiced by one person or by a group of persons.

To free Esse *primordial movement* or the Most High Soul's inner nervous system (Kundalini), giving freedom to the Esse or Holy Spirit, use the following procedure twice a week:

1. First meditate for approximately five minutes in sitting position.

2. Stand. Make yourself a receptive vessel for the movement Holy-Spirit Esse to flow down into the crown of the head.

Sound the *Esse* (Pronounced EsSEE) three times.

3. Feel the involuntary life currents of Esse taking action in various sensitive parts of the body as a desire to move, to sound, to laugh, to weep, etc.

4. Let the movement *happen.* For a few minutes, move the body, turning clockwise. Let the hands be free with movement.

5. Sit down for a second meditation of a few moments. Arise after the short meditation. Start second receptivity for the Esse movement with increased emphasis on movements: turn, whirl, spin; sound mantra *Esse.*

6. Sit for third meditation of a few moments. Make a resolution to heal someone in special need. If one should seek to heal the world, he should visualize thoughts of peace and world-healing.

7. Stand. Move with joy and happiness, jumping if inspired to do so. End with meditation and holding in the Light the one in need of healing.

Speak aloud with mantra-fullness. Hold a deep, inductive feeling. Stand receptively. Know the Holy Spirit as the Presence of God is the true and pure motivating power and the Presence in you.

Know that your own Most High Soul is the dwelling place of the Esse.

Feel Esse entering and pouring down upon the crown of the head. Release all in submission to the Will of God. Let the Esse flow, in, in, in; Esse, Esse, Esse, Esse, Esse. Move your body as Esse. As Holy Spirit moves you, move. End all movements of Esse with meditation.

APOLOGY ESSE

The Esse Dance of Apology frees and purifies the Undersoul accumulated energies of hatred and hostility.

A person who cannot apologize is sick in the gratitude levels of his emotions.

How does one approach God? — with his heart or with one or two mouths? In a two-mouth ambivalent approach to God, supplication is as a wilted stalk or leaking water. Approach to God through the heart can come only from a grateful heart.

To apologize for an undisciplined nature destroys the hardened shell covering the heart.

Begin the Apology Esse by visualizing the one to whom you would apologize.

For a single person: Speak aloud the apology stanzas in the following mantram before the circling movements of the Esse. Feel it. Know it is going to be heard. Send it toward the visualized person — and be free of the burden of lust, hate, greed, separateness, envy, and nontrusting.

In a Group Esse, one person should read aloud the following stanzas while the Esse movement is being enacted by the group. Those practicing the movement should extract the essence of the Apology: empty their hearts of hatred, envy, greed, separateness, untruths. Let each word in the mantram-stanzas sedimentize into holy charity, forgiveness and love.

*I have wronged you. Forgive me. Through my cloud of
self-darkness, I have failed to see your worth, your dignity.
I apologize in the spirit of forgiveness with a whole heart
for my sin against your soul.
You cannot harm what is real in me, neither can I harm
what is real in you.
I am no longer happy to be married to unreal things in
you or in any other. I portray the true. To find this, I am
emptying myself of hatred.
Where I have cultivated anger and separateness, forgive
me. I have not known what I have been doing to myself
and to you.
Accept my apology, and let us dance the Shiva
Dance in the Jesus Embodiment of Love.
La. La. La. Ha. Ha. Ha. Ah. Ah. Ah. Hyee. Hyee. Hyee.
Hyee.*

Scriptural Esse

*I move and center.
The Spirit of Truth moves,
frees, heals.
Esse. Esse. Esse.*

Speak the above mantram before reading aloud a Scriptural sentence or several verses of the Bible. Contemplate the essence within the Bible verse(s) while practicing the Esse movement.

If the Scriptural Esse is practiced by a group, one person should read aloud a Chapter selected from the Bible while the others are using the Esse movement.

For the Scriptural Esse, use the Esse movement as given for oneself. Know that in this movement of Esse movement, you are healing bigotry, prejudice, separateness; and that the Word of God through the Esse movement in you is free, dissolving the enclosure separateness in creed and cliques within religions; that the Esse Holy-Spirit Wind is moving into all religions as God, the One Power, the One Word free of dogma, of persecution, of division.

Feel the essence of the words in the Scripture. Know "This is going to happen, for the hour is at hand."

GROUP ESSE

The practice of the Group Esse is experienced in three movements. Each movement is preceded by a mantram and meditation led by a man or a woman.

Mantram before First Movement of Group Esse.
Stand and Speak:

> *Instant Polarization is through Jesus.*
> *He is the Door through which I have*
> *dominion in this world and a Kingdom in*
> *the Heavenly Kingdoms.*

The Group should assume the attitude of total receptivity. Following the speaking of the Mantram, all should be seated for meditation. Meditation should be practiced for approximately thirty seconds as a oneness with the True Self, as an invitation to knowing one's true being. Visualize these ideas with a deep contemplative receptivity.

All should rise, stand, and begin the first movement.

First Movement:

Following the meditation, the group is divided into two circular groups: one circle, male, to the right; and one circle, female, to the left. The women will begin to move counterclockwise; the men, clockwise. At intervals throughout the movement, all should say together: "La. La. La.

Ha. Ha. Ha. Ah. Ah. Ah. Hyee. Hyee. Hyee. Hyee." Shortly after movement begins, the two groups merge, everyone moving clockwise. This portion of the Esse is dedicated to *healing of one's self.* In this, one takes a leap out of the Undersoul-negativity. One should move with ecstasy and rhythmic abandon, taking a leap from the dark, freeing the self.

Time of the First Movement: One to three minutes.

Second Movement:

The group will continue as one; while standing, they will speak the following Mantram for World Peace:

> *The Omnipotent God-Presence is the Omnipresence in all worlds existing and nonexisting. Peace to all worlds.*

Sit and meditate, contemplating the mantram spoken. Each one in the Group visualizes a world of unity, harmony, love within the Oneness of God. Contemplate for 30 seconds. Rise. Begin the Esse Mantra: *La. La. La. Ha. Ha. Ha. Ah. Ah. Ah. Hyee. Hyee. Hyee. Hyee.* Move as one. In this movement, let the spirit of oneness move within you, taking command of the movement for the human race.

Third Movement:

After the World-Peace Esse Movement, the Group will continue by standing and speaking a Mantram for the Healing of a specific person or condition. Each person in the Group Esse will visualize the one he desires to heal, and speak an Angel to Angel Mantram:

> *Beloved, my Angel speaks unto thy Angel,*
> *and sees you as a perfected child of God.*
> *Be free in the Love of God*
> *   and the Will of God.*

Esse in Action

Come forth, and live with joy.
Peace.
I thank thee, O Angel.
I thank Thee, O Father.

Sit and meditate. Contemplate for 30 seconds the perfected body and life of the one you would heal.

Rise, and begin the Group Movement, speaking the Esse Mantra, "La. La. La., etc.," moving and turning in the spirit of praise to God. Throw off the sickness. Know that healing will come; that it is going to happen.

Continue in movement for a period of 2-3 minutes. Move with increasing joy. Give thanks for yourself as a unit of measure of God. Give thanks for the world. Give thanks that you can love; that you can forgive. Give thanks that you are free in the Esse. Move and turn. Leap in the happiness of the Group's oneness. Remember that what one man prays for happens; and that when many together set free the moving processes of the Holy Spirit, mighty things come to men in the world.

The only Healing Power is the Healing Power of God. He is the True Physician within. You are His sunset and sunrise. You are His lakes and trees. You are walking and running. You are His music.

Sit and end this Esse Movement with a prayer led by the third leader.

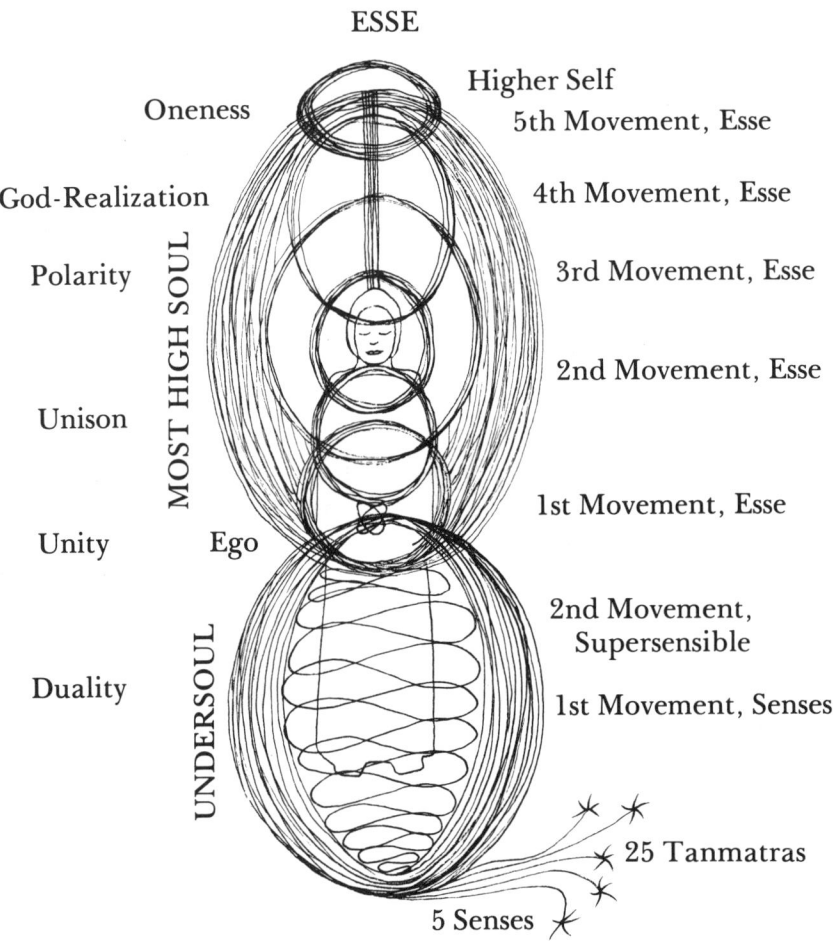

CHART: THE MOVEMENT OF THE ESSE

7

THE NATURE OF THE MIND AND THE EGO

What is retained of the ego when death comes? What is retained of the ego when birth comes? What is the life sustainer of the ego? How and why does it take on the mask of gravity-unknowing? How and by what does it gain the assumption that there is a Self? What imprisons the ego in ignorance clothed in fantasy? How may this illiteracy be made literate?

UPA-SOUL AND MOST HIGH SOUL

Mind strength is built through willing; keeping promises; correcting habits; marking and tracing the currents and interflows within the ego-mind and the Undersoul.

From Archetypal instruction received in the Buddhi light in meditation, one learns that he has an Undersoul. The Undersoul is connected by the Upa-Soul with the Most High Soul, which is deathless. The Undersoul presently is acting as a sentient functional vehicle for the developing processes of the lower mind, the survival and experimentalizing lower desires, the lesser etheric body, and the lower sense-faculties.

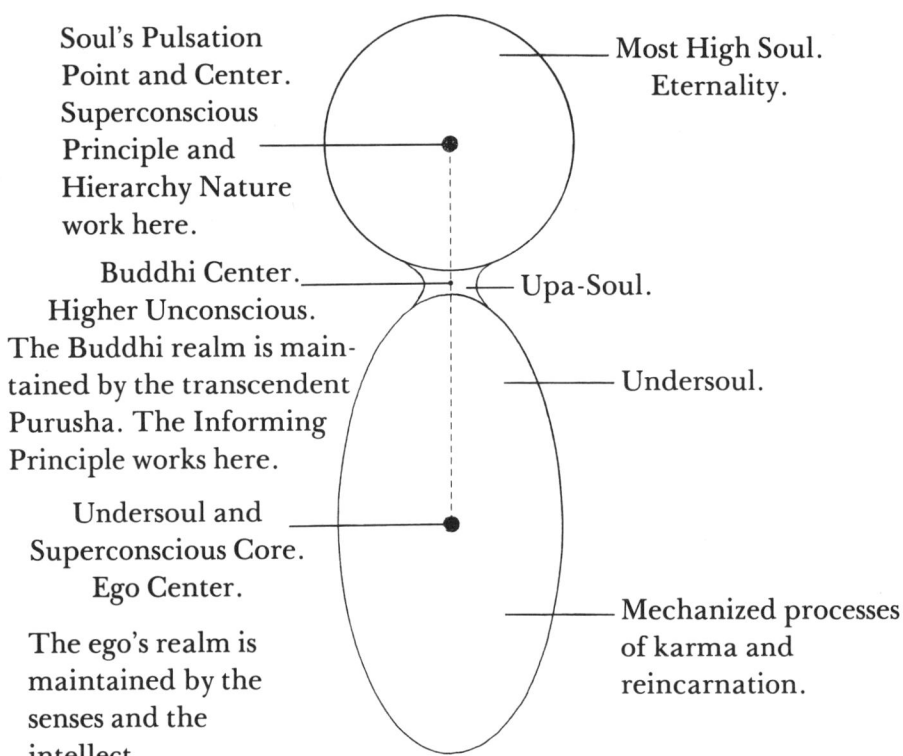

Chart: Most High Soul,
Upa-Soul and Undersoul.

The ego works directly with and through the Undersoul. One side of the Undersoul acts as the psychic brain for the ego.

As the Most High Soul has the ability to record and make known the Eternal verities of the Spirit, the Undersoul has the ability through the gravity states of instinctual phenomena to retain and learn through fixed ego-patterns and habits. This includes the past-life inherited memories of ego and of ancestral experience.

The Nature of the Mind and the Ego

The Undersoul is a Maya enclosure vehicle necessary for earth-plane expression. It enables one to keep within the law-enforcement system of Maya that he may develop a certain type of consciousness within and through the defense patterns functioning within the instinctual world.

The Undersoul has a psychic and psychological nature. It is automated through the lower-self or ego preservation for earth-survival.

The Undersoul is a mechanized corresponding vehicle for the soul, preserving varied projections of the ego throughout the ages. The Undersoul functions as an entity. This entity consists of countless earth birth-experiences of trial and error. One thinks of his ego falsely as the *self*.

To achieve the egoless state and to be master of one's own ego, one must function as a will-identity under the guidance of Absolute God. For this, he perseveres, renunciates, and makes union within the Eternal Patience of God.

In physical consciousness, one thinks to act. In the etheric sub-sentient energies, he functions to live. The will acts in the etheric body to build immunization. The defense system in each person given by the soul resides within the etheric bodies. The defense system in the physical body acts on the etheric planes. The defense system for the Spirit acts on the soul planes.

The mental life is a willing, creating life. All creation is in the mind. Mind, when free within the hierarchy nature of the True Self, creates with God.

The astral nature of the astral or emotional body gives the power to express love. All human love-hungers draw upon the reservoirs of love-knowing in the astral nature.

The ego is a necessary vehicle that man may represent himself as a person. In the present time the ego functions, to all appearances, as the conscious mind—drawing upon past karmas, or of good or evil.

The ego is a vessel for outer expression of the undeveloped powers of soul-expression. The record of the ego is a record of experimenting experience in the earth. Its frailty lies in the fact that it thinks it is limited to one life experimenting. The subconsciousness obliterating-faculty prevents one who is expressing only the ego from remembering from whence he has come, and prevents him from exploring the future.

The ego is tightly bound into karmic law, and must suffer every penalty for karmic deviation. It is the ego that suffers; the soul or the True Self does not suffer. That which heals suffering gives realization; it is the Divine within the soul and the Self that heals. All who aspire to the spiritual life and to enter the Path must escape the sin-tensions of the ego.

With right motivation come these good words: *inventiveness, innovation, incentive* and *transcendence*. These are accompanied by a unique insight, building for a creative future.

A state of desparagen (or constant despair) as experienced by the Undersoul obliterates motivation. The volatile principle of the will functioning as hierarchy nature comes from the Will Fiat. When the Life Fiat is absent from the will, there is no motivation. Where there is not motivation, the life-vital processes are dead; there is neither insight nor incentive in a deadened life-vital action.

Man seeks to become a volatilized spiritual Being. When Esse moves through a mantramic statement in conjunction with primordial etheric movement, this provides union with God through the Holy Spirit.

Esse as movement is Holy Spirit movement. The Esse acts as a Holy Gas giving virility to the physical; vitality to the etheric; holy feeling to the emotions; archetypal consciousness to the mental; and Holy Spirit Realizations to the spiritual.

The Most High Soul of man — the Eternal, deathless vitalizer for the True Self — is a Holy-Spirit manifestor automating the Esse or the Holy-Spirit Gas. The Most High Soul is a vehicle of superconscious energy in a state of unceasing movement.

The Undersoul of man is a gravity, energy projection or understudy of the Most High Soul. The ego, by which man expresses himself, lives through the energy processes of the Undersoul. The ego has been developed and automated from memory habit-patterns of thought and action as expressed through one's ancestry and from uncountable past lives.

The Undersoul is especially influenced by the Moon and the lower planetary energy processes. The Undersoul, as a vehicle for all ego movement, is subjected to seasons and to cycles, to physical birth and to physical death.

The Undersoul is motorized by the subconscious. The Most High Soul is connected to the Undersoul through the higher unconscious or Upa-Soul, which is a pure, undefiled primordial-matrix vehicle established by our Father in Heaven accompanied by the Hierarchy.

It is the work of the Initiate to call down through the mantra the Esse downpouring of the pure, primordial Holy Spirit of the Most High Soul into the darkened recesses of the Undersoul where it may circulate, cleanse and purify. Through the use of Esse and a sounding mantra in conjunction with meditation and movement of the body as directed by the inner primordial, higher-unconscious soul-compulsions, one adjusts, cleanses and frees the Undersoul, that it may become a suitable vehicle for transmission, transenergizings, healings, realizations, gifts, and holy powers.

Congestion in the Undersoul-energy produces sickness, frustration and untimely death. Congestion of the Undersoul is spiritual suffocation. Uninhibited Esse circulation in the depths of the Undersoul produces wisdom, creation, happiness, youth and vitalization of all processes of life while in the physical world.

Physical work requiring physical energy, when used with awareness of service to God, scours and cleanses the Undersoul. Soul-united rhythmic dancing or movement, when used sacramentally, purifies the Undersoul, giving grace and freedom, health and joy to the glandular system. The glandular system is the organism for the emotional or astral body. Movement used with emotional sacredness provides psychological good health.

All forms of movement create. Any form of creation, such as music or mandala art forms—when used as service to God and to mankind—gives expression to the Most High Soul through the mind.

When the Esse movement is given equal time to meditation, the Esse radiances are free, and the Undersoul potential of holy magnetism is expressed as a healing presence through which the Name of God may be sounded and freely used.

The most high state of grace of the human life is expressed when the Undersoul conjoins with the Most High Soul through the use of the Esse as movement equal with meditation to cleanse, to free, to receive, to expand.

Movement used to express the lower astral musics such as rock, or movement used in discoteque gyrations overstimulate the Undersoul sexual currents. The psychic tensions are thrown heavily upon the astral and glandular nature whereby one expresses the emotional through sex as lust.

The Undersoul is similar to the shell of and over the body of a snail. It is heavy and burdensome in the present era of Self-Genesis. It is heavy with the guilts of many devious turns and twistings along the way of earth life and earth struggle. A new vital life-energy substance is seeking to animate this hardened egotistical shell of containment built over the aeons.

In this Self-Genesis time, man of the earth is given the opportunity to unite his ego-gained faculties with the Most-High-Soul powers. This was made possible through Christ Jesus who came to overcome the world that man may know the world as it is in all aspects of human and soul life. Through interrelatedness, perspective is gained and the new man in Christ is born.

Everything that is in order is painless. Everything that is out of order is painful.

Awareness on the level of the Undersoul produces discomfort, astonishment, and, more often, unhappiness. Awareness on the level of the Upa-Soul produces peace, confirming of God, informing the meaning of life and the pursuits of life in earth. The Upa-Soul interprets God through meditation, prayer, contemplation on God, and through selfless service for God. Awareness on the level of the Most High Soul unites one with his Higher Self, assuring him of his eternality and limitlessness in the Will of God; reveals to him the Cosmos; relates him to Universals, Galaxy-Consciousness or Knowing—Niscience.

To spiritually utilize the Undersoul, one must know soul-awareness and become a soul-observer. To do this, one draws his consciousness upward toward the Most High Soul and the Higher Self. He thus is enabled to contact countless prototypal ego-patterns of the ages of the past and of the future. He will see the Undersoul as the servant of the Most High Soul. The Most High Soul contains the Archetypal over-plan; this plan is screened by the Higher Self onto the ego during certain sensitized initiatory periods to cleanse, recharge and direct the life meaning within the Undersoul.

In each incarnation or return to birth in earth, one takes upon himself the yoke of the Undersoul. Eventually he will learn that he himself has built the Undersoul as a Maya house.

Soul-observation tells the Initiate that in all of his sufferings the most frustrating and most painful is the belief that the Undersoul is the only Soul, and that the ego is the only self.

The ego is impermanent as a vehicle; it is perishable. In each life the ego continuously suffers partial annihilation or something of death. The soul and the Higher Self are imperishable, eternal. The soul and the Higher Self motivate the purest aspects of the ego and the Undersoul.

When the ego reincarnation-record reaches a state of painful sensualized density, it is unable to respond to the purity within the soul and the Higher Self. The Higher Self and the soul are aware of God at all times. The ego and the Undersoul are unaware of God when fantasized by present and past-life lower-mind and self-desiring.

The ego is impressionable to the physical world and to the astral world. The soul, the Higher Self and the Most High Soul live constantly in a state of transcendental, Purusha, God-awareness and Divine-suggestibility.

The ego — dependent upon the senses, the intellect and the suggestibility obtained for the limitation-span within earth experience — is a partial vehicle rather than a whole vehicle. It is the Will of God working through the downpouring of the Purusha, or the Supreme Soul-Consciousness through the Higher Self, that sends the ego upon the stage of physical life, and compels it ultimately to become a chaste vehicle.

It is in the Divine Plan that the ego be an understudy for the Higher Self; the Undersoul be the understudy for the Most High Soul; and the lower mind, for the higher mind. When the Undersoul and the ego become over-full of sensuality, the igniting fire of pain and suffering works to create

The Nature of the Mind and the Ego

a clean vessel so that the ego may respond to the Higher Self, and the Undersoul may receive from the Most High Soul.

In the Undersoul, believing is a substitute for knowing. In the Most High Soul and the higher mind, where the Buddhi or transcendent experience occurs, Niscience or Knowing is the full and complete Reality within the Esse. A free Esse is beyond beliefs. Beliefs survive only through habit sensing. Knowing or Niscience within the Esse places beliefs in right perspective.

All Reality begins in Truth. From the Spirit of Truth comes the Esse downpouring, cleansing and purifying, sweeping away the weakening ego-pinions or supports of illusive beliefs. When one can say, "I know God *Is*," he is in that second beyond death and birth: he is Eternal.

In the downpouring of the Esse, one experiences direct contact with God. In belief, one experiments in ego limitation. The Undersoul is an experimenting vehicle for the ego. The Most High Soul is the experiencing vehicle through which God animates Himself.

The Dwelling Place of the Mind

All judging, criticizing sides of the mind draw upon the instinctual, primal apprehensions of the Undersoul. All defense mechanisms in the mind supporting aggression are rooted in the subconscious nature flowing into and from the solar-plexus region to the downward gravity chakra-stations functioning as Undersoul.

The true dwelling place of the mind becomes *a holy place* when the mind and thoughts function within one of the three *Eternal atoms* supporting the Eternal One or God in the higher mind. These are: the *heart's sacred atom;* the *Indestructible Atom* in the center of the forehead; the

Eternal Sustaining Atom overdwelling the soul at the crown of the head. To meditate on any one of these atom points is to be liberated into the realms of holiness and spirituality.

The ego is the ruler of the *experiencing mind.* Deluded by the illusion that the sense testimony of the ego is the Self, the objective consciousness lives in the finite or limited rather than in the deathlessness of the soul.

The ego has been built from countless experiencing existences. The ego is limited in the mortal aspects of its nature, not as yet having manifested the whole of the Self. The ego is the "me" and cannot be true to what it is when claiming to be the "I." Only *The Self* is the I am that I am.

The higher or divine mind acts as a counterpart of Universal Mind. The *True Self* is the lawful and rightful authority over the ego.

The veil between the Self and the ego is lifted in meditation upon the True Self. When one meditates, Self reveals what ego and Undersoul conceal—and one moves beyond the misconceived, comprehending the Real in consciousness.

The True Self remains firm in Purusha or Supreme Consciousness, which is superconscient and transcendent. In the Purusha, hierarchy nature is free to will in the Will of God.

Universal Mind as Eternal Spirit gave to Self the power to project into gravity life the ego-side of the mind. Beyond ego, the higher mind, called *Buddhi,* is the chaste mental nature of the True Self united to Universal Mind.

The ego-engrossed mind or lesser mind functions through ego and intellect, sense, subconscious and Undersoul-impressionabilities. These aspects of experiencing-ego are phases of mind working to produce command and mastery over gravity, Maya energies (kinetic and atomic) on the physical, etheric, astral and mental planes. When ego has fulfilled its work, soul and Self will reign as hierarchy creators serving this eternity system made one with the Universe.

The *Kloshas* or veils spoken of in the Sanskrit teachings relate to the energy-field stuff or garment of the ego-undersoul. Undersoul-energy veils shut away the superconscious energy-field which is the natural habitat of the soul.

When the Undersoul energies reach the time to explode into dissolution on all levels of ego existence, one enters into an initiation called the *fiery trial*. All who are entering the Path undergo this to some degree. The greater the soul-work, the greater the fiery trial.

One should ask himself: *"Who is desiring to meditate — the ego or the Self? Who is seeking God, the ego or the Self?"*

The ego is an entitized vehicle for the Self. One side of the ego from time to time longs to be rejuvenated and revived by the True Self. In the core interior of the Undersoul, this nostalgia-longing comes as an aching desire to know God.

The ego is entitized to know and experience guilt, to know frustrations and impatience with itself. The conscience or Grand Psyche aspect of the soul is a vehicle for the ego and for the soul. Every hateful deed casts a Klosha or etheric shadow against the Light of the Self. From this Undersoul action, suffering comes; pain is experienced.

The Purusha, which is the Eternal Consciousness, works to pour down to the ego awareness of the True Self. The Prakriti or Divine-Mother power of Nature — which works without ceasing to stimulate all aspects of creation in Nature and in mind — circulates and stimulates ego as a servant for the Self.

When ego thinks itself to be the *I*, duality is but one half of itself. When ego knows it is drawing its life from the light of the True Self as mind-spiritual, the duality *me* in the ego moves beyond the two into the sacred three of the Real.

Undersoul builds for the ego, keeping alive the gross energy fields for the bodies used on the physical, etheric and astral planes. The higher unconscious or Buddhi — working with the involuntary systems of the body—restores the health of the physical body, keeps alive the higher energy states of the etheric body, and maintains the love attitudes moving as energy in the emotional or astral body.

The ego is fantasized to think it is not loved. The True Self absorbing the God Purusha is the center of inestimable love moving with God as holy concern and love. Thus, the True Self is supported by the absorption of love moving from every form and identity expressing Intelligible Love. Such love relates automatically to love those who believe on love and are loving.

The egot or ego is wrapped up in veils of self-preservation. Jesus, the Lord, came to tell man that freedom is in self-denial, and to explain to men that only through self-denial could one unwrap the coils choking and suffocating the Holy Spirit.

The sharp mind of a sharp intellect bruises the love-atmospheres. To one who seeks to love through the ego there is the continued shrinking of the love-nature. In the atmosphere of a sharp and criticizing intellect, this shrinking creates suffering, inhibition, lack of incentive, and death to the will to love.

The ego does not love. It works through its own attachments to things or persons.

The first sign of ego-deflation is when one is non-satisfied with himself. Dissatisfaction can be of two kinds: unholy and holy. Unholy dissatisfaction leads one to immorality and violence. Holy dissatisfaction leads one to humility, whereby the true Face of God can shine forth through the lampshade of the ego.

True humility is to know that one is an Image of God and is therefore devoid of any ruthless, passionate excelling over any other human being. One is what he is by the Nature of God in him; none can contest God in him.

The Nature of the Mind and the Ego

Humility is nakedness, purity, weightlessness. Humility is childlike, pure, and accountable at all times to law. The very essence of purity within humility assures lawfulness, rightness.

Humility provides an unchallenged authority which is experienced for the good of humanity in timing to the need to remember that God has given to every man the essence of goodness, rightness, innocence. Humility knows no compromise or complications stemming from the pristine light of goodness in God. Humility has a language which only the Saints can interpret and speak.

Transenergization

Energy as law is order.
Energy as movement is fire.
Energy as thought is creation.
Energy as love is life.
Energy as light is knowing, wisdom.
Energy as faith is vitality.
Energy as hope is restoring.
Energy as earth is power.
Energy as fire is initiation.
Energy as Knowing creates and keeps the Channel open.
Energy as water is union.
Energy as air is oneness.
Energy as silence is centering.

In the Undersoul, every dark mass of negativity has one penetrable point of energy. When the Esse Light penetrates this point, the complete mass is transenergized. The great Masters, seers, healers and the angels use this technique of Holy-Spirit light-energized power with freedom and with knowing.

Every situation of Undersoul ego-darkness contains a penetrable point. Healing is made possible when one has acquired the power of transenergization.

It is the work of the spiritual Initiate to free his Undersoul to a higher functioning state. Through the soul-therapy or spiritual art of transenergization, one reverses the obsessive currents in the Undersoul, that these currents may be transformed from the primal state to their original primordial state of innocence and purity. The transenergization of the lower-mind currents into the higher mind opens the remembrance of God and of the Omnipresent functioning within the Most-High-Soul state of mind as Superconsciousness.

Transenergizing is the Power Divine given to each soul that one may be with God as a builder, a mover of worlds. As a transformer, one must first transenergize, and thus become one in the Will, the Life, the Light and the Love.

Transenergization pertains to the deliberate cultivating of the soul-skill arts, such as: the creating of mandalas, meditation, the speaking of the mantra, the use of movement before and after meditation, as in Free-play and in Pleasance. Prayer, worship, Agape-creation, Marking and Tracing in self-research, and Logos speech used through transenergization techniques relax and free the Undersoul that it may become the future spiritualized brain.

The true Agape used in Healing Mediation and the Holding in the Light directs the higher soul-light purifying energies downward into the slower and fixed energy-processes of the Undersoul. The hierarchy-nature healing practices overpower the sin-body states imprinted in the Undersoul.

In the present era, the three most prevalent natures of man are: ancestral, individual and spiritual. A fourth nature of man—the archaic instinctual—is now being assimilated into the other three natures. The soul-nature of man longs for birth. The nature of the soul will come to birth

The Nature of the Mind and the Ego

or be recovered when all Kali-Yuga ignorance has been eradicated by the "Golden Yuga Day" seeking to be manifested through the Light of the Christ.

Until a person enters the spiritual Path, his ego-nature and his personality consist of 70% ancestral inheritance, 10% grace-inheritance from past lives, 10% karma from past lives and 10% of spirituality.

All things existing experience without ceasing an interplay between three grand or master life-forming energies. The fixed or constant structure in the law of energy-exchange is divided into three grand states or positives of interplay: (1) Omniform as forming energy; (2) uniform or uniting through Duality Polarity energy; and (3) bioform as procreative energy.

In Omniform energy, soul works with the transcendental. In uniform energy, the self as conscience works with the laws of polarity or the opposites, the harmonic in merging, blending and the fusing of minds. In bioform energy, forming ego works as sentience within the producing and reproduction energies of the collective subconscious.

While appearing to undergo many variables or variations, these three energy-constants are the ruling factors in the balancing structure of life as existence, life as sentient, life as consciousness. When any one of these energy functions is lacking in the body or form, the result is malformation.

The function in Omniform is sattvic, truth, perfection. The function in uniform is rajasic, acceleration, unification between all forms. The function in bioform is tamasic, instinctual, reproduction through polarity selection. The energy rates in bioform function in the Mayaic tamasic rate as units of measure controlled by the alternative energy processes within Time and Space.

Birth as consciousness in this eternity system began as

Sattvic-Heavenly. Birth to duality activity was experienced as gravity absorption, moving, rajasic, and astral. Birth to earth personal life-processes was experienced by sentient, karmic, and polarity selection within tamasic or Mayaic limitation.

The lunar laws of gravity work with the tamasic energy. The cyclic law of the planets works with the rajasic. The galaxy rhythmic law of the solar energy works with the sattvic.

The interplay of the grand three is never absent: in sentient, through which the intellect is formed; in the conscient, wherein one is self-aware; in the transcendent, whereby one is effulgent in spiritual union with God.

To be absent from consciousness is to be vacuous, non-existing as self. All energizing processes of life work to produce awareness as consciousness. To identify the state of awareness one is expressing, is to be whole and in command of the three interplay grand functions of energy, and thus learn that one is a creator with God.

Where do I come from? Transcendent in Omniforming or Sattvic reveals the Cause and the Source.

Who am I? The uniform emergent, the rajasic providing the quickened intelligible, discloses the all in the One.

Where am I going? The tamasic works within the action principle bringing the self-realization as to the place and the where in the purpose and the plan of God.

Consciousness begins first as soul superconscious-awareness; second, as mind self-awareness; third, as ego-awareness through sense experimentation.

In the tamasic, awareness works through the seemingly dense or the solid; in the rajasic, through the semi-solids of astral and gravity; in the sattvic, through the transenergetic, which is timeless and spaceless, unweighted and unmeasurable by sense or intellectual mind.

The Nature of the Mind and the Ego 139

It is the work of all spiritual persons through the use of the Esse to change the biotron energies in consciousness into the master omnitrons of light. Through experience and self-mastery, one accomplishes this, and is thus a presence for God in illuminative virtue.

Most people are living in the biotron consciousness or the gross consciousness—a slave to sense and sensuality. Through meditation, contemplation, mantramic speaking and the Esse movement, one moves out of the biotron gross consciousness into the superconscious or omnitron state of light. In all his associations, the hierarchy-nature healer uses the transenergizing power of light, illumining the situation and the condition—healing and comforting.

In the biotron consciousness one is ambivalent: he desires that his son or his daughter be an image of himself, but he also desires that his child become a hero in the light of other men. He passes on his conflicts to his child, who is divided as to his place of loyalty and as to his range of freedom in individuality. The parent desiring his child to remain in the parental encasement, and yet anticipating the projection of himself as a hero figure to the world, creates a psychic heat in his own mind and in the subconscious mind of his offspring or child.

A person living in the biotron light simply cannot understand a person living in the omnitron light.

The One-Constant is Spirit. The vehicle for the One-Constant is Light. The functioning of the vehicle of the Spirit as Light is *Energy*. When Energy works as sentient form through mass, this is the Spirit made flesh. Energy as density through flesh manifesting as consciousness is *Genergy*. Through the higher-mind energy expressed in the genes of man, the parabolic and archetypal-symbol functions desire to be utilized as revelation and creation.

Genergy, or gene-consciousness, functions first as biotron

energy; second, as unitron; third, as omnitron. All of these are developing phases of genergy-consciousness.

On the level of man, biotron energy manifests with the assistance of Nature through cycles within the hormonal system. Unitron manifests as psychology through the nervous system and as mentality in relationships of karma and grace. Omnitron manifests as soul-radiance, perceptions and illuminations through transcendence.

Biotron works with Time. Unitron works with confrontation with self and with the *other*. Omnitron works with Space and Spacelessness.

Christ is in charge of Space. The Father is in charge of Time.

The duality system of the earth is energized to polarities. Evil is the result of wanting too much or of having too much. Sin is the imbalance of polarity. Sin overloads the polarity-rhythm and harmony.

The mastery of sin indented in the Undersoul gives detachment. On mastering detachment, a third aspect is born; one moves out of duality away from sin. Conscience then is free to act as a chemical catalyst to devour sin.

Psychology led man away from his conscience. Niscience, or Knowing, leads man back to his conscience so that he may come into the perfect peace spoken of by Jesus. *"Peace I leave with you, my peace I give unto you: not as the world giveth, give I unto you." (St. John 14:27)*

Jesus manifests as the Conscience Principle, and Christ manifests as the Consciousness Principle. These are both in man: Consciousness and Conscience. They are the Holy Duo of God giving to man *Deus* or God.

Christ is the Great Exorcisor.

When one understands the atom in its relation to Consciousness, he will be electrically charged by Galaxy; his mind will function within the Omnitron Universe. He will reach beyond the regions and planes of Maya with his thoughts, and dwell beyond the solar, beyond the supernova, within the Atma or whole of Spirit.

The Fourth-Dimensional Consciousness

Persons sealing themselves away from the Esse or Holy-Spirit vitalities within the soul-movement are chronically resistant to God. They are perfectly contented to live within their own fixed ego-habit patterns. However, there comes a time through the progression of God that the former habits giving one access to the Pleasure Principle do not satisfy or succeed.

In this period of time, bitterness and resentment have discolored the soul-spaces of the mind. Presumptuous negativity exposes one to the uselessness and futility of self-made concepts and interpretations of life.

Tamasic inertia freezes one into irritations which are retained as the next-life karma. However, if one has within his nature a certain courage and strength, the higher rajasic will enable him to open some of the aspects of the higher-mind thinking processes. No matter how old one is, or how near to death one is, if there is strong selfless desire, the Will of God will provide him with a Third Vitality through which he will open himself to the realities of the Spirit within his own life.

When one moves within the Esse or the Holy Spirit, he enters into a Fourth Dimension. The Coinciding Principle within Buddhi unites him with the Informing Principle, and he becomes a seer and explorer of Kingdoms and Dominions beyond the biological, physiological and psychological. He who masters the Fourth Dimension is free to pursue the realities in other dimensional worlds.

The Grand Number of Creation in the present era, on

every level of consciousness, is the Four, signifying the Fourth-Dimensional Consciousness now available to man in his mental birth to Enlightenment. Accompanying the Four is the Three. The Three—God, the Father and the Holy Spirit—must act with the Four that His temple be formed and spiritually created in the consciousness of man.

Since the coming of the Christ, the Earth polarity shifted from the Two-Dimensional Consciousness and the Three-Dimensional Perception into the Fourth Dimensional. All the present groaning and wailing and weeping stem from this: that man is now coming to birth to extend the Third-Dimensional State into the Fourth-Dimensional State of Consciousness and thereby experience God-Realization.

Archetypal Knowing

The human body is a prototypal machine, and the mind is an archetypal machine.
The four aspects of the mind are perfect when used sacramentally and selflessly.

The majority in the world lean on Undersoul and ego thinking; their mind faculties automatically flow to the level of the Undersoul. Such persons have entered the world as laggard ego-bound souls. These have incurred mind-damage through failure to use their minds within God-guided creation.

Ego-mind persons are fringe thinkers dependent upon conceptualizing compulsions. These now are offered the opportunity to unite with their soul-tides and soul-rhythms.

The conceptual mind or intellect, which is the ego-mind, feeds the bigot; keeps alive the psychic arguments within the lower mind. Stagnant conceptualization produces Undersoul mind-heats, creating states of dissonance and mental-psychic tensions. The Archetypal mind, Buddhi, is organized to reveal and to inform; the Buddhi mind is beyond conceptualized opinions.

Men who live as ego believe only through the ego; thus, they know not when death comes or why birth to the world comes. Ego-ruled men live in the unreal, believing the ego to be the only real. In each life, the ego dies. Self dies never; Self is Eternal and deathless.

The Self as Wisdom knows birth, death and life as one. Back of every ego is the True Self seeking to smile through the mask of the ego; seeking to reveal the True and the Real.

The ego *does not know* what is coming or why it is to come. The ego acts, compelled by the repetitious ancestral and ego karmic compulsions of past lives and of the present-life actions. The ego cannot tell one what death or birth or life is; thus, the ego is limited in power, knowing only limited knowing. Only the Real can transmit the knowledge of the Real.

Through the practice of the Esse movement, one encounters the *nescience* overflow in the Undersoul. In the extended vibrational quickening of the Esse, he sees the energy masses contained in the Undersoul as portions of nonsynchronized, sensationalized, irrational forces causing sentient agony and suffering.

In the after-effects of the movement practice of the Esse, one becomes familiar with the undertow and tides of the Undersoul. He sees the Undersoul as a skeletal framework built by the countless sojourns of the ego. He learns that the structure of the Undersoul is yet to become a perfected frame for a greater sentience, consciousness and realization.

When egotism is absent, the True Self as the Real can enter into this frame or house called the Undersoul and live there as a shining being of the soul made of the first order of Spirit. As long as the need and demands of the ego in the energy mass of the Undersoul are predominant, the frame of the ego is an unfit vessel or house for the True Self. Rare are those in the world who have the structured Undersoul purification and chastity. The time is inevitable, however, when ego, having fulfilled the accumulation of earth-life requirements, will become a true house or temple for the True and Real Self, that the transcendent Soul and Mind may have their say and their voice.

The ego is continually sounding "Great self, Great self," thinking its mechanics to be perfected. The overthrow of fantasy from the throne of ego is attained when one, on entering Archetypal Samadhi, sees what is the Real and the True.

The True Self is of the Light; in the True Self there is neither fire nor flame. *Fire purifies; Light enlightens.* The Undersoul cannot teach of the Light; the pain of fire teaches only through the Undersoul and the ego.

The essence of the work and effort in the mastery of fire transenergized into Light is retained as treasure by the Self to be used as a gift or a grace in future spiritual expression for the Self. When death comes, this mastery-victory essence acting as a halo-covering of the soul remains as spiritual power to be used in the next day or birth to the earth.

The life substance for the ego is built by the senses and the intellect. The senses do always the same things, never changing, yet causing sense of change. The intellect operates through the repetition of no or yes, dark or light.

In Undersoul-ego functioning, one thinks and feels first negatively, then positively. Preponderance of the negative builds the Undersoul soils. Many lives of the negative produce the dark electricities upon which the lower mind within the ego feeds; thus, one is tamasic, leaning in inclination toward despair, heaviness, depression, inertia. When the soil of the Undersoul becomes the red electricity, one is then in the rajasic Undersoul state—violent, aggressive, murderous to self and against life. Clearing the Undersoul soil through the Holy Wind of the Esse brings the sattvic peace, the cleansing, the pure. Self as the Real then is free with the Masters, with the Beloved, with the Lord.

Holy longing must come before the ego becomes the server and servant for the True Self. Holy longing crosses the bridge of fire into Light. Esse comes as freeing grace. Esse as law sweeps clean the Undersoul. The Undersoul, no longer being a place of mystic dark, becomes a translucent center energized by the golden rays of the Upa-Soul and the True Self. The Self sits majestic in Reality, free. The countenance of God is seen. God is known. Then only comes Niscience or Archetypal Knowing.

There must be movement equal with awareness in Spiritual Knowing. He who moves is alive. He who moves not is a corpse. The circulation of the Atma or Buddhi Wisdom is indescribable, and can be perceived only through Esse as movement.

The Esse garment is the higher-etheric garment woven out of the Galaxy-substances of the starry worlds. In the movement of Esse, one is in Space as expansion, in the Reality of Timelessness.

The tuning fork for the Galaxy-dance of the Esse is the heart, the soul and the breath acting as one in the Divine Intelligible. Cares and weighted burdens are relieved and transenergized through the Esse movement that the Most Holy Lord may be known, seen and experienced.

Book Two
Hierarchy-Nature Healing

8

THE COINCIDING PRINCIPLE

The Coinciding Principle uses the unmanifest in Space to prove God as Law, God as Just, God as Love.

On the clear canvas of Space where nought has yet been seen or heard by sense, God reveals His rightness, His justicity.

Beyond the void of relativity, God as Omnipresence smiles as radiance, as Light equalized.

SPIRITUALIZED JOY

The joy of the Lord is your strength.
—*Nehemiah 8:10*

Joy as movement acts with the Coinciding Principle to ignite hope and vision, enthusiasm and health. The keynote to health is joy.

Joy has two relatings in the mind of man: sensual joy and spiritualized joy. Sensual joy feeds the lower mind of man. Sensual joy is rooted in man's desire nature to experience pleasure at any cost.

Sensual joy obscures and obliterates the conscience. Spiritualized joy stems from the true bliss-nature founded upon rightness or righteousness within the will or hierarchy nature of the Higher Self. One must choose between the two joys.

In sensual joy, one uses the pleasure principle to display or exhibit his ego. In spiritualized joy, one is used by the Will of God to bring peace, joy, health and enlightenment to all forms of life in the earth and in Heaven.

Spiritualized joy begins with trusting-love. To be born with trusting-love, one remains in the state of spiritualized joy in all conditions. Trusting-love opens the spiritualized love-portals in the heart.

As man develops more and more definitive qualities in his intellect, he is likely to crave sensual joy through wrong-sentiment attitudes. Through excessive pride, he draws upon the lower pleasure principle to obtain indulgences in every form of action.

Sensual joy is never satisfied. In passion, it increases lust. In appetite, it produces gluttony. In comfort, it fattens, making flabby the defense system of the body and splintering the instinctual system built throughout the ages for the physical protection of man.

Sensual joy inevitably reaches the dead-end of sensation. Saturated, the senses refuse to be manipulated or energized through useless repetition. One thus comes to disgrace or to sickness or to limitation through excess in sensual joy.

Spiritualized joy provides the Healing Presence. The holy magnetism keeps alive the soul's pulsation, gives vital exuberances to the play of the higher mind, and promises a continued state of grace, whereby God moves forward in mighty surges of His Spirit within creation.

The hierarchy nature is at home in spiritualized joy. The hierarchy nature as the Will of God in the Higher Self uses spiritualized joy to transmit the message and the tidings of God as Eternal.

Of all the elements manifested by the soul, spiritualized

joy is most experienced through the breath. He who has attained spiritualized joy cannot be moved, for the Constant of God in him is ever present, assuring his well-being, his health, his equanimity, his polarity.

Knowledge of one's eternality as a reincarnating ego is a product of spiritualized joy. The Higher Self in its hierarchy nature is buoyantly poised in the Eternals. Fixed upon the Constant of God, the Higher Self knows itself to be Eternal; it knows its function to be Creating.

Enter thou into the joy of thy Lord.
— St. Matthew 25:23

SYNCHRONIZED ESSE

The Coinciding Principle is the existing Intelligible communing itself through the function of Synchronicity. One unites with and assures himself of the proof of the Holy Spirit through the Coinciding Principle.

Every eyelash, every hair of one's head, everything acted upon by Holy Spirit receives its life vigor through synchronization. When one is aware of this, he opens himself to the Coinciding Principle, whereby he becomes one in the One and all in the All.

Failing to understand interconnectedness, interrelatedness and the intercorrespondences supporting the system of synchronization seals away the Coinciding Principle. Coinciding begins when one recognizes there is a mathematical Law of Order caring for him.

In the Coinciding effluvias, the tide of God is always in. God proving Himself is always present as Omnipresence. Through Omnipresence, holy wisdoms are available as *maha matra* or the twinkling-of-the-eye instantaneous revealing and healing.

In Spirit, Primordial is the pure Purusha. The Coinciding uses the Purusha, the Divine Stuff of the most high Unconscious, enabling man to have inward soul-experience while in the body.

The stepped-down Purusha stuff is the Primordial first-plasma within the auric fields. The first plasma stuff is used when the Coinciding Principle has its uniting play or field between the unmanifest and the manifest.

The energy supporting the play of Purusha-stuff is kept alive in its most-high revealing aspect by the Third Music or the great Archetonal Sound. This Music flows into the mind-retention faculty as a reinforcing Constant, that one may retain and sustain spiritual ideas and revelations in full consciousness while sleeping or waking. The flow of the Third Music sustains and keeps alive the coinciding, confirming, revelatory nature of functional soul. Soul-faculty powers or vibrational extension of the senses are experienced within the coinciding field, giving holy confirmation when one has done a right thing; is approved of by the angels; has made a right decision; has received a Passing or the Opening; prayer has had an answer; guidance is right; someone else is telling the truth; or one is protected, loved.

The Higher Unconscious contains the Purusha state of God-Realized consciousness. The Greater Archetypes dwell in the Higher Collective Unconscious or the Purusha of Eternal Spirit.

The Coinciding Intelligible acts as organizing grace. There is an Intelligible organizing principle existing between all life forms expressing equal degrees of consciousness. By this, men are more than objects or things or symbols. They live and receive the fruits of grace through synthesis.

Within the functioning of the Coinciding Principle, one is free in the Esse or Holy Spirit. The Coinciding Intelligible provides a language more than any language spoken by the tongue — a language using the reciprocity functions of the mind, whereby all men are obligated to function with integrity in their spheres of expression.

When the Coinciding Principle is opened, the true communion and communication begin, and all of the vital interrelated strengths flow together as an affirmative vehicle within the Will of God.

In the Coinciding within the Esse, God removes space from Himself and proves Himself in one trillionth second of time. Holy synchronization of the Coinciding assures one that he *is* and that God verily *Is*.

To be in the Coinciding is to confirm in a flash, whether one is doing right things, whether healing has come, whether it is a true thing or a wrong thing, or whether it is a waste of time.

After every Coinciding experience in Esse, one should give thanks to God. In this, he Passes the blessing to all — thus, the Coinciding continues as an unceasing movement and quickening for all. The Coinciding within the Esse is the Darshan and the Dharma acting as one.

He who Passes the Esse onto others is in the state of healing. The Coinciding Esse is a holy ricocheting, going as movement to the need as a Will-of-God touching, anointing and healing.

BEYOND THE PSYCHIC

To one having grace-timing, the Coinciding Principle opens. The first ethic is to respect the Law of Timing, the keeping of promises, the keeping of records and diaries. Stewardship of Time opens one to knowledge beyond the academic into Niscience or Knowing. All spiritual practices enable one to move beyond the gravity units of measure in Time.

He who has full expression of the Coinciding Principle

has the power to prophesy; experience out-of-the-body investigation; reverse illness for himself and for others; and, eventually, encounter the masterful mind-strengths of Holy Presences.

The Angels, the Saints and the Most Divine Devas live and function through the Coinciding Principle. When an Angel or higher Presence comes to minister, he comes in exact timing to the receptivity of the one in need.

Coinciding Principle functions through the fifth and sixth dimensional Bi-Polarity Laws. The mastery of gravity places one into the Time-free and Space atmospheres of the Coinciding Principle, whereby seeming miracles occur.

The first coinciding experience — or two synchronized occurrences — begins with the Yantra or the Mouth-of-God Center opening. The first phase of this is understanding the symbols through the Yantra Initiation. Accompanying Yantra-Initiation is Self-Realization and ultimately God-Realization.

The first sheath-covering for the Yantra technique is the Buddhi light, which includes in its action Mantra and Yantra. There are four *Yantra* phases or initiations. All pertain to a form of mergence of the Holy Spirit: (1) blood; (2) water; (3) fire; (4) Holy Spirit.

In the present era, the downpouring of archetypal spiritual wisdom is flowing into the souls of the initiated and the sensitive. Until now their Higher Selves have been silently immobilized as to the vibrations of the transcendental. The excessive vibratory hum revealing the frictionalized karmas from past lives has veiled man from his archetypal and hierarchy nature.

Presently, all souls who have been initiated on the Path of the Spiritual Life are ripe to receive the hierarchy side of their Higher Self and soul natures. To gain the hierarchy-nature powers of the Higher Self, one must use them consistently; the initiate must become aware of the Coinciding realities of the functioning nature of inner thinking, emotional and etheric vitalities.

It is regretful that the Coinciding Principle, when first encountered with awareness by the probationer or novice on the Path, is very often used psychically. To the untrained, the Coinciding Principle opens one to the mystical side of the pleasure principle. Mystical psychism is the cause of many green psychics believing themselves to be messiahs or saviours. Such persons in these psychic states are especially adamant, being inflexible and unteachable.

All mystical psychics carry with them a certain side of sensual magnetism which attracts the unpolarized mind; this activates dangerous situations. The psychic natures on the gross and green level of knowing very often expose those who are dependent upon and interested in them to set fire to heated karmic conditions in the Undersoul, whereby the one attracted is burned, scarred and disillusioned.

The green psychic functions within the lower first, second and third devachan levels of the astral world. If one of a psychic-matter nature has failed in his evolvement to understand the apparitional or pictograph side of the Siddhi powers, he will incite superstitions, fears and psychic frenzies in the natures of those dependent upon him.

In the study of green psychics, it is always seen that such persons carry with them a form of supernormal confidence, supported by the ego. Invariably, they transplant into the lives of those dependent upon their powers their own focus point or condensed side of phobia or weakness. Thus, a green psychic attracts to him persons who hate as he hates, who dislike as he dislikes. Hate thus becomes accumulative in ego karmic combines or cliques which operate to delay the receiving of the True and the Real.

The devachan green psychic uses his own fantasized

image of life, and places it hypnotically upon the suggestible minds of those who are unself-realized and unsoul-realized. Therefore, all projects formulated by and under the guidance of the mesmeric forces operating through a green psychic are fated to be confusing, misdirecting and unlasting.

Only a blind mystic responds to or depends upon a green psychic as the door to one's own soul-powers. To indulge this dependence is to invite a disaster worse than any hurricane, tornado or earthquake — for such exposure stretches the soul to unendurable limits.

It is the Will of God that each man make union with God directly. If there be grace, pure motive, sincerity and faith, the Holy Esse working within the Coinciding Principle will bring one to the source of instruction which will enable him to cross over the antakarana or bridge of the Upa-Soul into the precincts of his own soul-nature. In this, his hierarchy nature of the Higher Self will become the Buddhi interpreter of his eternal nature, which is the True Self.

The Coinciding Principle functions first by proving that there is a directing Intelligence superior to the outer consciousness mind. The outer consciousness mind or objective mind is but a partial vessel for the subconscious, the ego, the intellect and the Undersoul.

The four aspects of the mind are superconscious, higher unconscious, subconscious, and objective consciousness. Outer consciousness is dependent solely upon sense and sensory experience. The Coinciding Principle is the Intelligible side of the true-mind functioning within the four aspects of the mind so that they may become as one. From this, spiritual enlightenment is ever-present.

The green psychic seeks to master the psychic-matter phenomena not ordinarily seen, heard, tasted, smelled or physically touched. The green psychic is dependent upon the lunar subterranean subconscious flows centered in the lower quelle side of the subconscious within the darkened side of the medulla oblongata; in the vibratory hum around the nimbus of the brain; and in the solar-plexus psychic-fires center around the navel.

A green psychic without a Bhakti heart of love is confused as to ethic in demonstrating the use of the Coinciding Principle. Not understanding the mathematical and cyclic nature of the Coinciding Principle, the green psychic is dependent upon the darkened sides of the negative.

Pure spiritual functioning touches the unison points of light in the Coinciding Principle which spiritually support the synchronized system of the mind in God. A pure and true Coinciding revelation makes one aware in its higher level of an affirming and confirming God-idea and man-idea as being one at the same time.

When one has a Coinciding, he has a confirmation that he has fulfilled the energy in a Cycle; also, he is flowing virtuously with the Cycle. The conscience uses the cyclic law to remind one when he has failed to flow with the Cycle.

There is no fear in love, but perfect love casteth out fear.
—I John 4:18

Fear is one of the psychic powers. All psychic fears begin with cowardice. Agape or Holy Concern is the opposite and healer of fear. The giving person lives not in fear.

There is nothing more evil than a taker posing as a giver. This is a true wolf in sheep's clothing, a hypocrite of the first order.

All takers are take-over persons. They take over situations and persons so that they can take more, and therefore command more in their taking.

Courage, an open mind, open giving, and trust in God

move one beyond psychic levels of fear. He who is overladen with guilt must eventually have its companion, fear—fear of punishment.

Fear is the root-cause of many sicknesses. Lust is the root-cause of all evil. Lust-fantasy in a woman puts her into manipulation. Lust-fantasy in a man puts him into aggression.

Fear paralyzes the life force. Chronic diseases are caused by fear.

All persons having the lower-astral psychic experiences are impressionable to the subtle, demonic, subhuman worlds. No one is open to the suggestibility from the subtle worlds unless he fears these worlds. Persons having total faith in God close the doors of psychic vulnerability.

When a person desires to give all to God—and has any lingering psychic vulnerability—he will be exposed to the subtle regions. Only through total commitment to God and His Power can one move beyond the lower-devachan plane persecution. Courageous, true believers of God are protected from the demonic by the Angels.

Psychic vulnerability is built into the suggestibility level of one who has used the psychic black-arts in former lives. When one has used his psychic nature to persecute, manipulate, torture and gain—and turns toward reclaiming his spiritual heritage—he is persecuted by the very subtle forces he formerly consorted with and lived by.

Fantasized persons live always in the danger of being drawn down into the psychic subtle regions and being deceived by these forces representing the dark. To be a lover of the weird and the abnormal, to consistently practice or pursue life at the cost of others, is to attract the dark.

Reality for physical-plane man begins with honesty. He who has self-honesty and honesty in all relationships has little to fear from psychic manipulations. The hard-rock of honesty is the first protector against psychic manipulation.

To be honest with one another and with oneself is the first step on the Path. A little drop of honesty on evil is like a drop of acid on a sore finger.

Confession is the door to self-honesty. In the lives of some who reach toward the Path, the time will arrive to go through the door of confession. However, if their sense of shame and guilt is unbalanced, they will turn back or fall back. The over-emphasized and heavier weight of their burdens will lead them to that destination where they can work out their unfinished karmas. If one has a living Teacher in this time and has given service, respect and trust to the Teacher, the Teacher will take him by the hand and guide him over the abyss of his samskara darkness.

Confession is one of the greatest laws. It is connected with breathing itself.

Coveting and envy are close allies to build psychic atmospheres harmful to others in the world. Total faith and surrender to God attract the pure atmospheres where love abides and trust sustains.

A true seer or prophet looks upon the psychic aspects of the lower devachan planes as a nuisance, as intrusive. He sees the telepathic darts of energy as he would see a swarm of flies which must be sanitized and cleansed.

As Jesus met Satan, so must every person who would place his will in the Will of God also meet Satan. If there be any darkness left in one's mind and heart, he must be tried and say to that which is dark: "Get thee hence; there is no power greater than the Power of God." If the eye is dark and the hand falter in this hour, one will continue to reincarnate in the physical plane miserable and separated from the true Light which lighteth this world.

> *Finally, my brethren, be strong in the Lord, and in the power of His might. Put on the whole armour of God, that ye may be able to stand against the wiles of the devil.*
> —*Ephesians 6:10,11*

The Coinciding Principle proves God to man by imparting to him the Presence of God as the Intelligible and Caring Constant. Thus, man to be in the height of the use of the Coinciding Principle confirms God in his mind by knowing himself to be God-like in his own nature.

In the intricate side of life and of man's development within the inner Intelligible, one can prove for himself that his own awareness is accompanied by billions and trillions of correlating similar thoughts and actions in the total Universe. One of the first ways one sees the synchronized processes within the Intelligence of God as the Intelligence in All, is that he begins to experience certain confirming God-directed events in his life of the mind and the emotions and of his desire.

The Coinciding unities are available to every soul crossing over the abyss of his own self-illusions. The Coinciding Principle has functioned in man since the very beginning of this eternity system. All great sages and all great seers know God, experience Him and prove Him through the Coinciding Principle.

Every moment of the day, one lives in the Coinciding Principle, which cannot be seen by the physical eyes, cannot be felt by physical touch or tasted by the tongue, neither can it be heard by the outer ear or touched by the hand or the flesh. The Coinciding Principle can be proven and experienced only by Knowing or Niscience, which is beyond sensory knowledge.

The Coinciding Principle is a revealing vehicle through

The Coinciding Principle

Knowing. It is tangible with a substance of its own, which is an energy, vitality, semi-fluidic, similar to the fluid drawn to a wound to heal a cut. Every ignorance unanswered is as a nescient wound awaiting to receive the healing Ni-science revelation from God.

The Coinciding Principle substance, as close as it may be described in a tangible manner, is a pregnable stuff from the higher mind of man projected from the soul. It is the first stuff of the soul which has substance, which is not of the flesh, but functions by and through and within the flesh of man.

Coinciding Principle substance remains after death in the bodies which survive death. It may be likened to a soul-blood through which the arterial flow of the spiritual atoms are made flexible for the use of the soul-powers.

The fluid-like substance of the Coinciding Principle exists in the total earth, astral, etheric and mental. It is a soul-activity flow of communion which holds together all communicating sentient and impressionable consciousness life. It can be likened to the white of the egg holding together the yoke of the egg.

Everything man thinks, everything man does and everything he desires to do function through the gel-like Coinciding Principle soul-substance. The telepathic waves of all mind-flows have their play and function in this energy fluidic aspect of soul-blood, which makes man a contacting spirit while living in a many-bodied vehicle of a planetary system.

All in the earth cannot be separate. All are incorporated in the one soul-blood of Coinciding action of energizing, feeling and thinking. Thus, one finds upon opening to the reality of the Coinciding Principle that there is no separation. The thoughts and feelings of all living in this world are of one mind. No one can be separated from their energy flows of God-knowing or God-unknowing.

Everyone is more directly responsible for his own nature once he understands that he must make union with God Who motivates the Coinciding Principle. In this, he becomes aware of the Archetypal compulsions coming directly from the Christ.

Union with one's Teacher to find God is a step forward in initiation, whereby the development of the supersensible side of the mind is assured.

All persons believe to some degree that the Eternal Cause or God sends a person to a right place at the right time to find what he needs as a remedy for his knowing, for his learning and for his healing.

Prayer acccelerates the Coinciding Principle working through that which is asked for and that which is responded to out of the great synchronized polarity of God as Omnipresence in one's life. Prayer makes one a direct witness to the Coinciding-Principle functioning. Coinciding events show him that this Principle given of God provides him with an extended discovering process whereby God is proved as being the One knowing every need, every desire, every longing.

When one becomes spiritualized through self-discipline and acceptance of the trials in Initiations, the Coinciding-Principle vitalities are active beyond psychic grossness; purification is extended into the spiritual.

The Coinciding effluvias of the soul carry with them the holy magnetisms, the holy attracting, the holy shepherding, and the holy health. Healing comes to that one who lives within these interconnected veracities stemming from that which is One and cannot die, and which is deathless and lives forever.

THE COINCIDING PRINCIPLE 163

Metaphysicians call the Coinciding Principle *mind.* Psychologists call it the *subconscious.* Spiritual persons call it *Intelligible Omnipresence,* recognizing it as the holy perception and witnessing vehicle for the Holy Esse or the Holy Spirit.

THE HIERARCHY PASSING

In the earth, men are divided into twelve types. These are called the *twelve prototypes.* Each prototype is born to express one of the signs of the zodiac.

The zodiacal-constellations system is under command of great Hierarchy Imagers, who with the Father of this eternity system imaged and made man in their likeness. *"Let us make man in our image, after our likeness." (Genesis 1:26)*

The twelve prototypal expressions in this eternity system are seeking to become a thirteenth prototype or like Jesus, who with our Father in heaven are the Hierarchs in this eternity system. It is the destiny of all men of the earth to become first in the likeness of the Hierarchs and finally to become the thirteenth Prototypal Image or "like" Jesus.

Jesus leads all men of this earth system toward their own individualized hierarchy powers. This is the true and essential purpose of this eternity system to become like Jesus and our Father in Heaven, and thus use the hierarchy powers within the Christ Mind.

Each prototype has its ego-functioning format which controls its karmic fate; it also has its cosmic connection with the Higher or Hierarchy Self which controls its destiny as an eternal son of God. One must incorporate all of the twelve zodiacal or Hierarchy prototypes within himself before his ego-passage in this solar system is completed. He can do this by love of neighbor and love for one another. One does this first by becoming co-atom to Jesus.

Jesus makes it possible for men to break down the karmic veils between prototypes.

Every existing sentient mass, as in a church body or group living within one archetypal idea or Hierarchy-consciousness principle, represents one prototype. The first Church represents the prototype of Peter. A group or mass prototypal entity representing one prototypal inclination is under one Hierarch or one zodiacal Ray. Peter portrays Aries, ruled by the planet Mars; the first Church was sometimes called the church militant.

The Species Angels govern and maintain the animal archetypal patterns for species creatures, both wild and domestic. The animal kingdom moves and experiences life through the Species Angels. Animals are not prototypes; only sentient man is a prototype.

Every prototype has an ego and an individuality. Specie creatures have two forms of life expression: one is derived from the specie which they represent, and the other expresses the reflection of the life in their environments and surroundings. For example, a dog comes to look and act like his master.

An animal has the subjective power of mirroring and reflecting his environment. Man has the God or Hierarchy power of visualizing and imaging his environment. The angels use angelic imaging. The angels are one of the eyes of the Father; they can see into the Godly in man. Their vision is fixed always in imaging this God Potential for man.

For man, in the movement of the Esse, the Esse-Vapor Holy Gas comes first as an etheric Vapor. It next becomes a whirling fountain-like crystal emanation of multitudinous lights sweeping with the Divine Passion of the Lord Jesus through the Holy Spirit, to heal, to give salvation, to cleanse.

In the first phases of the Esse, one receives the *Passing* through an individual having the Passing. When entered into with surrender to God to receive His Almighty Grace with total releasing, one receives individually with each sequence of Esse more and more of the Passing. From the Passing comes the *Opening*. One must be alert to make himself aware of more of the Opening.

With the Opening, one finds himself in the vibrational energies of the Coinciding Principle whereby he enters into his own prophetic soul-powers. He becomes a builder and the cleanser of his own nature. He verifies himself as a steward and a channel for God, that he may also become a worthy channel to heal through the Passing Power within the Passion of Jesus.

When one is Opened, he begins to live through the Hierarchy Powers within Jesus; he opens the Coinciding Principle. One who Passes lives in a constant state of union with his own Buddhi, which makes him a revelator and a discoverer within the hierarchy state of spiritual powers.

All is movement in the Esse. The Esse synchronization powers give one transenergization powers. He thus becomes Niscient or Knowing, being directly connected with the Informing Principle through his Buddhi nature.

With each Opening, Self-Revelation comes first on the level of the ego. From the interflow of soul-realized rhythmic practices and instruction accompanied by the Esse fulfillment, one is made aware of the ego-nature and eventually of the True Self; he becomes a master of the spiritual soul-forces rather than the servant of the Undersoul forces. Everything from the Esse provides the mind with the crystalline purities of the soul.

In Esse, one breaks down the dependencies upon outmoded tradition, replacing these with dependencies on God. It is the destiny of each one, in the whole and true consummation of the Esse, that he make his Undersoul the servant so that the Upa-Soul may draw aside the veil obscuring the Most High Soul and the True Self.

With trust, devotion and the acceptance of the disciplines on the Path, the soul-thread between the Teacher who passes the Dharma and his chela or student grows steadier until the Esse functioning of the trust-love becomes no longer a tug on the chela's heart atoms, but a firm, reassuring, balancing cable-tow. The chela then looks upon his Teacher not as a separate entity but as a divine-companion soul living in a rare atmosphere which he desires to attain.

The heart-rhythms of the Teacher providing heart-rhythms for the disciple have been mastered by the Teacher through the Hierarchy-heart Bhakti Initiations. Through the Teacher, the stepping stones of the rise from the novitiate state of the disciple extend into the superconscious which is of the Infinite, and therefore limitless.

Each day the spiritual life bears the soul-record of effort; any limiting tamas inertias act as an irritant in the Undersoul, preventing extension of soul-powers. If one habitually expresses the rajasic, the electricities of the negative produce a fiery cloud, a lightning and a thunder. Only where sattvic poise and sattvic calm exist can the Teacher's quickening regularities for the student or chela be experienced.

The Middle Path of the Tao correlates to the Esse. He who was Lao-Tzu lived in the Esse or Tao. He walked

The Coinciding Principle

far beyond the microcosmic densities of Maya. Now coming to birth through the Cosmos Disciples in the West is the Coinciding Dharma. This is the Dharma of the Christ taking one over the duality seas of the microcosmic into the macrocosmic. The Esse under Jesus leads the disciple into dimensions beyond sense into the Divine.

The Masters and the Esse

In the earth today and living in the astral planes, there are gurus who will never attain mastership. These indirectly serve the Great Teachers. Beyond these in evolvement are master-gurus who are the channelled *servers* for the Great Immortals, Elite or Masters.

The true Masters walk the course of the Hierarchs. These are the Old Ones, the Elect, whose works of the Primordial Days still exist in their natures. Only the adept living in the world has communication with those who are star-charted. Only those who have made union with their own direct Constellation Star can reach or touch the hem of their splendored gossamer light of the Eternals. The chain of the White Gurus serves as a mind-wave network of interrelating velocities leading to the Greater Elect, or Immortal Masters.

Time, Space, motion, gravity-mastery are of the Esse or Essence. *The Esse* is the charted way. Only the *Sat Guru*, Jesus, knows the Star-Codes and the Guide Stars to the whole and Holy Esse.

To live in the Esse is to be a utilizer of Maya forces and electrical charges. Moving into dimensions extended beyond Maya fixity gives the Esse freedoms.

He who lived in the body of Jesus lived in the Holy-Spirit Esse. Joseph, who sired Jesus, came from the Sirius orb. He is the Temple Masterbuilder for the dimensional

Temple-Ark of the Esse. Before being Joseph, he was that one called *Noah*. As an Immortal Master, he is the Noah for all who prepare the way for the deluge of the darkened storm now entering the world of Maya irritation.

Maya-energy irritation is now as a gas bag of helium moving toward fiery currents beyond controllable compass. Earth-Maya cataclysms are close at hand; the thunder of warning has long sounded. Suffering sent onto the face of the waters is close to the reaping time. Cleansing in the Undersoul astral-natures of men in the world must come, that men of earth may return to renewal of the primordial light. In future cataclysms and disasters affecting the earth, those who carry the virginal procreative seeds will be kept sacred and safe in the cleansing time or darkened days of the post Kali-Yuga days. Kali-Yuga is the dark night of the soul and mind. This darkened state disconnects man from God, causing him to believe the ego to be all.

Pollution of sin now requires renewal and revival of the primordial Esse, that the strong Edenic light or first beginnings may once more emerge. Primal cleansings always come before the great emergings of Primordiality.

The Primordial One or Ancient of Days works with the Hierarch-hearts of the Inward Hierarch-Immortals. These are the crowned Kings or Elect over the children of men. The Manu or Law-bringer works also with the Ancient of Days as the Law-giver through the sons of man. He who was Moses acted as a manu or law-giver for the Self-Genesis Age.

He who comes to accent law is under the Manu, the Law-giver. The Son of Man, Jesus, came to transenergize the suffering-octave enforcement of the Law. Jesus transposes the sentient suffering of the body to the suffering of the mind. This occurs in the mind of man as *conscience*.

Ego-suffering is relieved first through outward or external helps; eventually all suffering must be encountered and mastered from within. Self as the healer answers with a joy beyond suffering; for life in truth is joy. Truth moves upon the conscience as right Law stemming from the Manu positives or firmness within the Law.

The unknowing in the ego is the cause of suffering. The True Self does not suffer. When soul as movement acts within the heavier electricities within karma, there is first suffering, and then joy resulting from cleansing. No matter how stable a situation may appear, soul-velocity in the twinkling of the eye moves to shift the scene of the play to rearrange the karma, that one may circumvent the fixities of Maya recorded in the Undersoul.

The Esse soul-movement is beyond Maya or matter fixity. Soul-movement is the ordained victor over Time, Space and matter. In matter, soul-velocity uses the Maya dense electricities to produce form; to keep a balance between mind and body; and finally, through acceleration, to destroy the negatives so that the True Self may keep apace with the white electricities beyond Time and Space in the Universal Cosmos while living in the Cosmic.

SPIRITUALIZED INTELLECT

The more one knows, the closer he is to the karmic enforcement laws. Spiritualized Knowing or Niscience provides the spiritualized intellect through which one masters karma and enters into union with God.

One should be alert to those who are brilliant in only one thing. To follow such an one is to fall into his pitfalls of karma. Spiritualized intellect is absent from obsession, being creditable within the flexibilities of God-Realization;

making no claims for omniscience. Spiritualized-intellect ones come to bring the Christ-Mind, all-embracing Cosmos-thinking.

The point of brilliance in the intellect is the point of danger, for he who is dependent solely upon a brilliant intellect rather than God-intelligence is on the edge of the precipice of madness, in danger of falling into Luciferic darkness of soul-abnegation.

Sooner or later, one must let love enter into the building of the intellect; the first desire must be to spiritualize the intellect through love. The intellect must be spiritualized before one can enter into the spiritual life. The Divine Eye can *see* in no other way except through a spiritualized intellect.

Thinking overweightedly on the past produces senility for the aged. Thinking entirely on things for the future produces non-reality and non-reliability for the present. Thinking on things and caring only for the present produces emasculation or lack of refinement of the senses. Thinking in the Coinciding Principle within the Esse gives the interflow of the past, the present and the future as unity. From this comes a spiritualized intellect.

The beginning of the spiritualized intellect makes one a philosopher. Philosophy flows down to the roots of mind-realization, and grows up into the fruits of the spiritualized intellect. From such fruits, one extracts the elixir wisdom-truths by which he heals, teaches, and expands God as enlightenment.

The flexibilities of philosophy make the intellect less brittle, moving the mind-faculties toward the spiritualized intellect. The spiritualized intellect is the natural state of the higher mind, whereby man thinks in dimensional grace, thus blessing all whom he teaches and serves.

Men in love with the play of the intellect are critics and criticizers. The prideful intellect keeps alive prejudice.

The Coinciding Principle

The subversive intellect keeps alive bigotry. The archetypal wisdom refuses to imbed itself in the soil of bigotry or prejudice.

The fruits of Niscience, or the Buddhi-wisdoms, offer themselves only to him who has spiritualized his intellect within the Ahimsa progressions of his heart. Ahimsa, or harmlessness in motivation, is the fertilizer for the spiritualized intellect and the spiritualized will.

Man cannot cultivate the Ahimsa through intellect, neither can he develop it through the many attributes of the intellect. Only through a desireless self-will can he know the true Ahimsa blessings and grace.

When the heart reaches the Ahimsa state of love, the fluidic matrix of the will in the spine is perfected through kundalini's action. Fluidic will is that which wills within the Will of God without thought of ego, claim or fame.

Marking and Tracing

Man by blindness has made his surrounding environment inanimate; he unknowingly lives in a meaningful world ready to teach him. Being self-centered in ego, he fails to register the animated Intelligences in every form of life supporting his existence.

It is rare when one thinks of saying to the stones making up the chimney of his house: "Where did you come from? Why are you here, and what are you saying?" Nor does he commune with the trees and the plants as contributing factors to his own energy necessities. Insensitive traits coming from lack of hierarchy-nature knowing keep man in bondage to his ego experience. All great Sages tell the initiate to unite with the energy life-processes in the stone and with the sentient life in the plant and the animal, using these as the springboard for his God-nature to function.

There are voices uncountable in this earth seeking to

sound into the mind and knowing of man. Men are dull and spiritually illiterate because they are inattentive to the Spirit side of their hierarchy natures.

Millions in the earth today are no more than sentient vegetables, living to eat, to sleep. Above all, they desire to be safe. The Teacher who asks such ones, "Safe, from what?" is met by bewilderment and hostility.

No one in the world is totally secure from the Maya unpredictability forces unless he has knowledge of what these forces are saying. To understand the language of the forces present in one's own Undersoul cycles and rhythms is to be secure as an eternal being protected by Caring Intelligences watching over the growth and development of the mind.

When one is seated at the feet of instruction, he must be at home with the Life Principle; he must love Life for Life's sake. Jesus looked upon the children of God as little children. He knew that only through a child-like wonder and gratitude for the unceasing revelations of the Divine through the commonplace could one truly escape his fantasized expectations.

When one feels that he has a privileged right to demand of God special things for the comfort of his ego, he is inviting the discomforts of aloneness, neglects, poverties and of being downgraded to the level of nothing.

To know that one is verily a son of God, having access to the abundance of God, assures him of all his basic needs. It frees him from the bondage of surfeit and luxury, that he may run as well as walk while living within the time-scale of limitation through materiality.

The Caring Presences are a part of our Father's Kingdom. These are the Divine Companions who stand by one's side when he has entered the Path. When one goes beyond the testing side of the guidance he receives from the Coinciding Principle, and has set up the Father's Kingdom in his own nature, he is in contact with the high side of his Coinciding nature; and his hierarchy nature is free to use all of the energies which have been transenergized through spiritual competency and the helps of Mediation given so lovingly by Caring Omnipresence.

One should practice in some portion of his meditation-times the art of receptivity given freely by the Divine Companions who have proved God in their own natures and are fed in their souls by direct union with the Guiding Principle of God.

To test the Guiding Principle, one must have as a Teacher one who has mastered his own life within the Guiding Principle. Trust in the Guiding Principle present in all forms of life expressions builds a perfect vehicle for receptivity. The Coinciding Principle becomes refined, quick, flawless, perfectly polarized through faith and trust.

In cases of karmic solutions for one who first enters the Path, testing the Guidance Principle is often painful and ego-deflating. In this, there is the danger of one cooling his efforts and spiritual aspirations. If he falls from the Path, he will lose touch with his Teacher for many lives.

St. Paul has said: *"Despise not prophesyings; prove all things, hold fast to that which is good." (1 Thessalonians 5:20)* The earlier part of the Path is a very sensitive and sometimes a seemingly painful way to walk. If there be any treachery in the heart of one who seeks to enter the Path, he will betray himself and his Teacher and also his Teacher's Teaching; he will become a dissenter, throwing the stones of slander against his Teacher. In this, he blasphemes his providence, and thus misses the opportunity to be a part of the Great Way, that he might receive the One Truth and the One Life of the Eternals.

One may liken some persons who enter the Path to a child of kindergarten age who resists his removal from the home securities of his mother. Such children, on entering school, are yin children. The yin child seeks to have a late weaning from its mother. So does one with an unprepared heart who would be an initiate resist—on entering the Path—the disciplines as represented by the Path.

All Teachers are fortified against the stone-throwing of treacherous would-be disciples. They are insulated, for they are God-related directly to the Guidance of God.

True Teachers understand that stones thrown against them can neither change their purpose nor divert their truths, for the Holy Spirit Esse is the Holy Wind of God. There can never be a throwing stone equal to the levitating power of the wind of the Holy Spirit.

God has made it so that over-zealous attentiveness thwarts receptivity. When a person is bent upon getting his own way at all times, he sets fire to his Undersoul, and must undergo the burning away of ego-fixities. Under the Will of God, there are times and cycles when one experiences the Burning-Bush Initiation, that his Undersoul may consume excessive preponderances in the ego. In this, he learns of the Commandments of life on all levels.

If a student or disciple finds his Teacher in timing to the explosion of the ego or the egotistical shell, this is a *hard way* for the disciple. In this time, it is a grace-necessity that he have a Teacher to work with him to free the psychic voltages flowing forth from the Undersoul.

To do this, the Teacher must Pass to the disciple the knowledge of Transenergization. The Teacher also must work with the disciple on the inner planes and make him aware of his hierarchy nature and how to use it, and especially give to him the ethic by which it may be used.

When the disciple responds to the knowledge of his own

The Coinciding Principle

hierarchy nature, he will be more and more aware of the Guiding Principle stemming from Omnipresence, which includes all of the Presences in the Kindgom of God who have mastered the awareness of God.

Transenergization begins with *Marking and Tracing.* Marking and Tracing are a very unique gift seeking to spiritualize the intellect, that one may serve God under His direct Guidance.

Grace provides hope; from Grace comes Guidance. Guidance is the Verifying Principle telling one that God is a caring God, a loving God.

The perfected nature in man is known by God. When one becomes Self-Realized, he claims his perfection — and thereafter he walks in the more perfected way. This is the Grace: man through the Will of God in his hierarchy nature is to become a perfected fulfillment of God's perfection.

All Telepathic Disciples and Cosmos Disciples have access to the techniques of Marking and Tracing. All ideas which come to the world to preserve goodness in man come through those having extended Marking and Tracing powers. Marking-and-Tracing nature makes man more than an existing particle dependent upon portions of Nature to feed him and to provide him with the meaning of life.

Marking and Tracing are more than a gift. They are the vital intelligible function in all of the gifts combined, that one may ultimately be chosen — that is, become a proportioned vehicle whereby God is served.

Knowing oneself, knowing others, knowing what is happening, and why it is happening — all are part of Marking and Tracing. Marking and Tracing are an Archetypal hierarchy-nature attribute. The ego attribute of the Undersoul also marks and traces what the body does and why the body does it.

The Archetypal mind of the hierarchy nature knows through long aeons of the use of creation overdirected by the soul. Marking and Tracing function in all instances and occasions in thinking in the body and out of the body.

The hierarchy nature is the will function of the Will of God in man. Through the Will of God, one uses his Archetypal mind to mark and trace each situation and event offered to him by life, by existence.

The Marking-and-Tracing attribute is the opener of all situations whereby one can know what is being said, why it is being said, in all functions. When the Marking-and-Tracing attribute of the Archetypal mind is active, one is responsible for his fellow man who is yet undeveloped in the use of the Archetypal mind. Marking and Tracing are therefore the most important and vital attribute needed in a life of service for God.

Hierarchy nature wills man to become a perfect self. Hierarchy nature moves man beyond the Time-limiting ego-experience.

The Marking-and-Tracing system and its procedures give to those who desire God-Realization a fulfillment of Soul-Realization. From the first practice, exercise and spiritual technique, one is led into his own Marking-and-Tracing nature as given through his Archetypal mind. Through the use of the higher suggestibles in his hierarchy nature, he works within the Coinciding Principle protected by the *Just Law* stemming from the Will of God, and thus serves in the world with insulation and protection.

He who marks and traces with hierarchy-nature techniques leaves an *eternal mark* in the earth, whereby those who follow him can make their way by *tracing* the thought processes of the mind of him who has marked and traced.

In Marking and Tracing, one lays himself open first to his conscience and second to his Constant. The Constant fixes the discovering aspect within Marking and Tracing. Conscience working with the Guiding Principle shows him the way to extricate himself from limiting conditions caused by omission and deviation.

The conscience is the research vehicle for the soul. He who has a healthy researching conscience has emotional health and moral integrity. A researching conscience enables a person to be wise with the wisdom of a sage whereby he researches and understands the nature of his desires, his motives and his weaknesses.

The researching conscience comes through Marking and Tracing. Marking and Tracing produce a true stability of emotions and mind. The Marking-and-Tracing system automatically uses the discarding principle or the neti-neti powers: *Not this, not that.*

The intuitive flow enables one to incorporate the consciousness-expanding states of the Informing Principle. The quickening of the intuitive flow makes one reliable as a steady, centered point of light. He who marks and traces the Undersoul volatile energies and forces develops the higher intuition through which he can view the flow and interflow within the creation powers of his soul.

The Marking-and-Tracing aptitudes, when united with the Cherubim flow of humor which exists in the Coinciding Principle, enable one to be resilient, tactful.

Marking and Tracing pull aside the obscuring hindrances which veil the realities so clearly seen when Marking and Tracing are used. True healing begins when one discards the judging and condemnation aspects which reside in the lower mind. Through Marking and Tracing, one moves out of Undersoul suction.

It is not that man is a fool; it is that he is unknowing and unawakened. One in the world having the aptitude for the use of his researching-conscience nature is a true

Marking-and-Tracing initiate. He moves beyond the enclosure tendencies of his ego into the dimensions of observation and insight.

Intuition is a natural product stemming from Marking and Tracing. Through Marking and Tracing, one trans-energizes weakness into strength, darkness into light, sickness into health, ignorance into knowledge.

The disciplined disciple uses Marking and Tracing first through Meditation.

Second: Through the keeping of a Dream Diary, he observes and opens the dream codes which contain the seed-knowledge related to the dream. He marks and traces the energy-processes which flow into his consciousness from the dream state or states. He utilizes this energy of his dreams to keep open the cognizant side of dreams. In this, he is always in the state of Guidance from the dream and also while awake in the physical portion of a day.

Third: He keeps a journal which relates him to the interflow of all things spiritual; things related to past-life knowledge being assimilated in the present life. He is attentive and aware of association and the *why* in shared day-by-day experience.

Fourth: He is aware of his conscience, enabling him to choose through right discrimination and discernment.

Fifth: He is aware of persons God-sent; and he is aware of persons sent to act as a *vajra* exposing him to his own faulty concepts and wrongdoing.

Sixth: He puts into practice the cyclic and rhythm system through adhering to worship-practices, study-practices, service-oriented creativities.

Seventh: He stands back from himself and observes where he is and why he is, and thus enters into Self-Realization, Soul-Realization and, ultimately, God-Realization.

Marking and Tracing are man's divine privilege as a

being of consciousness living in this world. His condemnation of himself produces abnormality in every aspect of his nature. When the judging side of his nature is spiritualized, he comes under the Guiding and Correcting Principle within his soul and within God.

The brief span of life man experiences is too short for him to bear by himself. He finds freedom when he comes to realize that there are *Clouds of Witnesses* and soul supports in everything, in everyone, and in dimensional realms beyond enclosures, tensions and separateness. Marking and Tracing make of one a spiritual giant walking above and beyond the limited, experimental aspects of the Maya physical life.

One may liken Marking and Tracing to the rainbow-bridge between Self-Realization and God-Realization. One walks over this bridge which expands from sea to sea, earth to earth, man to man, angel to God. He becomes part winged in the powers of the mind and part rooted in the earth in powers of the soul.

It is by no accident that all great seers and saints tell their little ones or chelas to *Know thyself.* The only way that one can know himself is by acknowledging what he *is not* and what he *is*.

The Pathway to God provides one with the dimensional space through Marking and Tracing. The living Teacher who comes to teach the Marking-and-Tracing way has been earned by the chela. If the chela or student is ready to move over conceptual-enclosure knowledge dependencies, he will turn the key to this way of enlightenment, which is the only way through which man can build a Pathway to Niscience or the Knowing of God.

If one takes hold and controls his fantasy, he enters into the true imaging processes to be gained from Marking and Tracing. To benefit to the fullest from Marking and Tracing, one must realize that he is dealing with forces and energies that are *Intelligible,* which by processes of Intelligence have taken over the mind and emotions.

The immature emotions of man make him a dependent being relying upon the pleasure principle. The law of the lower mind and the ego is that it is always seeking applause for its action. In the Undersoul spill-over or releasing, one dies to pride by entering into mortification trials. Comprehension with Marking and Tracing assures that the higher mind is involved in the tensions of the Undersoul, and thereby the beginning of freedom is near.

Marking and Tracing enable a person to recognize the interflow of energy-processes. One's own body becomes a laboratory.

The search is fine and sensitive. By constant diligence and turning inward, one comes to recognize the interconnecting relationships between every plane of forming and shaping through consciousness existence.

YANTRA DREAMS AND THE COINCIDING PRINCIPLE

Yantra dreams are a prolonged, combined observation and participation. In this phase of dreaming, one's emotions are extended intensely; codes are magnified so that they take on a sense of supernatural insight.

In the yantra dream, one encounters coming lives' potential, whereby he can incorporate into his coming-birth expectancies defense mechanisms. This mechanism retained for a coming birth enables one to enter the world centered within his Constant, and thereby protected from challenge, persecution or rejection.

It is the emotional body that extends dream tolerance. Dream tolerance may be defined as extension of length of time in dreams, providing a form of lingering observation in one point of a dream.

It is the emotional strength and will within the emotions

which enable the dreamer to practice Time-extension in a dream. One awakens from a dream of this nature with a profound and lingering feedback revealing the significant aspects within the dream.

The Coinciding Principle, in the right side of the brain, is fed and nourished by energies within the emotions which are utilized in such prolonged dreaming states. Thus, the Coinciding Principle and the prolonged yantra dream work as one in the Buddhi-chain of memory which is beyond physical memory.

The prolonged yantra dream maintains the stability between dreaming and the Coinciding Principle. When one has this facet fully organized in dreaming and waking, he has mastered to some degree both Time and Space. His emotional body—the main vital strength acting as the charge-vita—functions in the physical world within the Coinciding Principle. He is thus prepared for things to come in every aspect of his consciousness.

Time becomes one within the One. The Spirit of Truth, acting as the Esse, provides the master-reflex power within the Constant; a range of action; a way of foreseeing; a knowledge of the seeming unknowledgeable.

Dream insight and dream wisdom function in the waking state as well as in the sleeping state of consciousness.

One lives in a Timeless state when he is working, living and thinking within the Coinciding Principle. One lives then within astonishments without astonishment.

As one proceeds in the spiritual life, he gathers more volume. As the singer must cultivate the reflexes of his diaphragm to gather the higher ranges of sound in his singing, one who enters the Coinciding-Principle way of life increases a valid venturing into a form of knowing rated as unusual by those dependent upon the habit-mechanics of lesser-mind observation and participation.

9

HEALING WITH THE HIERARCHY NATURE

Come unto me, all ye that labour and are heavy laden, and I will give you rest. Take my yoke upon you, and learn of me; for I am meek and lowly in heart: and ye shall find rest unto your souls. For my yoke is easy, and my burden is light.
—*St. Matthew 11:28–30*

THE HEALER

Good seeks no victory in fighting evil. Good of itself is the enemy of evil. When there is true goodness and sincere manifestation of its holy worth, this is the Arm of God casting out evil with Good. Good is the true physician representing our Father.

The Lord does not desire His sons and daughters to be healers only in the physical world. He desires them to be healers in all dimensions. Therefore, all must be knowing-disciples of His Word and His Way to dispense His Word.

The healer must be aware of the Night Ministry and its healing resources, and he must increase his powers of visitation whereby he may heal in hell, in heaven and in earth. Hell on the physical plane is suffering in man. But there is a hell of equal nature built from the debris of sin and error in man which must also be healed, that it be not a continuing source of evil-fallout of evil-suggestibility upon the astral, impressionable nature of man.

Since the Kingdom of God is within all, the healer must be there, aware of the Omnipresence of God as being also there.

The Vibration of God in suffering is the key to the mastery of suffering. He who finds it is healed, and thereby becomes a healer.

There is only one disease: absence from God. There is only one healer: faith in God.

The Omnipresence of God enables one to bear life and its sufferings. The Omniscience of God enables him to understand life and its complexities. The Omnipotence of God enables one to overcome sickness, sorrow, suffering, lack and ignorance. A great belief will set these three into operation at all times.

A miracle is merely the raising of the consciousness, receiving the abundance of Heaven.

The first thing occurring in the life of a babe at birth is suffering. Its mortal cry caused by the pressure of the Maya circulations in air and in the breath expresses suffering. The shock of encounter with physical energies produces sensitivity to pain. Fear and apprehension accompany the first life-breath. If assuring love is absent in the mother and those who deliver the baby, apprehension for the total life induces overweighted fear, distrust and pain.

Hierarchy-nature healers are the product of many ages of empathy-initiation trials; they have attained the Holy Agape or concern for the unknowing sufferers in the world. Some of these healers appear in the world as Intentional Sufferers. Their sufferings link them to the pain waves of man's unrequited conscience. Intentional Suffering carries with it a certain kind of grace-immunity strength. A healer having this strength withstands his own pain while transenergizing the pain of others.

The hierarchy-nature healer works for the world-soul as well as the individual soul. His mental and heart atoms operate on the level of the eternal atoms of the higher unconscious, where the true Archetypes exist.

The hierarchy-nature healer's thinking and care for the sick see the illimitable grace provided for all souls in prototypal form. His hierarchy nature abides within a fullness of grace in total awareness of God's good pleasure and love for His sons of the earth and of heaven.

Any kind of disease that decays or disarranges the flesh is a mortification disease. Mortification diseases stem from the astral or emotional nature, leading directly to heart initiation to gain Ahimsa, or a selfless love.

All redemption sicknesses relate to the calling forth or the lifting process of the consciousness. Redemption sicknesses relate to the mental processes of the mind; through such sicknesses, one dies to the ego-delusion that the physical life is the all.

All restitution sicknesses relate to chronic, crippling diseases in which the bone structure is distorted. This relates to former-life gene ancestral-karmas inheritance. Restitution Grace enables the sick with bone diseases to unburden their ancestral inheritances. Through service to the human race, Restitution Grace is made.

Acute sicknesses are activated by one's Guardian Angel and Recording Angel to alert one as to the Law of Timing; to heal the procrastination tendencies; and to stir up and reveal the sediment tamasic tendencies in one's nature.

All sicknesses occurring in the spirit of redemption are

Healing With the Hierarchy Nature

the healing demonstrables or the proof of God as perfection. All sicknesses experienced in the spirit of restitution are illuminative, revealing the cause of omission. All sicknesses occurring in the spirit of mortification are humility births. All acute sicknesses are time-cycle sicknesses seeking to adjust or to return the one sick to cyclic order, harmony, peace.

The hierarchy-nature imaging power is most successful when one is optimistic. When one is depressed and negative, fearful and unbelieving, he is united with the destroying archetypes. One who is continually in a state of depression assures himself of a life of limitation and of failure. All healers are enthusiastic and joyful transcribers of their archetypal imaging power.

Healing Grace and the Constant

Return to the Constant.
Live in the Constant.

The psychic healer invades the biased and disorganized energy-process in the body of one sick, giving temporary stimuli to energies existing in magnetic levels in the astral nature. The hierarchy-nature healer pervades the imaged primordial Matrix containing the *true* perfected nature of the one sick. The hierarchy-nature healer heals within the vibrationless wavelengths or the enfoldment of the higher unconscious.

The hierarchy-nature healer's own spiritual atoms unite with the higher eternal atoms within the higher etheric body of the one sick. Through right visualization and mantra-suggestibility, the healer returns the one sick to his true Image or Divine Matrix. All healing is the return to one's *Constant* or the primordial Matrix where the imaged or archetypal design of the one sick knows not sickness or death.

God is the Constant. He is unvarying in man's variabilities. The Image Matrix in the Higher Self contains the Constant of God. All must seek to remain united with their Constant; through the Constant, God is realized.

Man is in a state of changing changelessness within the Constant of God. He is therefore God-like in his true essential nature, where the Holy Spirit or Esse has its free play.

Faith in God is the language of the Constant. As Job turned not loose of his Constant through faith in God, so was he redeemed. All who unite with their Constants are destined to return to God and to manifest in *fulness of grace* perfection, joy, happiness.

If it were not for the Constant in man, there would be no Consciousness. Man is only what he is *conscious* of.

Many believe that when one dies there is no consciousness. The Constant in man retains consciousness after death as well as in life. Through the Constant, one transenergizes his pain into consciousness.

He who is under *Absolute God* is in his Constant. He who learns through separative situations or specializes in one-pointed thinking and acting relates his consciousness and his faith to *Conditioned God.*

Our Father which art in heaven is the Hierarch of this eternity system; He is *Conditioned God.* Conditioned God as our Father is a *Being.* God, Absolute God, is not a Being—He is a *Spirit.*

God Absolute projects from Himself Being as Consciousness and ego as consciousness. There are many Fathers Who are Hierarchs. Saint Paul said: *"There be gods many." (1 Corinthians 8:5)* In the range of consciousness, the Fathers are first, next to Christ. Christ, being Spirit and the only begotten Son of God, acts in the minds of both Beings and prototypes. To pray to Conditioned God is to make union with the Christ Spirit and with God Absolute, Eternal Spirit.

He who worships God must progress through all states of consciousness to become a *Witness* of God, and thereby attain to God-Realization. Through the varied stages of consciousness in deep and uttermost desire to unite with God, one is omnipotently enfolded within the various stations of Omnipresence which, through states of consciousness, make one aware of God and His many and varying aspects and attributes.

Our Father which art in heaven is the ruling Hierarch of this eternity system; Jesus, who is one with Him, is also a Hierarch in this eternity system. All eternity systems have a Hierarchy Being or Father overdwelling them, who, next to the Christ, is closest to Absolute God, Spirit Eternal.

The majority of scientifically-minded men, the product of lower Self-Genesis, do not understand the difference between our Father and Absolute God. Those who are caught on the cross-walk of agnosticism and atheism bring to the world a lower degree of worship-rituals which divert the soul-expression and evaluate life-experience on earth through scientific, psychological and humanistic supports. If this continues, men will become laggard or tamasic, caught into Maya materialism, dependent solely on their senses for loving, exploring and discovering.

It is inevitable in the Increase of God that men will increase in both the supersensible and in the inner nature supported by the *conscience* or Psyche attribute of the soul. The very aspect of men pursuing and cultivating will of itself move them beyond the agnostic and the atheistic. Men, by the proving facilities through struggle in the earth, will prove that Absolute God and Conditioned God are essentially One and the same in the sense that the Spirit of God projects Himself through both sentience and consciousness.

Men are still very limited in God-Realization, especially so in lesser Self-Genesis. However, in the eternal Time and tuning-fork of God, it is an Ultimate that men who are created of Light must return to the Source of Light, which is God.

Man illumined is in higher Self-Genesis. He is a trans-energizer of the gross energies allotted by the senses.

Our Father which art in heaven and the Lord Jesus are true Constant-Vehicles of Eternal Spirit. To eat and sup with our Father and with Jesus is to unite with our Father in heaven who knows the number of every hair on one's head; who also knows the promises given through Absolute God, that men in themselves are to become that which Absolute God has willed.

Everyone contains in his nature twelve prototypal natures. These are his inheritance through and from our Father which art in Heaven and the ten Fathers or Hierarchs in command of the zodiacal system.

The two Hierarchs in this earth are Jesus and the Father, making twelve Hierarchs all together. Buddha worked with the ten Hierarchy powers. He had no knowledge of the two Hierarchs: Jesus and the Father.

The Buddha chain of the avatars ended a great cycle of Hierarchy functioning for mankind of the earth. With the coming of Jesus working with our Father which art in heaven, the Buddha knowledge flowed into the potential Jesus Hierarchy-powers latent in all souls.

With all of His perfection and insight, Buddha did not attain full Hierarchy potential in his own nature. Those who are dependent upon the Buddha-chain of enlightenment are limited to the ten Hierarchy prototypal powers in their natures.

Buddha came to prepare men for the Jesus Hierarchy-powers. To be enlightened in the Buddha-chain is to prepare for Jesus Hierarchy-nature in one's own being.

Polarization within the Constant

When one becomes polarized, he becomes alien to the whole society.

All forms of spiritual expression produce polarization between the higher mind and the soul. Polarity stabilization can come only through experiencing the Third Music within one's Constant. When polarized through the Constant, one moves out of the range of the multiplicities within Maya into the greater expansion of Light.

Due to the Maya emphasis expressed in the alternates of duality, men resist polarized ideas which contain the solution to their imbalances. One day in the valley and the next day on the mountaintop is the fate of all who live within expectancies of permanency in the Maya situation.

All men existing in the energy system of Maya are subjected to excess or to little. The lower mind suffers excruciatingly because it fails to understand the command of the alternates in duality.

Mental effort must be acquired through the use of volatile expectancies. Dependency upon lower-mind psychic excitation defuses spirituality.

There is no limit to the Bliss Principle. The Pleasure Principle, when practiced on the duality levels of Maya, produces tragedy and comedy. Man is one day a heavenly Pegasus and the next day a jackass eating the straw of disillusion.

The grace aspect given to man for his self-delusion pitfalls is humor and comedy. When one can cleanse himself of fantasy-expectations, he becomes a humorist of high order working with the Cherubim; he can see with Yantra insight the mountains and the valleys and accept them as part of the scene he has contracted for by coming to birth in a Maya system.

God as the Increase is a Volatile Stirrer homogenizing duality existence, thereby making Himself known in all situations. Where teaching is the main expression, one learns through the buffeting of God's Increase in the alternates.

Conscience is used to give man insight, courage and healing through right discernment. Fear, acting within the low-octave of karma, leans one in the direction of gene-tendency in disease.

"The thing which I greatly feared is come upon me." (Job 3:25) Insight and vision come from high perception, which is grace. Fear comes from photographing what one fears onto the subjective etheric computing system of the lesser etheric body.

The lesser etheric body is similar to a photograph negative. Fear imprints upon this negative fluidic substance of the etheric body, which in turn, through the Law of Increase, comes to ripeness in karmic timing in the physical body.

The photographing receptive-negative within the etheric body acts with the law of cycles in the progressive development of the brain. The brain is a responding Time-machine working directly with the negative imprints within the lesser etheric body. The brain sounds off the alarm for the lesser etheric body, producing psychological reactionary states in the mind—preparing one to receive the malfunctions of the physical body.

Healing With the Hierarchy Nature

All chronic diseases are first conditioned into the subconscious functioning of the mind. Until one is ready karmically to externalize a disease condition into the physical body, the warning signals from the etheric body and the subconscious are experienced in dreams and in dream warnings.

Only when one is ready to receive a sickness does the brain function to order the cells and the organs to sound off that which is to be suffered as pain and disease. Dreams are, therefore, prophets, foreseeing coming ailments, afflictions, accidents, and all things which have been incubated and prepared between the functioning of the etheric body and the subconscious.

Every sickness experienced on the physical plane has come to the individual by an increasing accumulation of deviations. The true method in the hierarchy nature of healing begins first by inspiring the one to be healed to know himself as a being of love. Therefore, the visualizing process or pictograph method of healing begins with love; visualizing trust, peace, worth, health and happiness pictured in a stream of visualized dramas into the receptive consciousness of the one to be healed.

The visualization procedure will automatically reach the inner receptivity and desire for the one to be healed. This automation will automatically flow out the mental and emotional Undersoul poisons to be eliminated, enabling the one to be healed to experience in his own visualizing-imaging processes all of the wrong he has done, producing his ailment. In this spilling-out process, there is relief for the one sick; there is purging and cleansing.

'The hierarchy-nature healing in the next stages of visualization sees this excrement of negativity and trans-energizes it into the true Image or the opposite of its negation—that is, if the spill-out contains guilts stemming from hatred, greed, envy, lack of faith in God, the hierarchy-nature healer visualizes at this time and transenergizes hate into love, greed into giving, envy into sharing and gratitude, separateness into acceptance. The collective negativity of the Undersoul spills out inevitably in the second phases of hierarchy-nature healing.

It is necessary for the hierarchy-nature healer to remember that sickness is only experienced in the Maya duality levels and planes of existence. Physical-sickness is not experienced in any other planes of existence except in the physical world. Sickness occurs in the physical plane because it functions through the duality polarities: one in the physical world is either sick or well, happy or unhappy, right or wrong, good or bad.

A hierarchy-nature healer always visualizes the opposite of a negativity, or only pictures for the one he would heal the opposite of its state. In this way, he visualizes and indents as a pictograph for the person to be healed the rightful balance in the polarity, and thus brings about the healing.

The mind is a visualizing and imaging vehicle or instrument. To visualize, one must literally see while in a spiritual state of God-awareness that which is the true Image or the Superior Vibration over a negative, limited vision in the lower vibration or the darkened side of polarity.

Health and the Sattvic

> *Seek with all thy heart to gain the sattvic peace. Unite with the harmonics of the Cosmos. Accept timing and space as the directors through which you may master life and life-forces with elegance, grandeur, glory and joy. Peace.*

In the study of the life processes, one must learn to budget his aggressions. His first phase of channelling his aggressions is through self-responsibility and support of one's self financially. Inclusive in this is his payment and obligation to life-supports for others for whom he is responsible. His second phase of budgeting his aggressions and channelling his responsibilities is his right as an individual. In this, he faces his true and only adversary—his ego.

All in the earth come with aggressions. As one evolves, these aggressions must be channelled into creation. As an individual, one must know himself, the meaning of himself. Through initiation he removes the mask of his adversary—the ego—to finally come to the time when the real of himself expresses all that he is in reality rather than what others think him to be.

There can be no health in the body when aggressions are wrongly channelled or misused. The very cells of the body working with the memory system of the will to live, the will to know, and the will to create—when out of balance—produce irritation, inflammation and infection.

Every cell of the body is aggressive. When absent from the sattvic principle of love, there is sickness to the body. When one has finally reached the state of true self-awareness, his body functions in a dimension of health, unity and harmony.

A sattvic nature supports the harmonies of the Universe. One must strive to accept the challenges of life, the demands of karma within his own nature, and within the nature of others.

One should learn to read his own Recording Angel's record, seeing himself as an impersonal, energized vehicle of moods and aggressions. He must learn the difference between the kinetic pressures within the cellular nature. He must see in himself the supersensible inclinations.

If his aggressions incline him toward intrigue, secrecy, manipulation, he writes his own epithet of existence, for he exists rather than lives—domiciled within ignorance. Life processes to him seem accidental, fortuitous.

There can be little meaning in a life of hatred founded upon the preservation of envy, jealousy, covetousness and revenge. The sattvic peace once gained assures health, intelligence, freedom.

A malignant disease reveals that one has a portion of the mind which is malignant. One thought, when statically fixed within the thought-making process of the mind, is obsession. Malignant diseases are the outer manifestation of one obsessed thought standing before the soul. The magnification of the soul goes down deep into the cesspool of obsession, reproducing the mind malignancy on a certain level of the cellular system.

In each cell there are three points of sentient relatedness. The lowest tonal rate in the cell is from the gene inheritance. The secondary tone in the cell is the individual ego-memory and Undersoul compulsions. The third cellular tone, when reached, is the healer of the two lesser, secondary tones in the cell.

To be healed of a malignant disease, one must unite himself with all things sattvic. To do this, he gives thanks for his disease as a blessing of revelation. He gives thanks for the self-honesty providing self-revelation. He gives thanks for the harmony of existence providing life experience. He gives thanks to God for His Correcting Principle. He gives thanks for the merciful anointing of the Angel for every phase of his pain and suffering. He gives thanks for the contraclockwise fires which are eating up the malignancies, producing the white fires of God-seeing and knowing.

He who is healed of malignancy has sattvic grace. It is the work of the therapist working with soul and body to teach to the sufferer the mighty power of Imaging, which is centered in the middle of the forehead in the Indestructible Atom, where death is neither heard nor known.

To visualize with the sattvic Imaging Power is to use hierarchy nature and to return as a pure divine soul to the God-Image fixed in the inner parts of his higher etheric nature. This Image cannot be sick, disturbed or distorted, or know sickness, disease, suffering or sorrow. This Image is whole. Its breath, its life and its light thrive upon the Will of God pictured as perfection within all persons, all things created.

The battleground presently existing in such large measure against malignant diseases is an inheritance of many generations passed down through the lower tonal cell-gate of the genes and the secondary cell-gate of the ego. He who knows the sattvic and practices the sattvic with his hierarchy nature is a healer of first magnitude, a master over the tumults of separation and dysfunction.

All healers must become sattvic hierarchy-nature healers. The hierarchy nature and the sattvic suggestibles are one and the same. Through one's claim upon his rightful and divine nature—which is to will within the embodiment of life—light and love must be the continuing state in the consciousness of the healer day and night.

The sattvic or hierarchy-nature healer does not look upon disease as an unreality. He looks upon it as a state of consciousness overburdened by sense or sentient relationships.

Image in man is perfect. All sickness is distortion of

Image. Distortion of Image in man is sense and sentient information based upon duality. The sattvic or hierarchy-nature healer does not ignore all of the functionings which have produced obsession and therefore distortion of Image.

Sattvic and hierarchy are of the divine three or third existing in all forms by and through which man is made perfect in the Image of God, in the atmosphere of perfect good, as realized by the Father for man and as sealed into him in the beginning of this eternity system.

Myopic sense revelation is biased toward disease. The vibration of Ahimsa moves one out of sense-related Image interpretation. Therefore, to be healed, the healer must teach the sufferer to rearrange his heart as a vessel of harmlessness, whereby healing moves beyond mercy or the bearing of suffering into total healing and return to perfect Image as given of God.

Hierarchy nature is a power nature functioning as the Will of God. Hierarchy nature has dominion over sentient nature. Sattvic perfection in the hierarchy nature provides peace, acceptance.

Preparation of the heart demands that one throw out the spoils of pride, overthrow ego-expectation of superiority, accepting the terms laid down by the divine nature to forgive all who have worked to frustrate one's holy and spiritual aspirations and expectations. These are the terms for one having any form of sickness or discomfort, that he may be healed. An Ahimsa heart clean, pure, sincere, returning to its own good and giving good for all regardless of all: this is sattvic; this is hierarchy nature functioning in the ever-increase of healing, anointing, illuminating.

The physical world is a great way-station of correction of karmas. It is a way-station for gravity experience. It is also a way-station of opportunity for creation, for it is the work of man to spiritualize the gravity-processes of the earth, and to extend the molecular processes of the atomic world.

Earth solar system or eternity system must undergo the duality processes. One who moves beyond the duality processes lives in the third aspect beyond duality, where the *two* are made into the *three,* and the *seven* into the *eight,* and the *twelve* into the *thirteenth.*

When men achieve the *three,* they function within the *fourth* and *fifth* dimensional consciousness, where the geometries supporting the Maya systems are made flexible and creative.

The *seventh,* by which man is initiated in timing cycles that he may become the *eighth,* enables him to move into the *eighth sphere* or the planes of anti-matter supporting matter, called the astral kingdoms.

The *twelfth,* by which he becomes the *thirteenth,* is the hierarchy nature within the *twelve* prototypal identifications.

Lord Jesus Christ opened the sattvic hierarchy-nature gate centered in the Indestructible Atom in the center of the forehead. Calling on the Name of Jesus opens this gate and moves one toward the *thirteenth* aspect of his hierarchy nature patterned after Jesus, who represented the *thirteenth* principle among His *twelve.*

Jesus was the Sattvic Presence of God in the midst of the suffering of man. He functioned and operated through the hierarchy nature within the *thirteenth* principle. All hierarchy-image forms created in the likeness of the Father and Hierarchy express themselves through *twelve* Prototypal forms: these *twelve* in the earth in the spirit of goodness seek to become in the likeness of Jesus and thereby express the *thirteenth* principle or their sattvic natures.

He who is *open* receives the power to Pass. The sattvic nature is his natural heritage spiritually given by God from the beginning.

God is the Creator. Our Father is the Maker. All Imaged in the likeness of the Father are makers.

The spiritual power of Making is made possible by Imaging. The power of Imaging in man is *visualization*. All vision-processes work with some level or degree of the suggestible and impressionable.

Man in duality is an automaton. Man with the third aspect is a maker and imager of high order of Spirit; the Holy Esse empowers him to be a healing presence in the midst of trouble, sorrow, death, affliction.

The entanglements of duality do not offer or provide full truth or enlightenment. The third nature of man, or his sattvic sovereignty, seeks to lead him beyond sensuality indulgences and testings to the holy certainties of proven righteousness. In this, the healer is healed, and the sufferer is made whole as a witnessing vehicle for God.

Everything man visualizes in the Spirit of Truth through the Holy Spirit will happen. The bad happenings in a person's life, the cause-and-effect chain of failure and success, make man a victim of unsettled polarity, imbalancing his body, obscuring his morality, over-emphasizing his ego-prominence, and under-cutting God as the Supreme in all.

The choice is in the heart: to choose the Way or to remain in enticements of an obsessed lower-mind living. The Ahimsa heart is a rearranged heart and a heart empty of devices, cunning and manipulations.

Life is in man. Manipulation offends the life-flow, short-circuiting its essential and first purity. Thus, the lower mind of man is in reality a false god, misdirecting him into the belief that he is the lord over all he can see, taste, smell, touch and hear.

A sattvic mind is not an impractical mind in its relation to the physical world. The sattvic mind sees all things in the dimensions of creation *coming down from God.* The duality mind sees all things as *going up to God;* he believes himself to be especially selected and chosen by God, which gives to him self-enlargement and authority.

Sattvic mind knows that it is created in the fore-times of Universal Spirit; therefore, its destiny is perfection. Sattvic-mind is going *toward* perfection at all times. By choice of Spirit-of-God *Willing,* one is moving always toward that which is perfection. His divine perfection seeks to perfect for God.

The sattvic mind knows it is a God-sent Imager, a participant in the hierarchy system of creation. In moving beyond duality thinking and acting, one returns to his true nature, which is perfect.

THE ARCHETYPAL KINGDOM

There is a difference between the Greater Unconscious and the Collective Unconscious. The Collective Unconscious is made up of the entitized humanistic-will experience; it is a *memory-body* recording experimental creativity in the earth. The Greater Unconscious is the Purusha or the field upon which God radiates His Spirit as *Knowing* for man.

The Greater Unconscious is the Spirit energy-field of the Unmanifest where resides the Archetypes. Christ, as Overlord of the Greater Archetypes, as Presence, is the Archetypal Omnipresence within the Greater Archetypal System of the Purusha Higher Unconscious.

Subconscious mind draws upon the past which is present as active soul-memory in the Collective Unconscious. Archetypal Presence represents the *Spirit of things to come.* All revelation, all prophecy on the level of the Greater Unconscious contain the future blueprint signals and portent for things to come in earth and in heaven.

He who has earned an Ahimsa heart moves over the bridge of the Collective Unconscious containing formats which men have proven and disproven.

The seer as a prophet crosses the bridge of the lower subconscious, which relates to gene-memory and the reincarnation soul-processes of the past. Having mastered these, he walks beyond the abyss into the Bridge of Light, where he makes union with his hierarchy nature and becomes an imager-creator for God.

Everyone who has been *opened* to the Higher Unconscious where dwells the Archetypal Light has the power of *Passing.* The Holy Spirit makes such persons into holy seers and revelators.

The System of Niscience was received from the Higher Unconscious within the Archetypal Light. This System is given in this ending of the Kali-Yuga Day to prepare mankind for his leap into God-Realization as ordained in the Archetypal Kingdom by the Will of God.

The Archetypal Kingdom is the Great Unconscious of the Unmanifest, or things to come. On the level of man, the Archetypal Kingdom functions in periods and cycles of 12,000 years. In 10,000 years of these, man is initiated through whatever Saviour provision is given to discipline him and guide him. This 10,000-year period is called a *Moving Archetype.*

The 2000 ending years of the 12,000-year period are interim years through which mankind makes union with God without resistance. In these interim 2000 years, whatever degree of faith one has is made perfect for him; he has a soul-respite from the Maya rajasic pressures and tamasic inertias. During this time, that which determines what he will do through reincarnation will imprint itself upon him as Destiny for the next reincarnation cycles in a virginal Moving-Archetypal timing or time. This is what the Scripture means by "the sheep and the goats." Man's own virtue or non-virtue places him into reincarnation polarities and functions where he fits or belongs. Always in man, however, is the promise of the Risen Christ and his hierarchy nature coming to birth.

During a dark Kali-Yuga period, as in the present, all Scriptural knowledge and all religiosity tendencies are veiled and darkened. In this Kali-Yuga time, men who desire a spiritual existence struggle in manifold initiation that they may produce the continuum cognizance with the higher unconscious or sattvic light.

All teachings coming to man in a darkened, shaded Kali-Yuga time—with the exception of a Sattvic Teacher or Seer—are astral, misproportioned dimensional revelations. From astral instruction, one is fed on husks rather than on the grain.

Mankind is presently moving out of a prodigal-son cycle and moving toward the interim time of the beginning of the scientific-spiritual tools extending dimensional consciousness.

All persons on the plane of earth through the laws of karma and reincarnation are not equal or the same karmically. All souls in the Archetypal Kingdom of the Greater Unconscious are equal in soul and soul capacity.

The great laws stemming from the Unmanifest use selectivity for that one who is worthy, pure of heart and hands, white as snow in Ahimsa. This selectivity is divine and cannot be utilized as an ego-vehicle for self-claiming or fame. The selective laws of Archetypal Power are by Eternal Law in the Spirit of the Eternal *bound to happen.*

Once one has developed the Ahimsa heart, which has been tried through the aeons as to faultless giving and serving to God, he is ready to experience the Greater Unconscious.

When one has some remaining pleasure for gain in his emotional nature—and has other merit states of worth in his nature—the higher unconscious Archetypal Light moves upon him and his karma as devastation. Intense suffering is the result.

Suffering begins first through the Second Chakra: someone is taken away from one; or something is taken away from one; or something or someone stands between him and what he desires.

Suffering begins as ego-initiation when one having knowledge of the Supreme Laws in a limited sense is tested for the use of power. This comes as a test as to sincerity in giving—for giving is the first use of power. *Giving is power.*

To give in a desireless sense without claiming set upon the gift is attainment of spiritual power whereby one becomes God-like or becomes a God-man. Thus, the releasing of all attachments and possessions is the first and cardinal law for rulership within the sattvic, Ahimsa heart.

Christ is the Diamond Center or Central Point in the Archetypal Realm. Jesus' dedication as the Son of Man in the world enabled the Christ to polarize the souls of men in earth.

Man receives the Archetypal System in three ways: the Greater Archetypes, the Moving Archetypes and the Destroying Archetypes. The Greater Archetypes occur in 250,000-year intervals. In this age, the three Archetypes sound their Tones simultaneously, and men of the earth are being created in the vision of the Christ—that is, given new birth-impulses within their souls.

Jesus came in the middle of a *Moving Archetype,* preparing men for spiritual birth. At the ending of each Moving Archetype, men are graded as to souls and degrees of consciousness.

In each Moving Archetype, men are on trial that they may develop certain stages of Genesis-evolvement. Reincarnation-evolvement determines what Genesis one expresses in a Moving Archetype. In each Moving-Archetypal cyclic portion of Time and evolvement, men repeat Tribal-Genesis, Family-Genesis, Lower and Higher Self-Genesis, and Cosmos-Genesis.

When 10,000 years have concluded in a Moving Archetype, men experience an opening to God. When one is in Tribal-Genesis, he experiences God through Nature. If one is in Family-Genesis, he experiences God through a Family-Atom, through blood relationships and through marriage. If one is in lower Self-Genesis, he magnifies his ego. If he is in higher Self-Genesis, he spiritualizes his intellect, seeing God as the One in All. If he has reached Cosmos-Genesis, he is a Cosmos-Disciple, and he has established a likeness of John the Beloved, the closest disciple to Jesus.

At the end of every Moving-Archetypal Interval, men return again to the shaping and forming process of a new Moving Archetype. In the present time, every man in the earth has something of Tribal-Genesis, Family-Genesis and Self-Genesis in his nature. This always occurs in magnified form at the ending of a Moving-Archetypal period.

At the end of each Moving-Archetypal period, the four Genesis-attributes in mankind experience an alchemization. When a Greater Archetype is ready for manifestation, it sounds its tones upon mankind; there is mighty chaos in the world regarding clans, tribes, clusters of men, families—and the individualistic nature of the self is searched as to ego-integrity, ego-value.

God repeats Himself through rhythms. God activates Himself through cycles. The Greater Archetypes work in rhythms; the Moving Archetypes, through cycles.

In the present time, the great rhythmic flow of the Archetypal Light is conjoined with the Moving-Archetypal energy and with the Destroying Archetypes which work to eliminate, to assess and to judge where one is, what he is, and how he can be used by the Power of God.

The Archetypal nature in man seeks to perfect the *hierarchy nature* in man, that he may move into his heritage as a willing and mind hierarchy nature.

God is not far off. He is *Omnipresence* in His rhythms and His cycles. The Archetypal rhythms work without ceasing within the Law of God. In the Moving Archetypal cyclic states, man knows this Law and experiences it as the Law of Karma.

Wherever there is an eternity system or a solar system, the Greater Purusha or Higher Unconscious, which is the Mind of God, controls the rhythmic and cyclic processes of life solar, of life planetary, of life lunar and of life conscient.

God uses His Elect to present Himself before men. It is grace to recognize Omnipresence as being present in a pure soul.

The most pure soul ever to take flesh in the physical world is Jesus. He came as a Prototypal Presence expressing a thirteenth Principle in the Mathematics of God. He is the Saviour of men. He mastered gravity in His Ascension. One who follows Him and becomes co-atom to Him also masters gravity and moves beyond the suction karmic-gravities binding man to time, blending him to rhythm.

Healing With the Hierarchy Nature 205

In the present epoch, or ending of a Moving Archetype, men are experiencing an overlap between their unknowing darkened past and their knowing or Niscience vision for the future. Men are now in stress, and for the next 3000 years will be in a state of tension caused by the equipoled coordinating processes of the three in the conjoined Archetypal Flow.

Over and over, men are reincarnated that they may realize their hierarchy natures to the fullest, and thus become creators in mastery of Earth and planetary forces.

The Initiate, as a Nisciene or Knowing One with full awareness of the Archetypal System, is an advanced Initiate who presently leans upon his innate religiosity and the scientific heritage manifesting for him in the present time. Every possible skill of the inward as well as the outward must be melded or fused in both the inner and the outer nature, that the Initiate may show by prototypal and soul example what life is in the earth, what is asked of him who dwells within and upon it.

To define soul stewardship equally with an earth-walk stewardship, one must be as a hierarch and dwell in his mental light within his hierarchy nature or the Will of God in him.

The first requirement for a steward of the soul-sciences is that he must make real other worlds, other forms, other states in the lives of those who thirst to hear, and who are specifically anxious with holy anxiety to do the Will of God.

A Knowing Initiate knows that the Earth is the forging iron upon which he uses the heat or fire of Nature to expand and spiritually entitize a solar system. He uses the system of Marking and Tracing, sharing it with those who are also willing to Mark and to Trace. One who has *aware* Knowing or Buddhi consciousness is destined to know within the effulgent Buddhi Informing Principle. In the Informing Principle, Omnipresence can be seen and heard.

The Destroying Archetype works as the arm of judgment within the Law of Karma. Everything that resists the Omnipresence of God is irritated and worked upon when the Rhythm of the Greater Archetypes coincides with the cycles of the Moving and Destroying Archetypes. That which is inanimate, tamas and inert is subjected to explosion; and the resisting in the rajasic, during the period of the coinciding of the three Archetypes, discloses in their functions all negative frailties and weaknesses. During this interval of time, advanced initiates and also novitiates of the soul discover unusual techniques, utilizing heretofore unused technologies—thus, science on the kinetic level has come to earth.

The present era is the atomic era in which new technologies will challenge the mental and will proclivities of man, and will recover some of the virginal, primal, instinctual powers from the past.

It is always the case in a great conjoining of the rhythmic and cyclic laws that men seem to be unwittingly cast into a cauldron of chaos. God is always the same, yet He never repeats Himself. God increases at all times, in all periods, epochs and aeons. However, he has given to man free choice which will ultimately become free will. It is not that man is God; it is that man is *within* God. The Eternal Spirit of God in man gives to him through the extension of free choice the power to differentiate himself. All of the various vehicles God has given to man to live in this eternity system develop themselves through differentiating processes.

One should evaluate every moment of his life. As a conscious functioning being, he should evaluate consciousness. It is consciousness which makes man more than an animal. The goal of every man is to extend and expand his consciousness while living in Heaven or in earth.

Man is what his consciousness is. His conscience and his consciousness seek to lead him to Niscience, and eventually to Omniscience in his hierarchy nature. In this present Archetypal period unfolding and flowing into one's hierarchy nature and his soul, spiritual aspirants hunger and long to make union directly with God.

God is the Power and the Imager. Man's hierarchy nature contains the Likeness of God and the Image of God. Whatever man reproduces through his hierarchy nature is destined to be in the Likeness of God.

God is Omnipresence as Mediation in all worlds, all galaxies, all universes, all solar systems, all souls. God has in His nature as Eternal Spirit Omnipresence-powers to Pass into each and every creation He has projected from Himself a key vibration point of light and a tone or sound.

10

THE CONTINUUM SACRAMENT

And as they were eating, Jesus took bread, and blessed it, and brake it, and gave it to the disciples, and said, Take, eat; this is my body. And he took the cup, and gave thanks, and gave it to them, saying, Drink ye all of it; For this is my blood of the new testament, which is shed for many for the remission of sins.
—St. Matthew 26:26–28

. . . this do in remembrance of me.
—St. Luke 22:19

The Healing Altar

With a contrite spirit
I pray to transenergize
all I have harmed,
all I have wronged.

I pray that my cursing
shall be changed
to a blessing to any and all
I have sinned against.

A right spirit may come only from a contrite spirit. A trivialistic contrition-thought is as a snowflake against the heat of suffering. Only a whole and complete *contrite spirit* can avail in the act of *restitution*.

Through a true contrition, all the Scriptures written can be synchronized into one experience of Niscience or *Knowing*. By fusion of all the particles of many realizations, the one realization comes and abides as a knowing beyond knowledge. Once this occurs, one is pinnacled as one point of Spirit and is empowered by God to do His Mighty Will through works—works making God available to all.

A whole and right contrition is the emptying out of non-virtue. The emptiness gained from a whole contrition is refilled with a right and true Apostolic virtue in which the grace of the gifts supplants the load of sin, changing sin into powers for the Holy Spirit.

To be anointed with an Apostle's Anointing is to be touched, that cleansing may come. To be cleansed is to assure that gifts will come, that the Power of the Holy Spirit may do its perfect work.

The accepted time for the many souls to coalesce their combined soul-powers is now. Only through this composite body of a whole and right contrition may souls be appointed as witnesses and activators for Omnipresence or God.

The angel energies work in horizontal spheres; these energies build unsullied atmospheres. Prayers within the reinforcement of the angel atmospheres are powerful and mighty. Angel grace-atmospheres should accompany all praying, all worships, all meditations.

In a body of worship, all members, ministers and worshippers should prayerfully entreat the angels to build their spheres of encasement, that all devotional, petitional acts—mental and emotional—may be conjoined, thus providing for those serving the altar the right energy to keep and sustain the contrition core-body of worship. In this manner, that which is consummated for the altar flows back into the congregation as encouragement and strengths of sanctification and consecration. This, then, is a worship evoking the holy choirs of the Third Music, cleansing, anointing, healing.

Through the Holy Sacrament, one is God-Realized. God is made flesh, and the meaning of embodiment comes to birth as a whole and complete incarnation for God.

The Bread of the Sacrament for the Saints must never be absent from the altar. This is that ever-present Epiphany which keeps alive the virtue of the bread in the Eucharist from offering to offering. Therefore, as the rising of the Sun is assured each morning, Bread should be present on the altar continually. The Wine, which is from the true vine of the blood of Jesus, should also be present, representing that which contains the effervescent changing changelessness of one substance into another by and through the chemicalization of the Christ.

From a continuum of the Bread and the Wine comes the perpetual Epiphany, and the virtue of Laying-on-of-Hands is made manifest.

A CONTINUUM SACRAMENT may be on the Home Altar or on the Chapel Altar. The *Home Altar Continuum Sacrament* or the *Chapel Continuum Sacrament* are to be eaten after remaining on the altar for a 24-hour period. The Continuum Sacrament remains on the Altar of the Home or in the Chapel as a symbolic worship-vehicle through which the Body of the Christ is present. It is left for 24 hours—from one sunrise to another. Sunrise for each person is when he awakens.

All of the victories one has made for the Christ during the 24-hour period are taken into the body as an offering directly from the Christ. Thus, each morning on arising, one takes the Sacrament offered by the Christ. He eats the

The Continuum Sacrament

Bread in remembrance of Him, and takes the Wine as the Life-Blood for his life in the world.

Suggestions: Place a small white napkin on the Home Altar or Chapel Altar. Use a small flat plate for the Bread and a miniature glass for the Wine.

Take a small portion of bread.

Take a small portion of *mixture* of wine, pomegranate juice and water. The wine should be Concord or Port. The water should be spring water. If pomegranate juice is unavailable, use grape juice. The wine represents the Spirit of Jesus; pomegranate, the pain suffered by Jesus on the Cross; water, the water that poured from the side of Jesus while on the Cross. In case of children in the household taking the Continuum Sacrament with their parents, bread is offered; a small portion of grape juice is used rather than the wine.

The mixture of liquids used for the wine portion of the Continuum Sacrament should be one-third wine, one-third pomegranate juice and one-third water. This mixture may be prepared once a month and put in a container.

Use 13 drops of liquid each day. The 13 drops represent Jesus and His 12 disciples.

During the 24 hours, keep the Wine and Bread of the Continuum Sacrament covered with a white napkin.

Each morning on arising, after having eaten the Bread and drunk the Wine, replace them with a new portion of fresh bread and wine in the Continuum vessels.

On partaking of the Bread and the Wine of the previous 24 hours, bless this Feast of the Sacrament as it is eaten by speaking the following words:

Every living atom embodied in you, I return to God in the Name of the Lord Jesus Christ.

To bless the new Sacrament, speak the words:

Lord Christ, let this Bread and Wine be a symbol of Thy Life and Light in my soul. This offering, chaste and new, is my offering unto Thee. Live in it, O Christ, that I may live in Thee. Amen.

The very special cyclic times, such as Easter and Christmas, give space to the Increase of God that His Will may thrust men forward into Enlightenment. In the Continuum Sacrament, this Time-Space provision also makes a day holy, a life creative.

The Continuum Sacrament keeps one in touch with his hierarchy nature and with the supreme Spirit which has created all. On taking the Continuum Sacrament, it is important that one does not eat before the Sacrament. It should be taken after the hours of sleep immediately on arising.

From the time one goes to sleep until he awakens in the morning, he has experienced a Lunar Fast during the night. The Moon gives magnification to the sleeping body during the night so that the one sleeping may experience the dreams of the night minus the desire for food. Thus, the senses which would be used to direct the digestive system are transenergized in the night to digest the myth-encounters and the spiritual realities of the night.

In sleep one moves beyond gravity into another vitality substance called *akash,* which provides his etheric body with life restoring and vital life-energy so that he may work in the day with vitality and vigor. All dream functions recharge the vitalities of the objective consciousness in the waking-day state of experience. One must watch his dreams so as to draw upon this vita-side of the subconscious overflow of the sleep and of the higher unconscious.

One particle of Bread transformed by Sacramental

Transenergization contains the Body-energies of Jesus, the Lord. The vital life of the Mother of the World or Feminine Principle is also within the Bread. She, the Mother, is the life within all the grains. She is also the leaven, and she works with the Holy Spirit as the yeast. In the Sacrament, one takes in the Life Principle through the Mother and the Holy Spirit with the first touch of the Bread on the tongue. Bread is therefore sacred.

There are 13th-hour holy occurrences in the 12 hours of the day. One is on the moment of awakening, and one is the one moment after midnight. These are 13th-hour stations. In these two periods, something of the miraculous occurs; in the morning, chemically; in the night, soul-wise.

In the morning after the hours of sleep, the *tongue* has been prepared by the soul at night to receive, in the 13th or waking moment, the Continuum Sacrament. In the midnight 13th station, sleep enters into the soul-currents that direct the Buddhi or higher-mind dreams. Through the soul-currents, one is gathered into the Power of God.

The Bread taken in the Continuum Sacrament is the life. The Divine Mother sends forth her child for the life of the day with the Bread of the Continuum Sacrament which is filled with the life-atoms of Her Son, Jesus.

To awake to the Continuum Sacrament is to enlarge the circumference or sphere of Eternity. To be aware of the Jesus-atoms in the Bread (body) and the Wine (blood) within the Sacrament is to remain in Jesus as the Way, the Truth and the Life.

The Seraphim

In the year that king Uzziah died I saw also the Lord sitting upon a throne, high and lifted up, and his train

> *filled the temple. Above it stood the seraphims: each one had six wings; with twain he covered his face, and with twain he covered his feet, and with twain he did fly. And one cried unto another, and said, Holy, holy, holy, is the Lord of hosts: the whole earth is full of his glory.*
>
> —Isaiah 6:1–3

All Sacraments on the Home Altar and Chapel Altar are over-directed by the great Seraphim. All rules of worship are given to man by the Seraphim Angels. The Seraphim Angels are the guardians over the worship on the Altars.

The Seraphim maintain the order of the rules for worship. The six wings of the Seraphim provide the six wisdom-nourishments regarding worship of God.

Worship of God through the Seraphim rules of worship builds all pure and true ritual formulas for worship. He who worships any other way has not a pure worship.

He who does not kneel in worship has not worship. And he who is in a constant state of standing up and sitting down during worship is making a declaration rather than worshipping.

To kneel through prayer is to invoke the Angels. To sit and to absorb through worship of God is meditation and contemplation. To stand in worship through song or praise is declaration. Declaration should be understood and experienced as a sense of mantra or statement for God.

Meditation as worship should be experienced as the Darshan or Omnipresence of God. Prayer should be known as the prophetic and aware creator with God.

The Continuum Sacrament as given by the Seraphim for the New Era is a symbolic Holy-Spirit vehicle. To

The Continuum Sacrament

practice the Continuum Sacrament each day provides a living offering of prayer unceasing which acts as a continuing soul-essence flowing toward God.

The Continuum Sacrament is a continual incense containing the essence of prayer. It is a continual flame of the light of the soul. It is a continual healing oil of the manifesting power within the soul. It is a continual holy wind of the Spirit, anointing, quickening, awakening.

The Continuum Sacrament is a first-virtue Holy Spirit worship practice.

Virtue and the Continuum Sacrament

The Continuum Sacrament is cleaning out the rusty nail holes of my unknowing.

The Continuum Sacrament is intimately sacred. The Continuum Sacrament assures each day as being in harmony within the Esse. He who takes the Continuum Sacrament in the spirit of sacredness, as if it were the holy seed of a new life each day — vitalizing all processes and demands placed upon him — is free in the Esse or the Holy Spirit. To be free in the Esse moves one over the duality issues into the third Acting Principle of Holy-Spirit Consciousness.

One should look upon his first partaking of the Continuum Sacrament as a beginning of a new ledger or record to be written out of the actions of the 24 hours before him until he once again partakes of the Body and the Blood of Christ Jesus.

Anyone taking the Wine of the Continuum Sacrament without virtue is depressed afterwards, dwelling upon his sins and the sins against him. Anyone taking the Continuum Sacrament with a whole virtue is enthusiastic;

filled with the Wine of God Intelligence, of Life; acceptable in circumstance; agreeable in association; and on time in everything and in time to his grace.

One makes the Wine of the Continuum Sacrament into bitter, sour vinegar when he doubts the efficacy of the Christ in the Sacrament. If the Sacrament does not quicken one's blood, it has not been taken with a whole virtue. It is a quickened blood emanating from a whole faith that the Christ and the Holy Spirit can use in redemption.

The Continuum Sacrament, on quickening the blood through virtue-faith each morning, enables the person to use another rate of blood vibration superior to ordinary physical survival. The quickened blood contains the Archetypal Dharma Light of the Christ Mind, regenerating negative thoughts and negative actions into spiritual associations and accomplishments. The cells in the blood are filled with memory-indexes from one's past instinctual climbing nature. A new vitalizing memory is built through the positive use of the Continuum Sacrament upon awakening each day.

This vital life in Christ is in you. Jesus, the Manifestor-Mediator in the Sacrament, embodies both the Bread and the Wine with the androgynous nature of Christ Jesus in the Bread and the Wine.

The Continuum Sacrament makes the complete day. All who take the Continuum Sacrament have the Christ Spirit in them through which they can organize their works, their motives and their love through service to God. In the spirit of the Passion of the Lord Jesus, they receive the Passing Power of the Laying-on-of-the-Hands in all situations.

The Continuum Sacrament

The Continuum Sacrament is a first-virtue act for the Householder Altar. When all persons in the Family-Atom partake of the Continuum Sacrament each morning without fail, the Christ Spirit takes possession of the Bread and the Wine during the 24-hour interval. The Power of the Passion of Jesus is taken into the four bodies—the physical, etheric, emotional and mental bodies—that one may offer his service, his strengths and his dedication to God.

The Continuum Sacrament is the staff whereby the rock brings forth the water of life, health, Agape. It is the hand that breaks the bread and gives the fish to the hungry. It is also the unique Sacrament of the Wine of Cana and the Bread in the Upper Chamber of the Lord's Supper. The Continuum Sacrament comes out of the Holy of Holies, the Shekinah, wherein transubstantiation and transenergization are set free in the life of the Householder.

The energy-process within Marking and Tracing goes hand in hand with the Continuum Sacrament. On taking the Continuum Sacrament, the Marking and Tracing begin, thereby enabling one to see his sins in the fourth-dimensional light. He no longer becomes a Maya victim of his own sensuality and the sensuality of others, for he sees in the true hierarchy-nature imaging light. The Archetypal system functioning through the hierarchy nature becomes relevant to him through its own revealing. He sees and knows and creates. The hierarchy nature has command of the causal system. The causal system and the casualty are seen in their fourth-dimensional realities.

Jesus said on the Cross: *"Father, forgive them: for they know not what they do."* So are all men enclosed into their sins in the physical world through the Maya system of the *Klosha* or enclosure. The Maya enclosure makes all men brothers in unknowing. The Maya enclosure is the Undersoul of the world. Each man must cleanse his own individual Undersoul. On being dedicated to God, one works to cleanse both his own Undersoul and the world Undersoul. By this he opens himself to the Esse Purusha of the collective Higher Unconscious, which in its pure state feeds his need.

Jesus came to loosen the chains of bondage to sins. He works now to free men. As in each life one cannot receive salvation until every "tittle" is paid in karma, so can no one single person find total happiness until all are free in God.

On taking the Continuum Sacrament, one should pray for the sins of the whole world. On taking each morning the Purusha food, the holy Prasad or the Eucharist Bread, one should pray to be relieved of his sins and to relieve all in the world of their sins. The Bread and the Wine of the Continuum Sacrament, having absorbed 24 hours of the Christ, feed the life-spirit that strength and vitality may be ever present to fulfill the Will of God through love, light, life and will.

Where the plant conjoins the stone, there is oil. Where there is oil from the plant and stone, there is fire in the oil. The plant and the stone are the breast of Mother Earth from which all sentient things must partake to endure and to survive. He who eats bread also eats the mineral fire and oil in the seed and the grain and in the stone. There is no life existing in earth that is not assisted by uncountable life-forms and energy-processes.

It is automatic for oil to give fire and light. To profane oil by stripping it for greed is to deny nourishment for man and fulfillment in the life-enzyme chain.

All the practicals for nutrition are based upon sound

Cosmos and Cosmic principles, in that God keeps and cares for His own. Teachers must return men to the true bread and the wine of living health and life as given of God. He who takes the bread and lights the candle and drinks as a Sacrament the fruit from the vine—wine—is a body of wholeness within holiness.

FREE CHOICE

Every person in the world has *free choice* to some degree. This choice works with the Cosmos and Cosmic rhythms of the Will of God.

Choice is presented in three phases to each person through the system of karma as Law functioning as the Will of God. Every first choice is a test between glamor and reality. Every second choice contains within it the opportunity to dedicate to God what is chosen. Every third aspect of choice provides right intention and right determination—that is, to acknowledge choice as a promise to God, that one may succeed rather than fall into the error of ego-choosing. That chosen through the ego, through which one climbs, is as a mist and unlasting. Right choice brings to him who chooses rightly the absolute Will of God and the whole Law of God as support and strength and certainty.

Time as grace provides one who has right motive with a time-lapse for inner introspection into wisdom: a 24-hour reflection or a 36-hour reflection or a 3-day reflection with fasting provides to one dedicated to God the three phases of choice with full perspective. Such persons, while intuitively and inherently leaning toward right choice, in being called upon to make choice vital to the spiritual life are given the opportunity to see the varied testing aspects which will inevitably come in the making of choice as a dedication in the service to God.

The history of man's suffering, particularly in the Self-Genesis Age, will be filled with tragic examples of those having little mind-strength and little heart-culture, who have made wrong choice as compromise impulse.

In the life of Jesus, Caiphas and his fellow priests *chose* to crucify and to curse Jesus. This curse is the epitome of an unholy example by which billions yet to be born can be affected by wrong choice in time of crisis. It is inevitable that an evil heart moves into evil choice affecting many.

One simple choice on arising, even seeming to be innocuous, changes the total day when leaning in the direction of indolence. The Continuum Sacrament taken in the morning leans one in the direction of right choice throughout the day.

The first awakening breath of the morning is as important as the first breath taken at birth, for each day is a birth to energy varieties given to man by God to develop a spiritualized intellect. When the spiritualized intellect is finally attained, one begins his work with the hierarchy nature and is thereafter one who works within the Will of God.

The Archetypal Path, as given in the System of Niscience, provides the initiate with insight and a choice leaning toward Will-of-God attainment through his hierarchy nature.

Choice and conscience bring one into the use of the higher-mind powers or hierarchy-nature powers. To behold one's conscience working in conjunction with choice is to see Godly fulfillment through the perfect works within the Will of God.

Each night before sleep one should saturate himself

with the mantram or mantra of the night that he might rise on the morning with full awareness with his right to choose that which is right and pure and holy. That which flows out of the night's sleep in a freed subconscious and a union with the higher unconscious is the soul open-door of conscience. This is free when one speaks the mantram before sleep. Conscience then on arising is united with choice.

All persons seeking to walk in the Light should be aware of what conscience says through dreams in sleep that they may use through the Continuum Sacrament the holy vow or sankalpa resolution taken with the Continuum Sacrament. Right resolution keeps choice vertical, in touch with the Will of God.

These two practices—the before-sleep mantram and the morning Continuum Sacrament—keep alive the lamp of faith and works.

Faith and conscience gain momentum through the night's sleep. In sleep, man returns to God and bathes in the cradle of the Great Unconscious. His faith in God in sleep is a grace given through the restoration-grace of God.

Faith and conscience work together in the night's sleep. Remembrance of this in the morning, in the deep-within side of the subconscious, makes it possible for one to meet the Maya tests of the day, which await as challenges. These challenges are presented to the initiate in his work, in his creation, in his building.

Dream recollection is vital in a spiritual life. One must stay close to his dream-wisdoms that he may grow in faith, in truth. The dream-wisdom remembrance is the kind of wisdom that builds the spiritual life.

The core of morality resides in the heart chakra. The

core of morality leans upon the conscience. The core of morality cannot manifest in the waking state of life until one has developed the Ahimsa heart and is fully aware of the Bhakti skills in the use of love.

If the heart is amoral or immoral, one leans away from conscience. He has no contact with dream-therapies or dream-wisdoms. All dream-therapies are soul-therapies.

Every initiate committed by his soul to expand his spiritual life by living in the physical world is tested by his use of his grace-attribute: Free Choice. During this time, one of the initiatory trials presented to him is the trial of the dissolution process—that is, dying to any remaining phases of amorality or immorality in his own nature. This is necessary because on entering the Path he must manifest an unsullied conscience, an immovable faith, and a right and crystal-clear ethic. The tumults of the heart in his emotional nature rend him during certain trials, that he may become proficient in cognizance; that he may use for the future certain prophetic apprehensional wisdoms and also comprehensible realizations.

There is no person, whether on the Path or off the Path, who does not in some time see that he himself contains the power of good and evil through the functions of choice and conscience. When one is aware of this, his own history-making of former lives, and of his ancestors, marches through him. From this he obtains both the bitter and the sweet so that he may make flexible his own judging nature used by his intellect. Charity-Agape and flexibility in viewing the suffering caused by evils enacted by his ancestors and his ego in the past enable him to move out of the seat of judgment into a sweet and unladen Ahimsa charity. God's Forgiveness comes forth to give him support in the building of his own spiritualized intellect.

REDEMPTION

But of him are ye in Christ Jesus, who of God is made unto us wisdom, and righteousness, and sanctification, and redemption.
—*1 Corinthians 1:30*

Jesus is the Redeemer of this total Earth system.

Partially-enlightened gurus testify that they will liberate their chelas and take them from the wheel of karma. Cosmically and Cosmosly this is an impossibility. Teachers and gurus making such statements do not understand the Law of the Cosmos, which is Eternal Creation. The Law of Karma, or Cause and Effect, exists within the Eternal Laws supporting all Creation. No guru or teacher can liberate a person from the Law. Law *Is,* as God *Is.*

The only Being ever existing in a human body living totally within the Law and manifesting it in its whole example is Jesus. Jesus came to *redeem.* He came to fulfill the Law and teach all others to fulfill it.

The word *redeem* means to reclaim, to bring back to its original state, to free that which it redeems to its right and purposeful function. Redemption means to be put into rightful place, to be returned to the Law, and thereby become creative within the Law.

On taking the Continuum Sacrament and the Altar Sacrament one is *redeemed.* He is called forth to be that which he is in his true origins.

Those who think they can escape the Law cannot escape the Law. The Law is in the star, the leaf, the seed, in all. When Jesus said, *"Take my yoke upon you,"* He meant, "Take God's Law which works through Me."

Before one can enter the Path, he must be redeemed,

reclaimed, re-called, that he may in full virtue walk the Path within the Law. This is redemption.

The desire for redemption comes first; repentance, second; restitution, third; and redemption, fourth.

Jesus is the Redeemer. Through redemption one lives and breathes in full virtue or rightful righteousness as a son of God. *"If the Son therefore shall make you free, ye shall be free indeed." (St. John 8:36)*

Each time one takes the Continuum Sacrament in full realization of redemption as given through the atoms within the Body of Jesus, he may be likened to a vessel which formerly had corroded its luster through neglect, carelessness, inertia. Each Continuum Sacrament acts as a redeeming burnisher to reclaim this precious object, this treasure which had been built out of the skill of God-creation. The Redeemer, Jesus, burnishes in each Sacrament taken, and draws forth the translucent lusters of the Divine whereby God can make His Presence seen, known and heard.

> *I thirst, O Lord,*
> *with a whole thirst,*
> *that I may be a vessel*
> *of Thy True Elixir*
> *and Redemption.*
>
> *May I shine*
> *within Thy Light,*
> *that my buried treasure*
> *may be seen and heard*
> *in the Name of God.*

The Bible story of the buried talents relates to grace ignored or misused. To retrieve grace is to be under the guiding Hand of Jesus. Jesus goes into our buried grace and talents. He opens the flood-gates of God's guidance in the way one may use his buried treasure of grace.

Jesus makes each man a steward-processor in the use of grace, thereby making him accountable to the Law through the Commandments, freeing him from the bondage of heritage-karma through the genes and through sin. When one takes the Continuum Sacrament, God through Jesus resurrects the misused talent and neglected grace which is the natural heritage of all created by God.

THE SECOND DEATH

He that hath an ear, let him hear what the Spirit saith unto the churches; He that overcometh shall not be hurt of the second death.
—Revelation 2:11

If one has failed to be repentant in life, there is a second death he must experience after physical death. The second death is an ordeal of the mind, the emotions and the soul, causing a prolonged, comatose or purgatorial suffering.

The emotional body of an unrepentant person has an *egotistical shell*. The egotistical-shell portion of the emotional body must be dissolved through repentance and through works on the earth plane if one is to be free to arise to the Risen-Dead planes after death.

If one has dissolved his egotistical shell while living in the physical world, he does not undergo the after-death initiatory trials which face the unrepentant after death. Prolonged stays in between death and birth are necessary if one fails to dissolve the egotistical shell in the emotional-body after death. If one is unable to dissolve the egotistical shell after death, he enters the world heavily laden with karmic debts, which must be absolved through repentance, restitution and redemption.

Every time one speaks the 23rd Psalm Introspection exercise at dusk, Marking and Tracing in contraclockwise fashion the hours of the day, he is overcoming the second death. Each time one fasts he is in the state of repentance; in making a penance and resolution he overcomes the second death.

The habit of making a penance with right resolution clears the Undersoul. When one sets up a system of penance—doing without certain things which have kept him bonded to his selfish nature—he overcomes the second death. Penance is a side of giving which means giving up or self-denial.

A continuity penance in the Name of Jesus and Our Father frees one to undergo the 90 days of contrition after death with full cognizance and spirituality, blessing all.

The Continuum Sacrament taken each morning on awakening makes the day a continuum offering through which Christ may channel His Light, purifying and cleansing the foul obnoxiousness collected in the Undersoul. All of the Continuum Sacraments taken day by day fortify one after death so that he may be aware and conscious within the Pure Light of the Divine Companions inhabiting the Spiritual Worlds.

The Stigmata

He who keeps faith with the flow of the Sacraments, as set down as a blueprint for the Path of the Soul, keeps open his Stigmata Grace.

The Continuum Sacrament opens one to the Higher Unconscious supporting the Archetypal Worlds. It is inevitable that one who *opens* will become an *Opener,* or one who *Passes* the hierarchy-nature willing through his healing works.

On making total surrender to God and to His Purusha Consciousness which occupies the Indestructible-Atom center, called the *Holy Cave,* one moves beyond imagination and fantasy into direct experience of God-Realization as consciousness.

One of the fallacies given to man from the Devachan level of partially-reflected archetypal truths is that he must strive to bask in the bliss-substances of the downpouring light. A realized sattvic person is at all times in a state of basking. However, basking for one's own self keeps one in the mystical inversions; in this, love of self gives access only to the lower-devachan light.

Sattvic as basking provides both action and absorption. Exercises offered to a chela promising bliss for now and for the afterlife are yet in the state of partial astralocity, giving eternity providences rather than *eternal* certainties.

In the spiritual life, one must play the game of the sattvic. Men in the world who do not know or remember their own hierarchy nature persecute, slander and throw stones on the sattvic who would serve God openly in the market place, in the temple, and in the home.

The first stigmata one receives on serving the Christ is received as a stoning or obstacles thrown against the light he carries. These stigmas are the beginning of the inner stigmata which must be opened in the etheric, the emotional and the mental bodies.

Every opened stigmata-point in the bodies of man contains a spiritual-healing power from which the sattvic flows. These stigmata open-points are matrixes of spiritual power which the Holy Ghost uses to distribute Himself and to make His Presence known.

Every sickness in the life of a seer is that he may open a stigmata point, whereby the Holy Spirit may use and manifest His Power. Therefore, the sicknesses which come to a spiritual person come that he may open a stigmata as a bleeding wound through which the Holy Spirit may function.

It is accepted by all sattvic seers that prophets suffer sicknesses and die even as other men. Wherever a stigmata of a prophet or initiate is functioning as a disease causing death or threatening life, there is the definition of what level or degree of healing power is being expressed by the initiate or the seer.

Saintly Ramakrishna died of cancer of the throat. His stigmata healing power was to speak the holy word as Logos, healing. Kahlil Gibran died of cancer of the stomach. His stigmata was based upon the Mother Principle. The stomach is the stigmata matrix-point for the Divine Mother.

Jesus, in dying on the Cross—opening all of His healing stigmata to the multitudes of the earth—gave to man His Passion through His suffering on the Cross, thereby giving to "whomever will" *the Power of the Passing.*

The agnostic cannot live in the Household of Jesus. He cannot know the code-key to the Passion containing the Passing, nor can he know the transenergizing of the bitter poison, of the taking of the Cup.

Every person who is agnostic and cynical concerning Jesus contributes to the thrust of the thorns on the Crown of Thorns. The agnostic is superciliously insensitive to compassion, mercy. His ego-environment is limited to self-supremacy. He sees the one who wears the Crown of Thorns as an idiot. He sees the one who must transubstantiate the rust in the nail holes into glory as stupid.

Jesus works as co-atom through those who take upon themselves Intentional Suffering. To clear the rust from the nail holes invites the crowning of the thorns, where mental pain as a fire frees the buds of knowing in the Crown of Knowing.

He who wears the Crown of Thorns as a householder in the Household of Jesus has made the bitter, sweet; has made the rust into living waters; has made the Crown of Thorns into Illumination.

As a householder in His Household, one walks with Him the Path of Intentional Suffering. He who walks the Path of Intentional Suffering must open the stigmata points of the nail holes through his own suffering.

Intentional Suffering takes many forms. It leads one into unusual situations; sometimes awkward, sometimes pure and holy.

If one is to follow Jesus, he must look into the eye of suffering—and, by His Divine nature which He has passed on to one—exorcise or transenergize suffering into the ecstasy of oneness with God.

This eternity system in which man dwells is a *pain* system. All eternity systems having a small Sun are pain systems. It is through the Resurrected Christ that one exorcises suffering into perception of the Infinite, the Cosmos, the Universal. The refining processes of suffering are the initiatory processes to produce the true and eternal happiness given to man through the Everlasting Covenant of Eternal Spirit.

To look upon pain and suffering as insurmountable or unredeemable is to be absent in faith from God. In this world, suffering is the path-way. Resurrection is the Path. He who walks with the Saints to exorcise his own suffering into divinity walks with the Saints in earth and in Heaven.

The only way one has the grace to move out of his suffering is to have cognizant-grace with his suffering. In the cognizant state of grace, one is illumined, and sees the cause of his suffering. Through right choice, he is free and healed, expressing wholeness and holiness, which is his true nature while living in all worlds, Cosmos and

Cosmic. A cognizant consciousness is an aware consciousness, whereby every degree of consciousness functions within the Will of God.

God as Omnipresence has provided for this eternity system the Spirit of the Risen Christ in man. This is the power manifested on the Cross through the body of Jesus. The heart-atom of Jesus, exploded by the Christ on the Cross, contains the Passion Illimitable. The Passing Power of Jesus through the Christ now exists in the heart-atoms of all men in the earth.

On the coming of the Christ Spirit, an uplifted eternity system is accelerated into soul-power actions among individualistic souls who, in the vibrancy of faith and quickening of the Christ within, are filling their stations of life as servers for God.

All spiritually-enlightened men are accompanied by the Angelic and Saintly Presences. They are reinforced in conquerings, in mastering — and, in the Power of Passing, they represent the Christ. To be co-atom to Jesus is to be embodied within the Christ Consciousness.

The Path of Virtue is the Path of the Saints. To walk the Path of the Saints, one is walking with the feet of Jesus in the world. To walk in the Light in the Virtue Path of the Saints is to be under the Christ Command: *Go unto the world and preach the Gospel.*

> *Grace is the total love of God as a Gift.*
> *Grace heals.*
> *Grace empowers.*
> *Grace stands eternal.*
> *Grace functions on immortal levels and on eternal levels.*
> *Grace from man to man is the human-spirit Gift given by God to man.*

Grace from animal to man is the Gift of unison between species and creature.

Grace as given through the angels is the dispensation of forces.

Grace as given through the mineral and plant kingdom is the Life Grace provided through the Shining Spirits or Devas in Nature.

Grace through the Bread and the Wine of the Sacrament is the Body and Soul-Memory of Jesus, who is deathless in the midst of death; who is resurrected in the midst of weakness; who is ascended in the midst of chaos.

Grace as grace is the Presence of God, which as the dove rises up through faith, with belief, with action within the Will of God.

11

HOLY CONSCIENCE

How much more shall the blood of Christ, who through the eternal Spirit offered himself without spot to God, purge your conscience from dead works to serve the living God?

—Hebrews 9:14

God is always sure that what He has given to man will be used eventually with a right ethic and a right duty, for He has provided for all things in this world with His Love. The greatest thing He has given to man in this world is Conscience, for Conscience is God in man—and Conscience as God in man takes care of His Universe.

God has implanted into man this *Holy Conscience*. The Holy Conscience is used by the Holy Spirit to bring man to God, to incite in him a craving to make union with God.

In this Kali-Yuga Age, every Teacher must teach Ethic, Morality and Conscience. This is an Age of Power. In the use of power, Ethic, Morality and Conscience must be at one. At all times aware of the function of the Holy Spirit, the Conscience assures purity, providence, security, for he who has a pure conscience and an undefiled earth-nature is secure in God.

Love is the oil which makes it possible for the conscience

HOLY CONSCIENCE

to function. The conscience is the preserving spirit in man, protecting him and insulating him from evil.

If a person is always late, he has no conscience. If he does not keep his promises, he has no conscience. If he does not make an effort to support his family and to properly discipline his children, he has no conscience. If he is amoral sexually, financially and socially, he has no conscience. This is how one gauges if a person is weak in these portions of his conscience.

If one is trying to impose upon others in any particular phase of trust through human association, his conscience is a frail vehicle. Such persons are open to karmic situations which reveal where conscience must be validated and strengthened.

The conscience of a man or woman tells where the karma is; it also identifies the Genesis level as well as the soul-age of a person. If one looks the other way when there is a human need and situation—and he knows it is his Dharma to aid or assist in a situation—he is existing in a subhuman side of his conscience.

The primal instinctual nature is devoid of conscience. Tooth-and-claw situations reveal that one must look to his conscience. If he is seeking to enter the Path, and these negative traits of conscience are present, he must enter into research as to Truth and the meaning of Truth. The Truth cannot be seen or heard without a conscience.

Persons who have the eye of stone are separated from their conscience. The mentalizer is never close to his conscience. An honest conscience is a true conscience in which one knows that everything that is wrong is caused either by his own actions or by his own ignorance.

A constantly criticizing mind is caused by a rajasic over-heated conscience. A rajasic over-heated conscience sees in all others his own dissatisfaction with himself.

Every sickness-disease is a conscience-sickness—if not

for oneself then for some other person for whom one has prayed.

Dreams are a conscience-vehicle telling one what not to do and what to do in the daytime. Those having prophetic dreams are messengers.

As the enzyme makes food digestible, the conscience makes life livable. The conscience devours sin, and produces out of the energies in sin the life-blood of the Holy Spirit nourishing and giving meaning to life.

The Holy Spirit is the true Igniter. When one moves in the right direction, he accumulates and collects a repository of energy. This energy is used as grace to meet all emergencies in the human life.

A right-directed man is a vehicle for the Holy Spirit. A wrongly-directed man is a vehicle for Satan or the Satanic forces. Right direction comes from total submission to the Holy Spirit.

A right-directed man is a man with a conscience. He seeks nothing for himself, nor does he follow the path of self-aggrandizement. Sincerity, trust, patience and faith are the attributes one must achieve to become a vessel for the Holy Spirit.

The Laws are adamant. Man must be flexible within the adamant Laws. Conscience is the only way by which man may remain flexible and fulfill the whole of the Law.

THE EXTERIOR AND INTERIOR COMMANDMENTS

But this shall be the covenant that I will make with the house of Israel; After those days, saith the Lord, I will put my law in their inward parts, and write it in their hearts; and will be their God, and they shall be my people.

—Jeremiah 31:33

In the beginning of the primordial order, the Ten Commandments were established in the inward parts. Through Moses they were manifested outwardly. The Ten Commandments exist both outwardly and inwardly as the conscience vehicle whereby man keeps in contact with the Law of God and with God.

The Ten Commandments are the watchmen over the conscience and over the soul of man. Who lives in the Ten Commandments as they are portrayed to man through Moses outwardly must also open to himself the full dimension of each Commandment and thereby live a noble, full and satisfactory life in the earth.

There is no other way to master Maya existence save through obedience to the Commandments. For he who walks by and with the Ten Commandments walks also with the virtue of the Hierarchs, the mighty Ten who gave to man through the Son of Man "the way and the truth and the life."

The Hierarchs are the Fathers of other eternity systems working with our Father of this eternity system. They would be poor Fathers, indeed, who on having made man in their Image would have failed to give him a way and sense of direction to live in a world in which men are to become creators.

It is folly to be heedless to the Law which is laid down in the Commandments for this eternity system.

The Commandments of Jesus are the etheric Commandments, the unseen Commandments. They are invisible because they exist in the inward parts of the etheric body. These are the Commandments one must live, for they are life; they produce and preserve life.

The Commandments of Jesus judge the world. Men hardening their hearts against the Commandments through Moses have shut themselves away from the inward parts of the Commandments, for the exterior Commandments as given by Moses are lifeless if absent from the inward-parts Commandments.

The exterior and interior Commandments curse men when they fail to observe them. Internal and external sickness occurs in a nation, a people, a family when the exterior and interior Commandments are ignored.

Every Commandment contains a strengthening for the frailties of the human life. Taking hold of the Commandments in the spirit of love through Jesus unites the exterior and interior Commandments. Nature as a Provident Mother loves him who lives through and by the Commandments.

In each life's allotment of karmas so that man may learn, one Commandment falls to him as his lot or that through which he learns. For example, one man must learn to worship God and God only through the First Commandment, or one must learn to avoid killing, adultery, stealing, lying or coveting.

In each life, this one-pointed way is that which shapes man. If he fails to recognize his theme of learning, he must return again and again to the Laws which control, shape and inform him. One should ask himself: "What Commandment am I expressing in this earth existence as the learning vehicle whereby I may learn, know and experience?"

Each Commandment has a Master Virtue. Each life is seeking to fulfill its purpose of commanding one Commandment, thereby obtaining a Master Virtue.

The Love-message in the Ten Commandments is stated in the First Commandment. All worship is kept alive by obedience to the Ten Commandments.

√ The first chakra relates to two dimensions. One remains on the initiatory thresholds of the two-dimensional world until he can rely on the power to say "Yes" or "No" as a choosing, discerning and discriminating vehicle.

Every disciple must incorporate the Grand Dimensional Scale into his nature. Spirit knowledge has not reliableness or trustworthiness as a system to live by until one has mastered the "Yes and No" Dimensional Power. This is why the Ten Commandments must be lived in the religious, moral and in the spiritual life. No one can reach the pinnacle of the Dimensional Scale until he has incorporated the Yes and No Principle which upholds the total Universe from atom to galaxy.

The first encounter with the Ten Commandments is in the first chakra. The first encounter with the Sermon on the Mount is in the second chakra, where one must work with the twelve prototypes or disciples-to-be. In this, he must master the third-dimensional knowledge.

In the third chakra or solar plexus, one must unite with the Saints and come under the influence of direct association with the Angelic Kingdom. When one reaches the heart or fourth chakra, the true work of the Prototypal knowledge begins.

Conscience is the vocal aspect of Law.

THREE DEGREES OF AMORALITY

Likewise must the deacons be grave, not doubletongued, nor given to much wine, not greedy of filthy lucre; Holding the mystery of the faith in a pure conscience.
—1 *Timothy 3:8,9*

There are three degrees of amorality. There is the suckling amoral person who is using immoral acts to perpetuate his sensuality. His main desire is to avoid unpleasant situations at all costs; discipline is ignored. He violates, through his greed for pleasure, the aspect of tender concern, which is his by nature as a child of God. He is engrossed in tobacco, drugs, alcohol and sex. He is a manipulator on all levels of his cunning mind. The suckling amoral person is prevalent in all stages of society. The total system of the economy, political and religious breakdown is caused by the suckling amoral person.

The rajasic or violent amoral person filled with hatred, absent from remorse, is the terrorist in the present period who has invaded the privacy and the possessions of the naive and unprepared.

The satanic amoral person is a representative of the dark forces. He is engaged in implanting into the minds of the intellectually insecure ideals which affect the downthrow of the collective grace given directly from the Ten Commandments and the Jesus Ethic. The satanic amoral person takes over one's mind, inhibiting the will, and indoctrinates one into the amoral. With persistent jargon of permissive ideas, he de-cultures one's nature into amorality, whereby one ends up in an immoral state expressing immoral behaviour.

These three amoral functions in the world have built a screen against the Light of God which is more powerful than thousands of the walls of China and thicker than the Berlin Wall in Germany.

As lambs being led to the slaughter, made listless by this constant barrage of immorality, it would seem that the principled ones of the world are doomed to go down into the black hole of degeneracy. The Power of God is the Only Power. The hour of God is nigh unto men, for His Son has come. And His positron-atom is vibrating to overpower the darkness in this world. Those who have the Light must keep their stations of Light. Conjoined with the Light of God, they shall not fail; they shall overcome.

Birth to Conscience

The Lord Jesus is the Watchman over our conscience.

Every probationer on the Path is in the fetus state when he meets his Teacher. He is in the womb of his own ignorance. The Teacher holds the umbilical cord to the subconscious. This door is the door to the conscience of the student.

Unless a teacher is full-grown to his own conscience, he lacks the tools to teach those who are coming to birth to their conscience. If the teacher ignores the conscience of his student, the student is still-born.

Multiple-millions in the earth are living in social conscience, family conscience and tribal conscience rather than individual conscience. Men having conscience are uniquely individual as to appearance, personality, mind and desires. While acting through the individual conscience, such persons are attuned to every level of conscience, be it continent, national, social, family.

Conscience is the vehicle through which one gains the virtues. The virtue life-threads are filled with the pulsating flow of conscience, for at the root of the thread of any virtue is also found the seed-root of conscience.

Rectification comes from repentance, confession and restitution nourished by a healthy and wholesome conscience. A clean conscience is freedom in soul and spirit, in body and mind.

There is no way anyone can outwardly enforce conscience. Conscience is born *within.* The spiritually illiterate are those who have yet to learn of the full capacity and working of the conscience.

It is the spiritual impulse and compulsion of the soul to build virtue. Back of this is the Grand Psyche or Conscience, which qualifies the virtue to live in the world.

Mankind can only benefit by such virtues. He who is virtue-oriented has in ancient times made his dwelling place within his conscience.

If man desires to be nothing, let him be without a conscience. If man would be holy or whole, let him lean on that Law which provides the soul-power of conscience.

When one meditates and comes into self-observation, he encounters his conscience. This can be done only with self-honesty.

Honesty with oneself is sweet paradise. One cannot get over the wall of the Cherubim unless he has self-honesty.

Self-criticism interferes with self-seeing. Self-honesty is a vehicle of the conscience adapted to work with the whole of conscience rather than the minor pricks in feelings of self-reproach and sense of guilt.

He who has no conscience cannot recognize Jesus. Conscience is the Grand Psyche—that is, the seed of rightness sealed into every soul-sojourner of the Eternals. If one is blind in conscience, he has offended cognizance or memory of the use of conscience in other eternity systems. If one, through desire to serve evil, buries his conscience, woe unto him, for he is crushed under the wheel of the Law.

Remorse without conscience is suicidal, and becomes revengeful against life, hampering the life-flow between souls. He who deliberates his heart against mercy has no conscience; step by step, he has used remorse as anger and separateness. Only with the *will* to rectify and to look upon oneself as a holy unit can mercy and conscience and virtue become one in human life and in human existence.

Virtue establishes conscience. It is the nature of virtue to establish conscience. One establishes conscience by being an example to others—and therefore virtue is born in him who listens or heeds.

He who walks the Virtue Path has a proven conscience.

ENCLOSURE POWER

And herein do I exercise myself, to have always a conscience void of offence toward God, and toward man.
—*Acts 24:16*

Man is an enclosure-maker. The enclosure power is a soul-power. This power makes it possible for one to have an ego and to have a form, also to develop the four bodies, which must in each incarnation improve and sensitize their versatilities.

The enclosure power creates and affects the Family-Atom. The enclosure power builds a tight matrix between husband and wife, sisters and brothers.

The enclosure power builds the egotistical shell. The *egotistical shell* holds one into the ego-body mechanics and animations.

The *after-death shell* built also by the enclosure power holds one after death into emotional omissions, immaturities and offenses. If one does not dissolve the after-death shell during the 90-day contrition interval after death, he falls into a coma, to awaken to consciousness only in physical birth. Prayers from aware persons who live with knowledge of the enclosure nature reach these coma-shell forms, and aid the sound-currents of dissolution to explode and dissolve more rapidly. Otherwise, coma-shell states of the after-death may linger for thousands of years, preventing reincarnation.

One living in the world can be in a heavily-enclosed

consciousness which is coma-like, and thereby bound to the Undersoul.

Pentecost is the fulfillment of the Ascension of Jesus. Jesus said: *"And I, if I be lifted up from the earth, will draw all men unto me."* (St. John 12:32) The Higher Self and the soul directing the ego repetitive patterns began to express through mankind through a Self-Genesis state of consciousness. With the lifting power of Jesus in His Ascension, souls having advanced consciousness through past-life incarnations entered into higher Self-Genesis expressions; spiritual powers and gifts surfaced, projected from their souls. The Esse poured down upon them the Passing Power, that they might keep open the processes of soul-awareness of God.

Lesser Self-Genesis men bent on having their own way at any cost, expressing themselves as being the only one, began a wreckage-way of life, assaulting the very morality which had supported Human-Genesis orthodoxy and traditional ways of life. The majority of men in this age and time are expressing lesser Self-Genesis. All are eventually, however, to enter into the higher Self-Genesis way.

When a nation is burdened in the conscience, the whole nation falls apart. When a family is burdened by conscience, the family is in danger of falling apart. If conscience is not responded to — and repentance is absent — the family falls apart. Family-atom conscience-sickness is prevalent in this age.

The world is presently in a state of moral cataclysm, seeking to bring to birth a new human race adhering to principles whereby conscience on a world scale may be activated among all men.

A rajasic criminality conscience active at the present time is in the hands of tamasic-minded and unrealistic viewpoints which subject the innocent as well as the guilty to suffocation as to incentive. Persons having the law in their natures and seeking a sattvic peace are seemingly helpless.

All animal life is expressing a Group-Soul with which they are identified as specie and creature. All animals are under a Group-Soul system overdirected by the Specie-Angels.

Man is not an animal and has never been an animal. Man is seeking to become an individual soul. His potential as an individual soul gives him unique and singular characteristics, enabling him to express his Higher Self and his hierarchy nature. To act and think within one's hierarchy nature is to be free as an individual soul.

The individualized soul has by divine right the power to think for himself. Working with the fully individualized soul, there is implanted a conscience.

Animals, in the singular state, are absent from a direct conscience. The Group-Soul over-directs their instinctual natures through the overdwelling conscience.

The Specie-Angels of the Group-Soul watch over all animal mating impulses which work to reproduce without variation the same specie in the life chain of the animal. Therefore, each specie has its own particular individuality, which is inbred by specie propagation.

In the Genesis archetypal formats for the individual soul of man, Tribal-Genesis works in a similar manner to the animal kingdom, in that the tribe as a whole comes under the conscience of the medicine man and the tribal leaders.

In Family-Genesis, conscience predominates through the love-nature in the family, individualistically expressed; if there is no love in the family, there is no conscience in the family-atom.

Man has in his nature a destroying power when he perverts his love-nature in any abnormal sense. He opens himself to subhuman life that is lower than the animal kingdom; a life which has lost the power to reincarnate in physical form. The subhuman life desire-nature enters into the life of all who pervert love, who deny conscience.

The subhuman exists in the grotesque level of the lower devachan planes of the astral world. On this level dwell also the earthbound dead, the comatose dead, and the wrathful dead who have through perversion failed to reincarnate. The wrathful dead are fixed in a shadowed purgatorial level from which they cannot escape. Having bound themselves to the fallen Lucifer influences while in the physical world, their hatreds and dark evils flow mirage-like into the minds of the living who use drugs, alcohol, or are engaged in sexual perversions.

Many persons caught into lives of perversion and deception—fantasized as to their ego-immunities, self-protections or self-righteousness—are influenced to do unlawful things. Their magnified cravings and self-indulgences are fed by the unsatisfied hungers flowing suggestibly into their minds and actions from the subhuman levels of the collective Undersoul. Acts of violence and hideous crimes are enacted upon the innocent, the naive and the unprepared by psychic-voltage persons who are receptive to the subhuman suggestible thought forms.

When a humanity has reached the end of a civilization spiral as men are experiencing in the present, perversion and dissipation surface; evil reaches a peak that its opposite—good—may come. In the lower dualities, these Undersoul trials are inevitable. However, it is the task of all spiritual persons in such times to stand for the Light, to speak for the Light, and to act in the Light, that the accumulated evil may be purged out through the Power and Will of God.

In the life of everyone comes the time when he must

make the decision or choice whom he will worship: ego or God.

It is true that man has by the Grace of God been given individuality as a vibrating soul tempered by degrees of singleness as to appearance. However, it is also true that just as a fine part is essential to the lifting of an airplane, so are all other parts necessary, or there would be no flight, no rising in the air.

Man is necessary in the scheme of synchronization as given of God. Man, as a united soul with all life and with all souls, is a coordinating vehicle which, when singularized, would set fire to itself, for that which seeks to be the one and the only—the ego—is accompanied always by the Destroying Archetypal Principle which determines its death and its limitation.

This is the one Law of Life: one must lay down his life for his friends, and he must lift up his soul for God.

Ego-man is always in the state of accumulating things and persons because he is intoxicated with the ideas that more things and persons make him *more*. When he truly enters the Path of the spiritual life, his travel is light and his burdens are few, having detached himself from the ego-commitment to collection of things.

The true walker on the Way leaves his collective attachments, fantasy sentiments and rigorous claimings outside the entry of the Path, for the voltage and vibrational energies on the Path will not accept that which possesses or claims or holds. He who would make a leap into spirituality should make his most holy possession habitual prayer, habitual service to God, for God.

As an ego, man is a Time-machine. As a Self, the soul is a spiritual Timeless vehicle, an open conduit through which God may make His Omnipresence known and seen. He who walks the Virtue Path is a creator of this conduit.

He uses the Transcendental stuff of his soul to build and to make of himself a channelling instrument for God.

Two things happen when one prepares to enter the Way, the Path. He must become loose, letting that which is unreal fall. He must be prepared by prayer-buoyancy and devotion to make a leap into realms unseen and unknown by the intellect and the senses.

When the senses are ready to bud with the Aaron's Rod Initiation or kundalini experience, and one is to represent God as an Omnipresent vehicle, he must enlarge himself in every level of his nature to give room for Omnipresence or the Presence of God. By self-denial in the ego, he masters Holy Space and Holy Timelessness. He is not as a leaf in the wind, for a leaf must fall with the first wind. He is a rooted-in, God-oriented, circulating vessel for God.

The Teacher and the Conscience

Conscience is as a white light appearing to the eye of one having conscience as a fixed star in the constellation of existence.

When one comes into the aura of the Teacher, conscience becomes a vehicle of omniscience. Conscience coming directly from omniscient prescient power of the soul knows the right or wrong of the past, the present and the future.

Conscience sees without a tremor the truth, and falls upon the heart chakra, causing earthquakes of fear and apprehension when truth is denied. The heart chakra is a cup of truth wherein conscience becomes the preceptor for the future.

Conscience becomes the judge and the accuser in the heart center or chakra. An omniscient conscience comes only to one who is pure in heart, undefiled by sense lusting, sense hating, sense greed, sense non-chastity, sense envy.

Conscience is a portion of the Holy Ghost in man; the more conscience, the more Holy-Ghost action. The Holy Ghost is the activation spirit within the world-conscience vehicle.

Wherever there is soul, there is conscience. When the conscience is unclouded, the soul becomes a golden revealer.

The conscience is made up of the finer atoms of the soul and spirit. Conscience, as a vehicle for the soul and spirit, provides the soul-light when the conscience is pure.

Man has inherited the conscience principle from other eternity systems.

The Prototypal Initiations are in the heart. Back of the prototypal zodiacal circle is a linking chain of Saints who have mastered the prototypal constellation soul-powers. It is the work of the great Bodhisattva-Saints to produce the pure prototypal man who will ultimately be as Jesus, the Son of Man.

Conscience is directly connected with Saint-hood. The conscience of a Saint is a pure omniscient soul-vehicle. Each prototype is aligned with a zodiacal Saint. Such Saints have been God-men of the past living in the earth.

The conscience is a mind-soul vehicle. It is only when guilt enters into one's thoughts that conscience can function. People who are all feeling and willing, without conscience, are not united with the Father. Those who have united with the Son are exposed to their conscience. One having all feeling and willing thinks of his evil as good; but when the Mind of Christ rays itself through the mental atoms, conscience is born. Contrition and restitution follow.

When the mind is first quickened by the Son, and thought becomes a vehicle for the conscience, irritating diseases may appear in the physical body, such as infections of the glands, cells, tissues and blood. These outward infections and irritative conditions are appearance-diseases demoting one as to his pride and over-ego inflation. All inflation of ego is the result of neglect of conscience.

The after-death experience for those who do not face their conscience in the physical world is a terrifying and painful ordeal under the eye of their Guardian Angel.

The disquieted soul is the restless mind driven by a tortured conscience and fiery resistance to the Spirit of God. The only way one can know Truth is by letting the Broom of Truth sweep clean the lies and fantasies in his life.

If one cannot bleed for others, he has no conscience. And the first one he should bleed for is God by being willing to give to Him his whole and complete physical life.

One commands Time by fulfilling the Law. When one has mastered the Law, he goes beyond Time—and he becomes a healer. One cannot become a healer unless he has become a master of Time; he has to be in alignment with the Ancient of Days to master Time. All karma and suffering pertain to misuse of units of Time and energy. Observing the Law brings one into Timing.

The Holy Ghost brings one into remembrance of all things. The Law in the beginning of this eternity system was sealed into man's "inward parts" or into his higher etheric body. When one offends Law or abuses Law, the etheric body sets up suffering.

From the very beginning of Time, when the Law was sealed into man's chakras, Conscience began. A poor memory and loss of memory are the result of having offended Law and Conscience.

HOLY CONSCIENCE

The Holy-Ghost Illumination provides world-soul memory, akasic memory, memory of the day's action, and memory of dreams or dream-cognition. Illumined souls live in the four streams of memory in consciousness supported by the three aspects of memory within the Law: the past, the present and the future.

A sin against the mind is a sin against the Holy Ghost. The key to overcome the eye-for-an-eye admonition of the Old Testament is: "Do unto others as you would have them do unto you," and to keep at all times the Commandment: "Love ye one another."

The temple of the soul knows nothing of chains or slavery. Only a free soul can live within the soul-temple. Only through love may one be free and liberated.

A penalty on the body is a penalty reminder from the conscience.

The Bible tells one to shun evil-doers. This also concerns one's own self of the past who has sinned. When a person is in a state of Light—keeping his spiritual, rhythmic practices without variation—he is in a constant state of Light and is insulated.

One must have contrition for sin, and he must make every effort to be free from the sense of sin through perfect trust in God's forgiving Love. One cannot plant the seeds for a new life in an old sin-consciousness. As long as one has an empathy for those who were involved with him in sinning, and keeps this door open to the soiled karma of the past, he cannot live in the present nectar of God's Omnipresent Good.

The Teacher is the conscience of the student until the student makes union with his own conscience. The student must be alive with the desire to escape his problems, and he must see that instruction is the door to the escape from suffering.

If the Teacher sees that a student is heedless, being laden with tamas inertia, karmic law frees the Teacher — and the student is removed from the environment of the Teacher.

CO-SIGNERS IN THE SPIRITUAL LIFE

When a Teacher takes a student, he becomes a co-signer to a note which is dependent upon the virtue-collateral in his chela or disciple. If the student fails to pay his part of the note, it falls upon the Teacher to be responsible for the debt.

A Teacher, with his observation powers earned through spiritual processes, must assay the collateral he is signing for. If there is no character in his student, the door is closed between him and his student. If the Teacher co-signs the note, he becomes a co-signer to the karmic debts of his student.

If he is a teacher untrained as to the ethic of succession in Dharma, he will be blind to the significant responsibility between a teacher and his student. Under the karmic law of balances, if the teacher blindly or emotionally accepts the karma of a disciple through any degree of preference, he takes on the debt of karma of his chela. Such a teacher exposes himself to the personalized issues in a student's life, and thus directly learns through the reproduction of his student's karma in his own personal life.

A Teacher must *see* clearly; he must observe the spiritual potential of the disciple weighed against the debts of the disciple. Jesus understood this law when He took unto Himself His disciples: Peter, James, Thomas, Jude, Andrew, Nathanael, James the Less, John, Philip, Matthew, Simon Zelotes, and Judas. Jesus' Power of Exorcism of karmas of His twelve was used in two instances: in the Lord's Supper during the washing of the feet; and in giving the Fire during His Ascension at Pentecost.

A Teacher having absolving powers of karmic debts is under the Holy Fire through Jesus. No other Teacher in the world has had the total exorcism obliterating of karmic debts save Jesus.

As long as the Teacher and the student are bound together by the vow of instruction within the Holy Dharma, the Teacher remains bound karmically to the chela from life to life. In each return to life, the chela finds his Teacher, that his karma may be revoked and cleared. The teaching side of the Teacher remains in this bond; and the chela, no matter what portion of life he may live in his return to the earth, hears the voice of his Teacher as his conscience.

Judas entered Jesus' life to seek to knock Him from the Path. Satan used Judas to incite the satanic evil causing the Crucifixion of Jesus. Jesus' standing firm against all temptations laid down the blueprint for all Teachers in associating with their chelas and disciples.

To His disciples who asked materialistic favors from Heaven, Jesus showed clearly the pitfalls of ambition. To Peter, He showed the karmic debt the chela takes on himself when he denies his Teacher, as did Peter on denying Jesus.

If one would be a Teacher of the spiritualized truths, he will be always a chela whether he is a Teacher or a chela; always in the state of soul-expanding under the direction of the One who had full command of His Most-High Soul Powers.

Jesus loved all of His disciples. He understood their frailties, but He knew that their essential characters must be ever pounded upon the anvil of the fiery shaping, whereby as disciples they could through total submission to the Will of God serve the Christ Spirit in the transforming processes of the earth and the soul.

The Dharma and the Vajra

The Dharma is accompanied by the Vajra: the Correcting Principle. A teacher failing to have the Correcting Principle is working with the Pleasure Principle. He is seeking only to inflate his own ego. Such teachers are harmful; they stimulate and stir the karmas of their students, but by their own selfishness fix their students into karmic relationships.

A Teacher carrying the Correcting Principle rearranges the karma of his student so that the student may make restitution for his errors, and thus provide for himself a way to reassume the true responsibilities gathered through Initiation. However, a Teacher carrying the Vajra never uses it in excess or exhibits it to humiliate his student, or in any manner looks upon it with any form of judgment or satisfaction.

The Vajra sometimes comes from the Teacher as one word, which acts as a self-disillusion electric-blast upon the fantasy forces operating through the disciple or chela. Or the Vajra may come through the Teacher as a sealing-off anesthesia, blocking off the heart channels between the student and the Teacher. Or a Vajra may work through the Teacher through the Divine Supreme. If the student's karma be heavy, some act of the Teacher or choice of the Teacher may set up a roadblock upon the path of the student, that the student may work upon a situation which is antagonistic to his spiritual life. Thus, the Teacher is sometimes, through higher or divine authorization, used to set the student to work upon a neglected issue, possibly in family or finances or certain aspects of lust in the disciple's sentient nature which stand between him and his progress on the Path.

When the student meets the living Teacher, he must be aware that such Teachers work with the Living God. Living God, or our Father, represents the Life Principle.

The Teacher comes first to show the Way. That which is concealed within the Way is the Life; and that which keeps the Way open is the Life made plain or free. Truth which follows the Way and the Life is the Thunderbolt Vajra. Anyone having true authorization from God as the Living-God power to teach and to educate must also heal. Truth as the Vajra is the surgeon's knife cutting aside the chains and the bonds binding the disciple.

The responsibility of the disciple to his Teacher is the first requisite or requirement in the spiritual life.

The Ethic in the seeking of union with God; the Ethic within the seeking of life-purification; the Ethic in the use of the mind and the will; the Ethic in the use of love — these are the four doors to initiation on the apprentice level. When one moves beyond the apprentice level, he must be wholesomely united with the Correcting Principle or the Vajra aspect of the Dharma.

If one has retained any form of hypersensitivity regarding the Admonishing and Correcting Principle, and flinches from the Vajra, he is yet an apprentice, and must be taught again and again the Ethic. Finally, when he acknowledges to himself the wisdom of the Vajra and gratefully accepts the surgeon's scalpel freeing him from fantasy infections, he will become a whole initiate in the state of adeptship; he will take up the shepherd's crook, and his sheep shall follow him.

A Happy Conscience

The camaraderie between souls comes as a joy-linking to one who has a happy conscience, finding others also plowing the clover fields of joy, of peace.

A person cannot be happy unless his conscience is happy. In this era, a happy conscience is a rare and unusual jewel.

As long as one has smoldering guilt in the Undersoul ready to be expiated—and he does not respond due to procrastination—he remains in the boundary states of neuroticism, seeing all things in a multiplied complexity. Blaming everything and everyone, he produces in himself some form of affliction, ailment or suffering.

Men have lost their sense of true and pure fun and humor. Such men are reverting to the sardonic side of laughter on the levels of vulgarity or of obscenity-distortion.

Laughter and joy and happiness come from a happy conscience. He who gives his unknowing to God—to His Omnipresence through His Angels—will be free, content, happy, blissful, joyous.

Conscience is not a muscle. Therefore, when it functions in spasmodic states, it creates energy-crossed challenges, teaching and reminding one of the need for balance and rightness. Balance can appear only when there is a happy conscience polarized to God and His Will rather than to one's own unknowing will.

In every hour and moment of the day, something or someone will hold up the mirror of conscience to him who is aware that he has conscience. One should be alert to those who bring karmic issues to a head in his life. Truly, he has been in the presence of an angel when he is reproved by someone for his lack of ethic and integrity.

One cannot have happiness at the expense of conscience. If one consents to evil, he is an accessory of evil. He must bear the burden of what he *takes on* in his life.

When a child is born, the parent takes on the karma of the child and the child takes on the karma of the parent. When the child enters school, the parent must undergo with the child what is speaking in the karmic environment of the school and schooling. When the child enters puberty, the parent recapitulates his own unresolved adolescent irresponsibilities. If the parent has not been firm in discipline of himself, he will look permissively and passively on the deviations in his child without sense of involvement.

Conscience in all souls having physical bodies appears outwardly and inwardly as a full-grown potential during puberty. If in this time a parent having no conscience rejects his child and himself, new karma is made and recorded in prototypal and soul association. This is fixed by the Maya computing system as wrong motive in the Undersoul.

If a parent can pass the grace of good to his child through the Passing Power of God in his own hierarchy nature, these are sacred times in his life as a parent and as a responsible being.

Should one live in the world without parenthood, he will re-enter his puberty state on the astral or emotional level when his glands lessen the biological flow in his sexual nature. He will recapitulate all of his undisciplined offenses in his teens. Between his 42nd year and 49th year, he will revitalize all of the uncaring instincts primally alive in his emotional nature. Thus, both men and women in these years—if they have moved over adolescence without union of conscience—must return to their conscience and be relieved of the weighted burdens recorded within the

Undersoul. In this time, men and women in the lower-Genesis states recapitulate in some degree adolescence drives and impulses; unrealistic, fantastic daydreams surface, demanding fulfillment. Though men are unaware of this, this is an *abyss initiation,* requiring that one face the dragon in his own nature and master it in the clear light of a pure and cleansed conscience.

The 42nd to the 49th are the years of the *Great Examination* given by one's personal Recording Angel and the Recording Angels on other levels working with the conscience of man and mankind. If one passes these disciplinary trials as to conscience through the needle-eye of the Law of God, he reaches his 56th year as a worthy, wisdom, mental vessel for God.

A cool conscience is a balanced rightness within a person who has looked his own evil in the eye and has confessed through contrition that he has erred, that he has offended himself, others, and God. If there be no mercy, no compassion awakened in this time, the record of the past will appear in the next ego life-existence as afflictions of the soul and of the body.

Gratitude and Conscience

> *I will wash mine hands in innocency: so will I compass thine altar, O Lord: That I may publish with the voice of thanksgiving, and tell of all thy wondrous works.*
> —Psalm 26:6,7

Conscience and gratitude flow in and out of one another, for he who has the attribute of gratitude is fully alive and awake to his conscience.

Closest to the conscience aspect of man in the animal

kingdom is the dog, representing conscience on the specie-angel level. A dog will lick the hand of its master in gratitude; in doing so, the dog reveals the conscience principle in the animal kingdom. A dog in the house or home of a person having no conscience becomes vicious, taking on the likeness of his master.

The Conscience Principle is Niscient, knowing God is in everything. Conscience moves automatically to be present in those who seek to be good and to do good.

One must search his conscience each day. The most effective way is not through self-recriminations, but through the act of prayer.

He who prays has a conscience. The more faith-filled the prayer, the more conscience can work with the Guidance System which is connected with the practice of prayer and devotion.

In the lower aspect of the Undersoul, sex and hunger have no conscience; thus, sex becomes an offense against choice as good. Sex violation without conscience is evil against all things God has established as good. Hunger, which is a side of greed when unlicensed, is gluttony, obesity.

A nation can be obese and gluttonous even as a person. Such a nation has lost touch with its conscience and its people—and its people enter into lawlessness and self-destruction. In times of national irrationality, there are magnified psychic electricities which seek to burn those involved without conscience.

Conscience is a camera. It is constantly recording with its lens one's own shortcomings and the shortcomings of others.

In the human spirit which thrives and survives upon conscience for one another—or caring for one another—

conscience leads those who are yet weak in conscience toward those who have no conscience. Thus, conscience, the teacher and voice for God, fulfills its work.

A million lessons in the day for each soul in the earth: The bird singing, the fish in the water, the lizard on the rock—are all speaking with the tongue of conscience to man. Every other living thing is saying to the Other: "Let me live; be kind to me; give me space; join me in the compendium of life." He who has conscience is united with everything and everyone by the bond of union in God.

Tears and weeping are a conscience vehicle. Regret and remorse are conscience outpourings.

The collective unconscious of humanity must be accepted in a comprehensible knowing that a rectified conscience acts as a mirror, revealing sincerity and truth and trust.

Anger at one's self is the conscience speaking. Without rectification, anger is poison to one's self, to his ambition and to his very life. The vitriol of anger lives in every person who fails to accept the signals from his conscience.

A million prayers a day from the lips absent from the heart as love will not suffice when conscience is absent in prayer. Trivial prayers keep one in superficiality, surface issues of life.

The true state of repentance comes before each prayer, that one may adjust the lens of his conscience. Prayer is answered after repentance is established. Such prayers act as a hologram producing millions of faces of good intent, telegraphing to the world that one is in this world to reproduce Godly ideas and Godly works.

It is better to have a terminal disease, the carrier of ages-long conscience-deviation, than to have insincerity, hypocrisy, cutting and grating against the conscience. That which comes out in the body as sickness is conscience revealing the deviation and omission. That which is mastered through pain, suffering and sickness is birth to the Light — a Light which only a clear conscience can reveal.

A clouded conscience prophesies sickness, unhappiness, failure. A weakened conscience cripples initiative and protection.

Two most valuable things the ego has been given are: Choice and Conscience. When conscience is absent, choice is inevitably faulty. That which one searches for in prayer and meditation for harmony and peace will not manifest itself if conscience is absent.

REPENTANCE AND RESTITUTION

Repent ye therefore, and be converted, that your sins may be blotted out, when the times of refreshing shall come from the presence of the Lord; And he shall send Jesus Christ, which before was preached unto you: Whom the heaven must receive until the times of restitution of all things, which God hath spoken by the mouth of all his holy prophets since the world began.
—*Acts 3:19–21*

True repentance produces a holy abhorrence for cheating, lying, manipulating, conniving and twisting. The face of evil seen in the world by one will be as his own face in other climes and times. Restitution enables the new-born honesty to vitalize itself in purification and in diligences outpicturing a conscience eased of burden and guilt. A person who works with honesty in his own self-exposure will work with honesty to cleanse the world.

Every man by grace — regardless of his evil — has the gift hidden within him. This gift, by the grace of God, stands with him to rise above his evil, that he may befit himself, through and by grace, for the procession of gifts accompanying his needs in restitution. The gifts to be manifested through repentance and restitution are like invisible suns, making for themselves new horizons.

In the evil of man, he is dazzled by his own ego-light. In the true self of man, he receives the true light, and comes to birth in the true sunrise of the risen self accomplished by repentance and restitution.

Man is not in this world to wreak vengeance on his fellow man, to commit murder or violence, or to oppress the Spirit in man. Man is in this earth to create. His true gift or holy virtue of grace in him is present in him. Love is the freeing of the grace.

If one reaches the state of repentance, and by any singular or multiple action points his finger in judgment at any person, the opportunity to make restitution will be unreachable. *"Judge not, that ye be not judged"* in the moment of repentance is magnified in the conscience. If one ignores this, he becomes an outcast to his own conscience. He who lives without judgment is in a state of virtue-grace.

Perfect balance in karma is righteousness. Righteousness, rather than judgment, is given to man through Christ.

Criticism is the beginning of judgment. Seeing the hope in each thing is the beginning of righteousness.

A person who truly stands for Repentance on the spiritual Path is making penance for all mankind.

Restitution is the transforming power in the soul. A true restitution is that one give more than the payment of his debt with a willing heart and without thought of sacrifice. Forgiving and giving with a magnanimity, and without thought or expectation or recognition for what he is and how he forgives, are true restitution.

Restitution means more than payment in full. It means beyond payment — a magnanimity-insight.

Penance is another side of giving; it is a giving up of all the things that stand between one and God. By giving up, one makes restitution.

It is false restitution to think that one should receive virtue-returns for restitution.

The hierarchy nature in the sign of Scorpio is the sign of repentance; in Leo, the sign of restitution; in Pisces, the sign of confession.

Confession without rectification is hypocrisy.

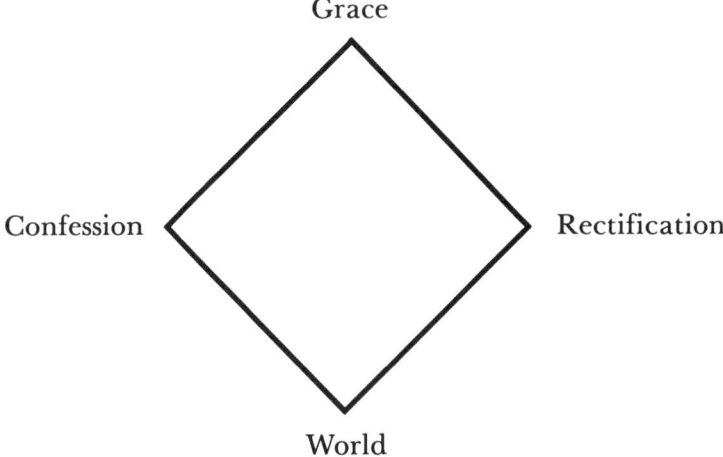

Title: *The Diamond of the Christ*

RESTITUTION AS FREEDOM FROM THE SATANIC

A man is a faithful and prudent servant (Matthew 24:45) when he is quick to atone for all his offenses, interiorly by contrition, exteriorly by confessing them and making restitution.

—Saint Francis of Assisi

The Lord is continually *re-certifying* His servant or server. The dedicated server is always in a state of the new in revelation and transformation. The Lord does not stand still—and anyone who represents Him cannot stand still.

Static electricity of unknowing and non-growth is of the satanic. Satan adores the apathetic, the lethargic, and the tamas mind. The satanics prepare their own the way the Christ does—over many lives.

Karma offers one the opportunity to make restitution; but it also offers him the opportunity to sin. Therefore, one should pray the Lord's Prayer: *"Lead us not into temptation."*

One cannot *exorcise* karma; he can only mitigate it through restitution for his sins.

Judas started his restitution when he became contrite. He began his restitution in "outer darkness," where he presently dwells. In aeons, he will retrieve his soul through serving those who suffer the torments of their evil-doing.

Restitution is paying off the debt of past wrong actions which were inspired by Satan. Every time one does good, he is disconnecting himself from Satan.

God does not ask one to make restitution to Him, because He is always in the state of Forgiveness. One does not make restitution to God, because the Love of God and His Forgiveness have erased his debts.

It is God's Forgiveness that gives one the strength to make restitution for the satanic errors in his nature, for having listened to Satan. One must give restitution as a payment for his debts or sins; therefore, he pays off the satanic in himself, and thereby disconnects himself from the influence of Satan.

When one ties himself to Satan's influence, it is as a gambling debt. One must pay off his debt.

God is a Certainty. Satan and the satanic are a gamble.

The heart of restitution is to overcome evil. When one

overcomes evil, he cuts the satanic chains of malice and sensuality, which are Satan-directed and Satan-controlled. Once one makes restitution, he can walk in honor and freedom with lightness.

By renunciation and restitution, one lives the past in the present. When restitution is made, one blesses the present, the past and the future.

Guidance comes only when one has a relieved conscience. When one has spilled out the memories of his deceits, guilts and deviations, his conscience becomes the receptacle of holy grace, whereby guidance and conscience are one.

If a man be found in fault, and he continues to provoke others to sin, he is close to the boundary of the pit. Having abused his nature to the end of endurance, he falls into the hands of the satanic—and he suffers the scourging-trials.

In the Niscience Ministry of Healing, the one who is healed is united with the Conscience Principle and the Revelation Principle through which he is given the way and the manner by which he can make restitution. Healing is made secure through restitution-grace. Within restitution-grace is resurrection power to exceed that side of one's nature which attracted sickness.

When restitution begins its work through the person who has been healed and has become a cleansed temple for God, great things are manifested in the Name of God. Restitution-grace gives resurrection power—and the power to Pass or to give Passing power to others.

DIMENSIONAL RESTITUTION

Restitution is made possible for man as a *soul-experience* and as an *earth-experience*. In the inner planes between death and rebirth, restitution is made to relieve the soul's record as to one's attitudes toward God. Restitution is always accompanied by guidance and placement in life and in death. These go hand in hand.

Conscious involvement as an act of restitution is necessary in the world after death, in the world of sleep and in the world of waking. The act of restitution must be given with conscious awareness. *Unaware* restitution inflicts one who is blind to karma.

The spiritual phases of restitution begin with awareness of wrong-doing and of evil. Offering oneself to God provides the way of restitution. From such an offering, Omnipresence sends the Divine Companions to ease the way and make bearable restitution.

Intentional Suffering is restitution power.

Restitution is the arm of Mercy in the Law of God. The Mercy aspect of the Law enables one to pay off physical karma through acts of restitution in the physical world. However, offenses *against God* are paid off in both the physical and in the Inner World of consciousness, as in dreams and in after-death contrition periods.

The only way one can *act out* the karmas he has made on the physical plane is by living on the physical plane, which provides him with the opportunity to physically face his karma.

One has the opportunity through the *Night Ministry* to make restitution for his errors. While in sleep, he receives instruction for the daytime solution to his problems and the problems of others. The Night Ministry is for all levels of restitution: world and personal. Such restitutions bring the karmic scales into equilibrium for offenses made during the daytime by the many in the physical world and also for the one opening the blessings of restitution.

Some offenses are worked out at night and some in the

day. Both night and day are action-oriented. The fourth degree of the subconscious mind makes it possible for all to work and serve in both the physical plane as well as the inner planes in states of restitution.

The karmic levels of restitution in sleep enable one to act out the energies in his karma through pictograph symbolic dramas of his physical acts. In this, he reproduces the potent instruction regarding physical acts.

The more one advances in the spiritual life, the more he can equalize his own assumption over karma—that is, work to rearrange the karmic patterns laid down by unknowing and unlawful men.

There is a prison sentence and penalty for every unlawful act. He who would steal Time, honor, monies, possessions or the will of others must endure time limits and frustrations.

Man is his own jailor. He serves *Time* when he has offended on some level. If he has offended any of the gravity laws, he is held to the lower rates of reincarnation to serve out his time. If he continues to choose the unlawful way of life, our God is the Law Eternal. Finer than the microscopic vision in an atom, greater than the telescope seeing the farthest star, is the Eye of God and His Will in All.

The Path between the gurus of the East and Jesus branches off in two directions. Gurus say: "Go into Nirvana and disappear." Jesus says: "Go *into* your troubles and lift the world."

Billions of souls in the earth understand in a limited degree the Law of Karma and the Law of Reincarnation. Such persons are chained to the heavier sides of their karmas because they are unwilling to use the energy of the knowledge of Reincarnation and the Karmic Laws through acts of Restitution. Wherever one is seen in the heavier states of karma — responding blindly, passively and irritatingly — he is unwilling to take on the yoke of Restitution, which is the yoke offered by Jesus.

> *Come unto me, all ye that labour and are heavy laden, and I will give you rest. Take my yoke upon you, and learn of me; for I am meek and lowly of heart: and ye shall find rest unto your souls. For my yoke is easy, and my burden is light.*
> —St. Matthew 11:29, 30

Every man has his own equated format of karma; thus, no two men make restitution in the same way. Willing restitution brings a holy joy and moves one into a third vibration within the Coinciding Principle, where dwells the Omnipresence of God.

Restitution is demanded of one until he takes hold of the Commandments, inclusive of the Golden Rule and the Commandments of Love given by Jesus. One becomes the victim of blind karmas until he possesses the golden treasure of restitution with a whole heart, whole mind, whole strength.

One's desire to make restitution is God's desire in man to correct what man has done wrongly. The greatest compassion comes directly from God as *Grace*. The more one has instantaneous reproving, the closer he is to the receiving of his grace.

A tree that is pruned in its season is a healthy tree. He who expects to not be corrected becomes a jungle and a wilderness unto himself. Refusing to be corrected and ignoring the message of Restitution which follows correction, is to be a laggard, a foot-dragger, and eventually a distortion of life itself.

God has given life. Life has one determiner: to make itself useful and beautiful. The useful side of life gives healing and health. The beautiful side of life is the fulfilling of the law of order, where everything is proportioned according to the exact nature and Spirit of God.

He who learns beauty at the expense of others is a parasite. He who reveals beauty for the Glory of God is an avatar carrying the first and supreme message that God Is.

> *I am in God, the One Consciousness.*
> *I am in Supreme Consciousness.*
> *I am a Supreme Consciousness entitized Being,*
>   *a divine unit of measure.*
> *I am the one in the One Enlightenment.*

Book Three
Exercises and Practices

DESCRIPTIONS OF TRANSCENDENTAL CENTERS

The *Constant* is located in the Divine Thalamus above the medulla oblongata in the back of the head slightly below the crown of the head. This is the dwelling place of our Father and the dwelling place of one's own Constant.

Buddhi has its homeplace center in the Indestructible Atom in the middle of the forehead.

The *Higher Self* has its dwelling place in the soul energy-field above the head as far as the hands can reach and touch. The Higher Self is centered within the Eternal Sustaining Atom, which is the vehicle for the crossing over from one eternity system to another.

The *Soul* is centered in its pulsation point within the crown of the head.

The *Third Eye* dwells directly beneath the Soul's pulsation. The Third Eye flows its light of vision outward between the eyebrow center, which is called the Jade Gate or the Cave.

The *Christ Consciousness* is opened through the Third-Eye canal. Christ Consciousness is experienced between the eyebrows.

The *Indestructible Atom* in the middle of the forehead was opened by Jesus when He ascended.

The medulla oblongata at the base of the skull, in proximity to the brain stem, is the *Mouth-of-God Center* or the Logos Vibration of the Holy Sound.

The *Hierarchy Nature* is experienced as consciousness in Buddhi, which is the Center of the Informing Principle in the center of the forehead.

12

THE MIND AND THE HIERARCHY NATURE

> *As the birds are flying, I am free to soar —to soar into Spacelessness, into azure states of Paradise, of peace superb.*
> *Peace and Space are one, for only in Space unrestricted is my soul free. In God, free am I.*

To have holy powers, one works in the company of those having the holy-grace powers, the Saints. To have divine powers, one works with those having divine attributes and grace manifestation works, the Hierarchy or the Fathers.

To know one's own hierarchy nature, one must move beyond fetishes or dogmatic names or titles which identify God as limited or as punishing. The hierarchy nature of the Higher Self assures man of his own destined way of his direct responsibility as a creator in this earth or eternity system.

In the hierarchy nature, the first vision is to create, to sustain creation in the Will of God. One finds his most dependable vehicle for his hierarchy nature in the sustained eye-single state or the Image-of-God power unceasingly fixed upon the Constant or Will of God within his own nature. Hierarchy nature lives in the Purusha Constant or Enlightened state of *God-awareness,* knowing the nature of the Plan.

The hierarchy nature uses the technique of the *Ward made flesh* through Christ Jesus to see the ultimate manifestation that all men be lifted up—and that all men become like Jesus or to *see Him as He is.* One side of the hierarchy nature *uses* its destroying archetypal powers to wipe away the guilt memories in the Undersoul and to clean out the negating fixities that produce the climactic states or cosmic traumas upon men.

Hierarchy nature sees with its imaging faculty of the Divine the cause of illness, loss and betrayal. Hierarchy-nature healing faculties heal all of these within the creative uptides of revelation sealing in a new vision for the future.

The hierarchy nature is the mind overlord over the ego and the Undersoul. It will not be moved from the Plan, neither will it die nor cease. Hierarchy nature maintains the matrix needed for the birth to life and to space. Hierarchy nature creates the atmospheres within the timeless eternal powers given of God.

Presently, man is using four sheaths for the mind; a fifth is now coming forth. All sheaths for the use of mind have been made by the hierarchy nature of the Higher Self within the Will of God. The hierarchy nature at work is the Will of God at work. Hierarchy nature determines all healing and lasting health. Hierarchy nature has ordained *health.* To will in the Will of God is to freely flow with the Esse within the hierarchy nature.

The Esse is energy used by the hierarchy nature to expand and extend the vibrational velocities of the Divine. A conscious flow of the hierarchy nature is realized only when one crosses over the vibrational duality grossities of psychic force and play.

The higher mind consists of Light. It is the carrier of the Light seeking to become the Life. There must be Life in the mind to heal. If Life be absent in the mind, mind is drawn downward by the force system of the sentient.

Life in the mind is moved by the Holy Esse or Spirit. He who has obtained the Esse flow in the mind is a healer. Life as movement in the mind automatically assures that Light shall reveal and also heal. Innocence abides where perfection as the archetype is ever-present. Life in the mind with the Esse is as a vine—climbing ever higher toward the Light of right resolution, right solution.

Life in the mind is the Life of God. Life as God in the mind comes from experiencing God as the Life, the Power, the One. To heal, one must have had God-proving experience through Life experience with God in countless lives.

Life in the mind heals. Light in the mind reveals. These two must have agreement with one another that healing may come, for there cannot be healing save revealing reveals the cause of sickness.

Life dwells in the heart of the disciple. The heart contains many corridors where life is experienced and tested through love. Where love is, there is more life, that Light may shine and illumine all mind expression.

The gift of the mind as consciousness is the gift of God's Love. Who loves lives, and in living is in the Presence of God.

The mind since its beginning has had its home in radiance, radiance directed by God who makes His home in the mind as a portion of Himself. In the Higher Self is the hierarchy-nature mind. This is that mind which contains the Will of God, the Life of God, the Light of God and the Love of God—all contained in the Atom called *Eternal Sustaining Atom*. This Atom dwells as a jeweled center in the Higher Self.

God as Creator in the Higher Self divides and diversifies Himself in the four major attributes of His Eternal Spirit Nature. As the Will, He is the One willing. As the Life, He is the Life living. As the Light, He is the Light revealing. As the Love, He is the Love loving. In the Higher Self, Will is Will in God; Life is Life in God; Light is Light in God; Love is Love in God.

The Higher Self contains in its hierarchy-will nature a mind sheath supporting the archetypal design for that which is to be. Through the mind willing of the hierarchy nature, the archetypal design will not change or be changed from that design. *It will be:* This is the Divine Constant. The True Self is at home in God; not one particle willed by the Creator can be moved. It will happen. It is going to happen.

He who finds his own hierarchy nature cannot fail. In each incarnation, his creation when responding to the archetypal plan in the hierarchy nature assures that he will succeed, for God is present as the Omnipresence in all his affairs, personal and spiritual.

The chief desire in the disciple is to find God and to experience Him directly. In each life or incarnation, he must express God as Will in all of his affairs. He must express God as Life. Through the Light, he must reveal Him as intelligence, and he must see and know the Omnipresence of God as Love.

To come close to God is to be initiated into the four unchangeable attributes of God; in each life this occurs without variation. The more sensitive one is as to what God is, the more he will become God-like. Not one life can accomplish God-likeness. Many lives are necessary to grow more and more into the Archetypal design planned for that which is the Nature of God in him.

Guidance

Guidance in the Will of God is a first versatility grace given of God. The Will of God acting as Guidance is the natural nature of hierarchy power in each soul. To explore one's own willing to be a hierarchy creator within the Guidance Principle of the Will of God is to do rightful and just things within the Law of God. For the disciple the Will of God is seen in his own *action versatilities*. To act for ego is to build; to act for God is to create.

One can see the perfection of the guidance within the Will of God when one creates. He can see the ego-guided will when he builds on the temporal scale of time as limited. The ego-guided will is under the control of sense and sense-enlargement rather than God in everything.

In the life of the ego, one builds to receive. In the life of the hierarchy nature of the mind under the Guidance Principle as creator, one immortalizes good by giving. By giving, one is in the Presence of God present in all planes of creation. Giving is a will act directly connected with the hierarchy nature, which is omnipotently magnanimous. By its own nature, hierarchy nature knows it is limitless within the abundance of the Eternal Creation. Hierarchy nature knows not poverty or impoverishment.

Hierarchy nature understands completely the difference between choice and willing. Hierarchy nature knows that choice is a gift loaned to those who are yet to learn that willing is a *right*. Only those who observe willing as sacred are within the guidance of the Will of God.

That which moves lives; that which moves with *awareness of God* creates, heals and manifests. There are no boundaries in Spirit. Spirit by its nature unites. The disciple moving in the Esse Holy-Spirit conscious awareness moves in the hierarchy nature resounding to the Archetones of music unheard by the outer ears. In the nature of the sentient or lower mind, one is deaf to the inner music supporting the higher mind and its hierarchy power of willing in the Will of God.

In the sentient or lower mind, the life compulsion may be stronger than the light compulsion; therefore, darkness of the mind becomes darkness against the soul. The hierarchy-willing powers of the Higher Self are slowed down; then, only the lower music can be heard, crying "Self, self, self," or "Me, me, me."

For light destined to come, life must become first fire as pain or suffering. Thus, the Undersoul, which has been a will receptacle for the draining of the lower mind and ego, must become the fire of pain. All through the canals of the glands, the nerves and the blood, the sounds of grief, pain and suffering are heard; the energies of pain in the lower mind become the energies of doubt of God, of life, of self.

It is not the nature of the Most High Soul directed by the hierarchy nature in the Higher Self to dwell in or upon darkness; therefore, the hierarchy nature of the Higher Self created for its vehicle for the finite world an Undersoul. In the raising power of the Holy Esse experiencing the hierarchy nature as the Will of God, the Undersoul is destined to ultimately function as a vehicle of Light; for God is Light and His Nature is to bring all of creation into awareness of Light. The Undersoul is to become a sheath or mind-expanding vehicle for the Light of the Higher Self. Presently, the Undersoul functions to work as a receptacle of the unknowing and the unfulfilled.

Connected with the sensory system of the mind, the Undersoul acts as a vortex for the nerve energies, sensory energies and lower mind energies; all are under control of several degrees of the subconscious mind. The Undersoul is a foremost will instrument for the ego; in this, it is an indirect or secondary willing instrument for God who gives the constant will to survive.

The Undersoul acts as a forming, energy, primal brain matrix. The subconscious is the motor for the Undersoul. The subconscious mind works also within the conscience or Grand Psyche of the soul.

Subconscious mind receives all orders as to its correcting function directly from the Higher Unconscious, which is the Buddhi aspect of the hierarchy nature. The Higher Unconscious is the gateway to the hierarchy nature.

The energies of the Undersoul are presently working to move mankind as souls into the clear light of the higher mind whereby the hierarchy powers can function for man in the earth.

All that man can know of the Nature of God and of his own extension power of God while living in the earth must be learned by opening the Higher Unconscious. When this happens, he is no longer a sentient, motorized, mechanized habit-bound creature. He becomes a Wisdom Knower of the indestructible vision implanted by God, the Eternal Spirit and Governor over all.

SIMPLIFY AND GLORIFY

The hierarchy nature is free to function when one simplifies and glorifies.

The terms for the spiritual life and for the hierarchy-nature willing are: Simplify and Glorify. Simplify and glorify begin the spiritual life. To be unburdened is the greatest of grace.

To many, it is more difficult to take up the virtue-grace

of simplifying and glorifying than it is to remain in the habit sin-compulsions. The greatest healing of all comes when one transenergizes and steps over sinning into Truth. By this, the intensities within the Undersoul are slowed down. The habit patterns are atrophied and eventually are burned in their own fiery energies.

The most challenging condition and function existing in the Maya system against the spiritual life is *sinning*. Through the Maya tenacity of claim and attachment one holds to his sins more than any possession. His errors, his mistakes, his denigration and his ego-encherishment are greater than any house, home, castle, nation or person.

Sin is supported by the habit culturing development in the Undersoul. One holds onto his sins, for they represent the pattern, ego-design and will of his psychic-matter nature. This being set and molded into the Undersoul directs the modus operandi, or his method of learning as a way of surviving.

A person can be as possessive of his life-style as he is prone to be possessive of a person or an object. The power of enclosure in him in certain times sets up a wall against freedom and liberation. Being overpossessive in any aspect of life keeps one fixed in the illusions of the ego and the Undersoul. True Self does not claim, bind, tighten, or hold onto any relationship or any possession.

THE HIGHER UNCONSCIOUS AND THE MIND

The Third Music is the natural play of the Archetone provided by the Archetype.

Where the spiritual world meets the gravity world, there is a spherical realm of pure mind and soul atmospheres.

With extended senses and soul-faculties, man living in the gravity world can explore the archetypal realms of bliss. He can make himself an experiencer of this bliss-vicinity by purification of the chakra light in his nature.

The Archetypes and the Archetones presently are functioning in the hierarchy nature of the Higher Self and the Buddhi nature of the higher mind. This is the realm of the *Higher Unconscious,* or that place of stilled quiet which sounds the Audible Hum of the Cosmos within the Eternal Spirit of God.

All who seek spiritual experience are destined to retain something of gravity in their articulating what is seen and revealed. In the search for spiritual experience, one seeks to pass on what he has seen, heard and experienced; it is his work to pass on to others that they may also know and experience. One works that he may move over the gravity obstructions, that he may be united directly with God, and thus learn of the spiritual mysteries at first hand.

There are billions of souls inhabiting the physical world. Each soul of the earth is a part of the collective Higher Unconscious.

Archetypal knowledge is available to those who have moved beyond the gross gravity energies in their lower chakras. Beginning at the heart chakra, one relates himself to the Higher Unconscious through Meditation, Prayer, Contemplation and the Holy Practices. In the Higher Unconscious or Buddhi light, the Archetypes flow directly and rhythmically into the souls who seek to know and to experience God as Eternal Spirit.

The first phase of initiation into the Higher Unconscious bliss-realm is perilous. In this, one must encounter the struggle aspect of the Undersoul that he may still or quieten the frenzied energies of the ego, the intellect and the lower mind and will.

The hierarchy nature is at home in the Higher-Unconscious experience. When one becomes an adept in the use of his own hierarchy nature, his Undersoul becomes an unshadowed instrument; his Higher Self then may take possession of all appearance and apparitional aspects of the ego.

One may think of the first step in initiation as a struggle and also as a trial through which the senses are tested that they may become flexible, and thus changed into soul-faculty powers. The hierarchy nature within the Higher Self, once reached, enables one to undergo the more profound initiations through which he becomes a master of forces.

The Undersoul's greatest power is the power to draw upon the gross electric forces existing in the elements and especially upon the gross atomic system supporting Maya existence in earth.

Each life in earth is a Time-experience. Earth life is limited by Time and by karma. The ego is the burden-bearer of this karmic limitation. The ego utilizes the energy forces within karmic limitation, that it may eventually experience through spiritual transenergization the functioning process of the force system. The task of the ego in this present time is the greatest the ego has ever known in its predestined reincarnation cycles.

The Higher Self in the effulgence atmospheres of its hierarchy nature is the creator. The ego as the builder uses the force system through gravity and the atomic. The Higher Self as the creator uses the akash side of the *spiritual atomic* system to energize the ego and spiritualize the intellect.

Each ego life-existence contains and retains something built by the ego experience in other lives. Each life has some form of victory achieved through the transenergization of mind energies.

Man in the earth presently has reached the place in his evolvement to where he can no longer totally lean upon the ego. The Archetypal downpouring within the Higher Unconscious is now giving to him a mirror whereby he may begin to understand the necessity to unite with his own and true reality.

In the coming Dwapara-Yuga time, all in the earth will respond in some degree to the Archetypal flow of the Higher Unconscious. The present stirring in the earth is caused by the downpouring of the Archetypal flow from the Higher-Unconscious realms.

The subconscious is the dual gravity twin of the Higher Unconscious. Men who work with their lower chakras are presently receiving the Archetypal flow through the subconscious. The subconscious contains the memory of ego experience in the earth. The present spilling out of exaggerated violence, terrorism and subhumanism is caused by the Higher Unconscious stirring the sedimented memories in the subconscious.

He who destroys one's will destroys the vital creative side of the mind. The mind cannot function without the will, willing as a self. The satanic mind is a will-killing mind. To render one's beliefs in God useless, one invariably encounters during the first phases of initiation a satanic mind which seeks to take away from the mind all mental-initiative, all mental-incentive and all mental-creation.

To mentally accept a doubt-implanted inference of a satanic mind assures one that his higher mind will become vacuous and useless, where the Presence of God cannot enter in. He who surrenders his mental will loses touch with his higher mind; he becomes a mental-vegetable functioning through the lower or animalistic mind.

The Mind in God is the centered point of the Eternal Atom where dwells the Spirit of God. The Mind in Christ is verticle thinking, one-pointed thinking of God as the

One Omnipresence in all and in everything. The Mind in Jesus is the Mind of mankind, whereby man is crucified, resurrected and ascended.

The Mind in soul of man is the individualized mind. In its highest state, it is ever-present with Omnipresence, in Jesus, in the Christ, in the Father, in God.

Consciousness is a Space-Vehicle. *Time* determines how Space is used for God.

Whatever one's consciousness is, he *is;* one is no more than his consciousness. That which pushes consciousness forth is mind. That which tests and examines consciousness is sense. That which knows as consciousness is Self.

In the ego, one is what and where the consciousness *is*. In the True Self, one is the consciousness.

Billions and trillions of suggestible and impressionable mind and emotional influences have built the ego consciousness. Consciousness on ego levels occurs first as experiencing; second, as serving; and, last, as awareness.

> *I am aware; therefore I am conscious—*
> *not, I am awake; therefore I am conscious.*

The New Mind-Sheath

The brain is not a spiritual vehicle; it is a mechanized vehicle serving the senses and the intellect. Mankind is presently forming another brain. This is forming through the work of the Undersoul.

In a two-plane understanding, with a Third-Dimensional consciousness, man little understands his own involuntary systems of forming and shaping. The involuntary system in the background of man's development on the conscious level is rarely experienced by the conscious mind.

The Mind and the Hierarchy Nature

The subconscious mind uses all involuntary systems to circulate and keep alive the action in the Undersoul and the ego. The Higher Unconscious uses the Eternal and universal involuntary to work with the soul of man that he may assure his destiny as a creator in the earth.

The Higher Unconscious moves man beyond his subconscious dependencies upon the ego or gravity-bound involuntary systems. The involuntary system working with the subconscious on the physical plane keeps men sealed into the cyclic habit patterns of everyday existence.

The involuntary system in creation begins with God; this is opened through Initiation, Meditation, Mantra, Prayer, Devotion, Worship, and service to God. All of the most-high virtues work directly with the higher involuntary compulsions which are part of the Absolute Will of God.

In the fifth-dimensional state of consciousness, man will be *aware* beyond ego-consciousness. The fifth state of consciousness provides the hierarchy sheath for the higher or Buddhi mind. The most prominent state of the Higher Self is the True Self; its nature is the hierarchy nature which works directly with the Will of God, the Life of God, the Light of God and the Love of God.

The Undersoul and the ego presently are working to build the higher-mind sheath through which the hierarchy nature of the Higher Self will be available and expressed by the objective or outer conscious mind. When this is accomplished, man will function mentally and emotionally through his own divine hierarchy nature, and thus be aligned at all times with the Living God rather than the duality aspects of God. The fifth sheath, giving freedom to the hierarchy nature of the Higher Self, will function as the new mind in Christ.

All the struggles in the body, all the contestings in the etheric plane of energies, all of the tumults of the emotions, and all of the mind dependencies upon the ego-conceptual mind working through a persistent duality will no longer predominate, for man will have mastered his Undersoul, having reached the Most-High-Soul state of unceasing God-Realization.

The new mind sheath man is working upon is ordained by the Will of God. The Higher Self in its hierarchy nature is moving man forward toward a God-Will progressive consciousness.

The Higher Self is a hierarchy pilgrim. The Christ came to enable man to be a full hierarch or son-of-God being. God in His manifesting powers is presently heavily-charged in the hierarchy nature of man.

Many advanced souls in the earth have used their hierarchy natures before coming to this eternity system. Those having the hierarchy powers have attained their fifth sheaths and beyond. They work with men now on the inner and outer planes, that they themselves may add to their own hierarchy natures and powers.

It is the natural state that mind as the first vehicle for creation must gain all of the powers latent within the nature of the mind. Thus, man on earth will become God-like and a son of God.

As a hierarchy pilgrim immersed in the earth, it is destined that man be a builder and a creator with God. He uses his ego to build and his hierarchy nature to create. To do this, he must use and explore his divine nature, experiencing various states of consciousness from life to life, age to age.

The hierarchy nature of the Higher Self is the ordained creator for God at the divine level of consciousness. God as Omnipresence resides in the hierarchy nature of the

Higher Self. Hierarchy nature neither languishes nor waits; it exists in eternal compulsions of going, becoming and creation.

The earth presently is polarized upon its axis to function within the vibrational *four*. The axis of the earth is now facing a major shifting of its poles whereby the earth will move into a fifth vibration.

During this era, which men intuit inwardly, the Sun of this eternity system and its planets will enter into another Archetonal beat of energy processes. Nature, as men know it, and physical nature which man possesses, will move into other gradations of refinement and development. These occurrences will begin at the ending of this present Moving Archetype, which will be 5,000 years after the birth of Jesus.

Jesus, as the Messiah functioning as Christ Jesus, used all twelve chakras within a thirteenth dimension. It is inevitable in Time that all men will be like Jesus. The earth is the crucible for the sons of God, all seeking to become hierarchs or mind-creators with God.

God is Spirit in the hierarchy nature of man. Man is ever-creating new sheaths or energy fields for his divine nature.

In the lower nescience state of duality, heavenly powers are misinterpreted, abused and misused; nescience creating powers are out of the range of God-awareness. When one creates for his own possessive nature in the nescience state, he comes into the range and influence of the fallen archangel powers, or Luciferic telepathies.

The hierarchy nature of man assures him that he is a creator. When he is *nescient,* he creates the unlasting, the painful and the separative. When he is *niscient,* he creates with his hierarchy nature within the Plan and Will of God.

The Undersoul, working with the subconscious, acts as a sponge to absorb the wrong desires expressed in the nescience state. In regular cycles coordinated with the cleansing processes of the hierarchy nature of the Higher Self, one must spill out the faulty debris within the Undersoul. This affects man individually and it also affects the world. In the present time, the world's Undersoul spill-out and man's Undersoul spill-out are simultaneously working upon each other. This is the cause of world-chaos, of hatred: hatred of self, hatred of others, hatred of life. This is also the cause of every man being separate and divided and untrusting.

The hierarchy station for the use of the hierarchy nature is at the Buddhi Point, or the Indestructible Atom, which is in the middle of the forehead. When one uses the Niscience method of healing, he is using his own hierarchy nature within the Will of God to heal. In this moment of healing, he gives a *Passing* to those in need of healing. The Will of God takes the need into the command of God, that the situation or person one would heal will receive instantaneous correction or healing. In the Niscience techniques of healing, miracles occur, which are in reality the Will of God at work.

All persons entering birth to the Maya system controlling the Earth come to earth that they may gain the Realized consciousness and thereby use their hierarchy imaging powers. The terms for birth for the Maya system supporting the world are many: one of these being possession and possessiveness; the other being the power to enclose and attach to oneself an area or territory through which he may feel rooted and supported.

The body thrives upon repetition, demanding it unto the day of death. The mind thrives upon changing, being dependent upon the versatility-essences arising from the reservoirs of the mind. The mind to live must be always in a state of change, of movement.

The contest between the body and the mind creates the tumults which the soul must master. The soul is seeking continually to move the body into movement beyond repetition so that the mind may live in its natural life of hierarchy-nature creation.

When one first cries out to serve God, or to assist God in helping His children, he begins a long stage of *Incubation* and initiatory trials played upon by the Undersoul. In this, his ego-pride and vanities are gradually pulverized and pounded by the angelics assisted by adversaries on various levels, wherein his ego-power is demoted that his soul-power may increase. Many years may transpire in Incubation to enable one to finally reach his true hierarchy nature of the Higher Self and to work as a will-instrument within God.

The will is essentially a mind-instrument. Therefore, the initiate seeks to have a mind unsullied by fantasy-thoughts based upon competitions. He works to have a mind free of rivalry.

Self-denial as taught by Jesus, whose Soul watches over the soul-power of the initiate, is the basic keynote which must be adhered to with sincerity and with valor. The timid, the weak and the vacillating cannot receive the high calling of the Christ until they walk the eye-of-the-needle Path—that is, enter into the straight Way of Truth. The words in the Scripture, *"I can of mine own self do nothing . . . The Father that dwelleth in me he doeth the works,"* are the sign-posts which the initiate is given on the Path of Self-, Soul- and God-Realization.

Egotistical-shell bound metaphysicians of today, using the ego-charged thought patterns for self-improvement, are entering a new phase of Self-Realization. Initiatory trials for one schooled in the former metaphysical conceptualized patterns, themes and formulas are now outmoded by the Archetypal system supporting the hierarchy nature within the Higher Self.

Metaphysical formats inflating the ego are but mentalistic toys heavily loaded with the psychic charge of neglected ethic and practices. These are presently to be overhauled by the greater sensitivities of the mind now pouring into all student levels from the greater Archetypal system supporting the mind building and also accompanying the developing versatilities of the hierarchy nature. The enlargement of the ego as provided by former metaphysical systems must now enter into a total reversal of ego-inflation into humility-attitudes.

Arrangement of the Heart

In hierarchy-nature healing, one first arranges his heart by speaking the mantram: "God is the Perfect Love in me."

Visualize the closest person to you as being one with you in the Perfect Love of God.

Visualize your fellow disciples or those with you on the Path as being one with you in the Perfect Love of God.

Visualize your work earning environment as being one with you creatively within the Perfect Love of God.

Visualize all the peoples of the earth in the Perfect Love of God as being united, harmonious and happy.

Visualize the Perfect Love of God keeping Perfect Order with His caring Love for His Universe and for His Creation.

Return the current sent out. Reverse through visualization God's Perfect Love blessing with His Grace all of the Galaxies, all of the eternity systems.

Visualize God's Perfect Love for all peoples of this Earth and all other Earths.

Visualize God's Perfect Love blessing all nations.

Visualize God's Perfect Love maintaining the prospering for all who serve His Word.

Visualize harmony in God's Perfect Love for friends in the Name of Christ.

Visualize God's Perfect Love manifesting through all relatives, all blood ties.

Visualize God's Perfect Love through fellow disciples.

Visualize God's Perfect Love through one's own personal beloved.

Visualize with gratitude one's own faith in God as manifesting happiness, peace and joy.

BUTTERFLY OF THE INFINITE

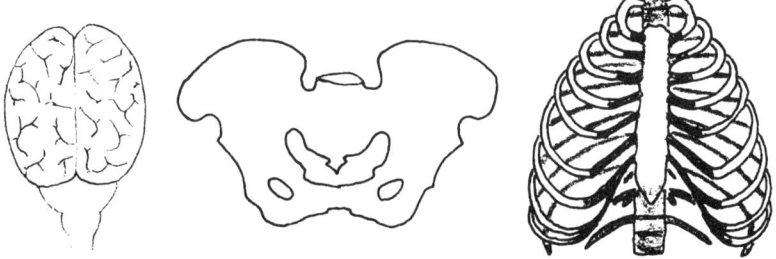

The physical anatomy correlates to the butterfly, which is the offspring of the eternal and the immortal structure. The architecture and archetype of the butterfly are repeated in the ankles, the hips, the rib cage, the wrists, and in the skull.

These are the Esse-currents centers where the great

chakras meet in the body. These are the permanent atom-points in the body which survive after death so that the energy-matrix format is not lost after death and in coming births.

Where these butterfly-points meet are the permanent atom polarity-points. When they are perfectly united and equalized, a symmetrical physical structure upholding the energy-processes of health is achieved. In the angelic kingdom these are called the angelic rosebuds through which the filtering of holy-kundalini nectar flows.

The butterfly pattern contains the retentive matrix energy-pattern living after death, holding together the structure of the incorruptible body. Before the physical body ever existed in the earth, this incorruptible matrix energy-body existed. It is the body one lives in before physical birth and after physical death.

To the seer in the physical world, this body, when seen, appears as a lightning flash of quickened vibration. When the seer extends his sight into the higher astral luminosities of the First Heaven, this body appears luminous, glorious in color, magnified in light. When the seer extends his sight into the transcendental, this incorruptible body appears as a radiance-body, having etheric vibration, astral luminosity, and spiritual white light radiating from all dimensions into all dimensions.

BUTTERFLY POSTURE EXERCISE

When one stands in butterfly posture with his heels together and his feet outward like butterfly wings, he opens the core-atom in the center of the heel. He is polarized with the core of the earth, the axis of the earth, and the star Polaris—and he is healed in the bone marrow. This mediation posture brings polarity and equanimity to all of the permanent atoms in the energy structure of the body.

Hold this posture for approximately fifteen seconds and feel life flowing upward into the seventy-two thousand nadis canals of the body.

Feel the energy flow upward from the core of the earth, between the axis point of the earth and Polaris star, which is in command of the molecular atoms in the bone marrow of man.

At the end of the posture, bring the wrist bones together, the hands, palms open, outward in the shape of a butterfly, and seal in the Polaris permanent-atom healing flow. Visualize your most peaceful desire as you exhale a long breath and say, "It is going to happen." Then relax your hands.

The Polaris energy takes possession of the cells in the brain, quickening the etheric brain so that the archetypal images of greater dimensions may remain active; superimposing the prototypal energies, thus giving man prototypal guidance within the Christ Mind.

This exercise may be done once a day or on special meditative days, such as, the Levitation Day, the tenth day after the New Moon.

THE GREAT MANTRA NAMING

God.   Christ.   Jesus.

Jesus is the Sat-Guru of the Human Race. All Masters are in alignment with this Guru of Gurus, Jesus. Jesus is the cross-over or cross-bow to the Christ Spirit who seeks to make real the Omnipresence of God.

The Mantra—"God. Christ. Jesus."—is a japa practice. Repeating these three Holy Names frees one to open the Buddhi or Informing Principle.

In the use of the japa practice, one should: First, breathe up, saying mentally, "God"—thinking of God as the One, the All. Second, while holding the breath, one should mentally say, "Christ"—feeling in the center of the skull the Light of the Christ. Third, one should exhale, saying "Jesus"—softly letting the flow of the Jesus Love permeate all parts of the heart center, and finally the body. (Use this Mantra practice not more than ten times at each sitting.)

The *Name-of-God Mantra* is appropriate for the Western Initiate because Western terminology is used. However, this does not exclude certain Sanskrit Mantra-sounds if they are fully comprehended and understood in the *feeling world* of the Western Initiate.

The OM, which is the sacred sound of the Word, is the mighty Mantra inviting God-Realization. Due to the submerged spirituality of many souls in the West, there are many Mantra-sounds which Western or Anglo-Saxon logos is yet to experience. It is the work of the Initiate to attract to himself his own Naming-of-God Mantra. His living Teacher assists in this, as it is a gift from the Teacher to his student to give the Holy-Name Sound of God, and thus free the archetypal hum in the soul of his disciple.

OM is the Name-Sound of God.

In the advanced instruction, one is under the tutelage of the living Teacher who is in the White-Line affinity to the Maha Guru residing behind the eyebrow center of the spiritual student. Awareness of this soul-affinity is an absolute necessity for soul illumination in the spiritual life.

The Maha Guru—the Great Immortal or Master—is present and in accord to each spiritually-awakened soul. He is a familiar presence *inwardly* known by the disciple. The living Teacher of the disciple is also known and recognized from "old times" or past lives. The Maha Guru's point of telepathic appearance back of the eyebrow center is sacred to the Initiate, as also his living Teacher is known and familiar to him. With a natural trust, he knows both the living Teacher and the Maha Guru. It is his grace on entering the Path to become aware of these divine companions of his soul-life. In some instances, he unites with them first in his dreams during sleep.

The living Teacher works to assist his disciple in the control and dissolving of his present-life karma. One is in a state of astral confusion until he acknowledges with gratitude the ones who come forth to show him the way and the why of the soul.

The soul is the mediative vehicle for the Spirit of God. The soul has neither organs nor organisms. Due to the interweaving action of the mind interconnected with the soul, the soul is the vehicle through which man knows of heaven. It is also a vehicle of perspective through which the action in the body and the action in the mind can be interpreted and transcended into spirituality.

The soul is the transcending vehicle pulling man up to God. In every human experience, man is soul-destined to eventually utilize every human experience in a spiritual way.

As self-creators, men use a mighty function given to them by God. This is the hierarchy-nature will. Men literally are creating themselves with this God-Omnipresence power. It is their heritage.

All of the Esse practices lead one toward the freeing of static brain levels which are content and seemingly complacent. To be caught into one of the brain-repetitions is to be obsessed by thinking one cannot change.

The total science of life is realization through trans-energization. These kinds of awareness produce healing and enlightenment.

The deathless part of man is his breath. Even though the breath seems to cease when physical death comes, breath continues in the soul's pulsation.

A mantram or mantra, when said while watching the flow of breath, produces actual forms in the physical world. The breath works as a coordinator with the involuntary systems of the nerves and the glands, and all of the so-called involuntary processes of life and existence. When speaking a mantra—such as, *God. Christ. Jesus*—the involuntary systems immediately vibrate the Bindu-seed of fire in the mantra.

One should watch his breath flowing on the exhaling-breath to see what the breath and mantra are doing and saying.

1. God. *(Bring breath up.)*
2. Christ. *(Hold breath.)*
3. Jesus. *(Breathe out; observe thoughts and images. Give thanks. It will happen.)*

From redemption comes the Passing as provided by the Passion of Jesus on the Cross. One should become aware of the Passing Power in his own hierarchy nature, and of the Passing Power he is receiving through grace from others. If the Passing Power makes its presence known through a Vajra, or a correction, one should bless it, and thereby receive the power to heal himself and others.

If the Passing Power is witnessed as revelation, one

should take care to use revelation with ethic. In each thing, he should make life sacred. He should share his joy of Knowing or Niscience with all—being ever a freeing channel.

In the flow, I Know the Esse.
In the jewel, in the tide, I abide
Eternal, free. Esse.

DIVINE MOTHER ROSARY

Divine Mother,
Take our prayers;
Place them in the Will of God,
That His Will may be done
In earth as in Heaven.
Om.

Almighty God,
Pour down upon us Thy Grace,
That we may see Thy Face
And know Thine Omnipresence
In all souls, all situations.
Om.

Our Father which art in Heaven,
Let us know Thy true Image in us,
That we may be like Thy Son Jesus,
And go in this world
To heal, to teach, to serve,
And Spread Thy Holy Word.
Om.

O Lord Jesus,
We sit at Thy feet,

> Taking the dust from Thy feet,
> Kissing the dust from Thy feet,
> That we may go in this world
> To heal, to teach, to serve,
> And spread Thy Holy Name.
> Om. Om. Om.
> Om. Om. Om.
> Om. Om. Om.
> Om. Om. Om.
> Amen.
> Om.

The Divine Mother Rosary should be spoken every day at Noon. At Noon, the Forgiving and Mercy aspect of God through Divine Mother may be made active in the personal, religious, family and spiritual life of the disciple.

The Noon time each day is the hour in which one turns to Divine Mother. Petitioning to become a mediator with a forgiving heart, one clears away his own karmas, that he may serve God within the Yin or Feminine Principle, which is at its most active at 12 Noon.

The OM's sounded before and after each mantra stanza build the steps to God in perfect mediative sequences. This necklace of mantras chanted, sung or spoken at Noon produces harmony, union, blessing. It is especially effective in making perfect union with God.

The twelve OM's at the end of the Divine Mother Rosary represent the twelve Disciples of Jesus. Each Disciple knew Jesus in a different way, as each of the twelve prototypes in the earth also know Jesus in a different way and must speak of Him as he sees Him.

When one uses the twelve OM's at the end of the Divine Mother Necklace, he is uniting himself with the eleven other disciples who go forth, even as he, to spread the Gospel or the Word. The twelve OM's represent the Prototypal Hierarchy potential repeated over and over in the earth through the twelve zodiacal signs.

The ending of the Rosary with the *Amen* spoken unites one with our Father. The final OM sound, which is the thirteenth OM, unites one with the Christ. By this, a perfected ladder or mantra station-points have ascended and descended into the needs of man.

ANCESTRAL ROSARY

Visualization Exercise: To be free from the burdens of one's own sins and the sins of his ancestors or "fathers."

Once a week, preferably 11:00 A.M. Saturday, repeat this exercise to cleanse the subconscious compulsions inherent within the automatic processes of gene-memory. This exercise is a confrontation with the genes on a cosmic level. It is automatic that once one steps out of gene-memory karmic tensions he makes union with the True Self, which is centered within the Great Atma or God.

This exercise is to free one of the burdens of guilt saturating gene-memory. One moves out of his own karma and gains the higher gene-selecting powers, that he may reincarnate, by choice, through parents of high evolvement.

1. In your thoughts, visualize a chart of your ancestral line, first placing the names of your father and mother. Then add the names of your grandfathers, grandmothers, great-grandfathers, great-grandmothers, and all other relatives that may come to your mind (sisters, brothers, aunts, uncles).
2. Speak these words to each ancestor separately:
    I ask forgiveness of you and I forgive you.
    I pray for your prospering wherever you are.
    I pray for an easy birth and an easy death for you in all worlds.

THE GENE FORGIVENESS DIAMOND-TREE

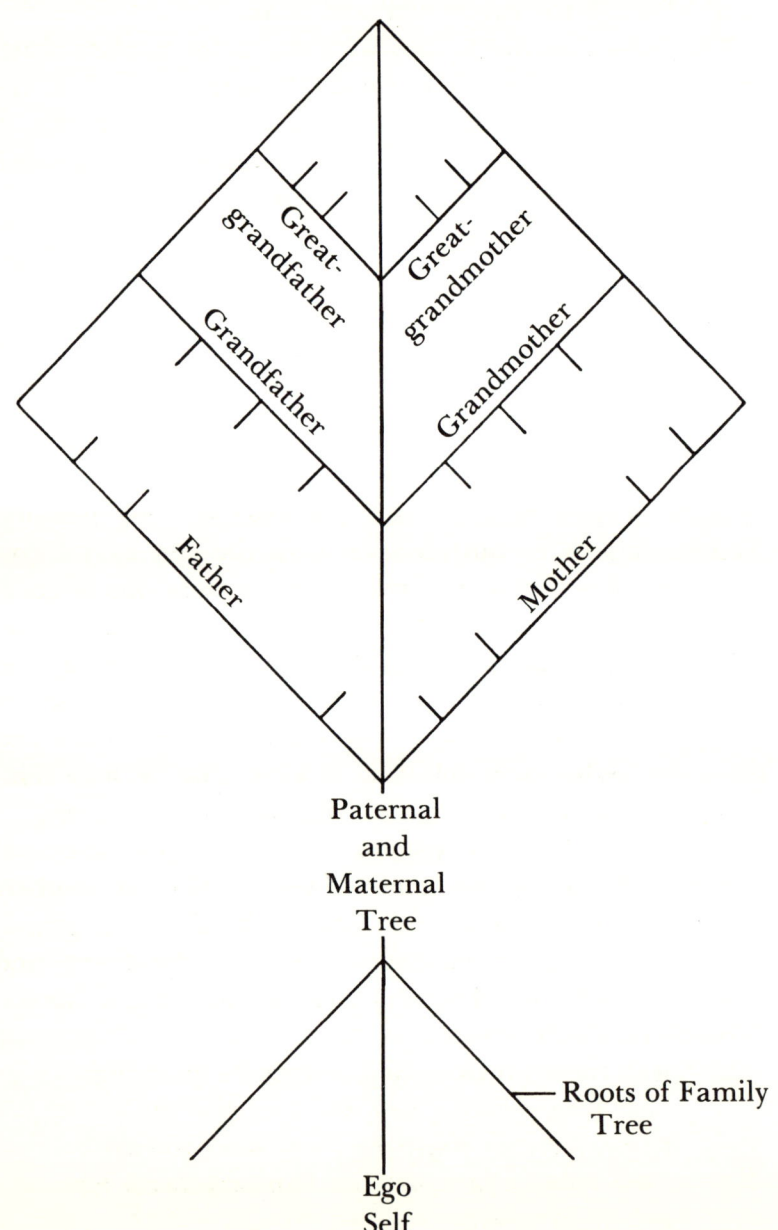

The Voltage of God protects His Plan for man and for every existing, living thing in this world and in all worlds.

In the present time, the commercializing aspect of scientific knowledge surfacing in the scientific discoveries of man regarding gene-inheritance will go "so far and no farther."

Knowledge of the gene structure of man and its tremendous inheritance controlling the karmic life-flow of mankind is in possession of the Angels and of God. Who dares to step through this line of Voltage and to redirect the course of the gene-memory flows directing man's growth in the physical world and in the spiritual will step into a vacuum of unknowing which will refute any further progress into the altering of the God-directing human state existing in gene-functioning, nurturing and progression.

Factual science supported by agnostic minds is routed upon a dead-end course. The commercialization of gene-knowledge into a dollar-obtaining structure will defeat itself.

Gene-memory is man's inheritance through which he grows to mind and soul stature within the Increase of God. Gene-memory contains both virtue and darkness. He who seeks to transenergize gene-energy memory can do so only through spirituality.

It is the Law of God that the sins of the fathers are erased by the progeny of the fathers. The sins of the fathers are overcome through spiritual transenergization processes. In every Family-Atom, souls incarnated together are united to increase their virtue and to master the negatives or the sins of their fathers.

In every third generation in a Family-Atom, there comes to birth one soul who has the power to transenergize the sins of the fathers. This person—through sacrifice, love, forgiveness, within the innate purity of his own heart—comes to birth as a saint in disguise. He works with the Saints, the Angels and God to release his bloodline from the sins, the errors and the lust in the family line. Being pure of heart, he stands as a point of Intentional Suffering who literally takes on the burdens of sin, and thus grace is enacted in a family, that all souls who are attracted through the karmas of their evils may be transformed into grace.

The Ancestral Rosary is to free the gene-negativity and to produce the quickening of the virtues within the Family-Atom. This Mantram produces miracles within the Increase of God. Families blessed with the use of this Mantram respond with unusual changes and quickenings in love for one another. The virtue-grace in the using of the Ancestral Rosary blesses the one who speaks it, aiding him to overcome self-hatred, separateness, competitiveness, jealousy.

Speaking this Mantram once a week will give, within a short period of time, a perspective as to placement in family. All blood relationships will be seen in a pure emotional dimension. Long-held sibling hatreds and hostilities will be healed. Parents and children will come closer together.

13

HEALING THROUGH THE CONSTANT

Radiance is a giving-maintenance of the Constant. Radiation from radiance is the state of Dharma in the act of Passing. One radiates energy or light from the Constant's use of supernatural energy in the soul. A radiating energy is the healing presence of the Constant.

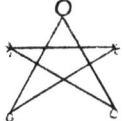 The Imaged, Perfect Matrix in the Constant. The Hierarchy Nature.

 Lotus Asana Man. Higher-Etheric Matrix. Soul.

 Embryo Man. Psychic-Matter Matrix. Ego and Undersoul.

Each person in his Constant is in contact with the energy of his direct star. The direct-star energy in the Constant correlates to the fixed star in one of the constellation bodies from whence he came to this earth system.

The five-pointed star is the symbol for the Grand Man in the Constant. This relates to his direct-star nature which he brought to this eternity system.

The Image of the Grand Man is in the Constant. The Grand Man is the Cosmos Man.

The Asana Man is in the core of the higher-etheric-body matrix.

The Embryo Man is in the core of the lesser-etheric-body matrix.

The Psychic-Matter Matrix is the matrix that holds together the Undersoul.

Hierarchy-Nature Healing through the Grace Name and Sacred Name

Behold, I give unto you power to tread on serpents and scorpions, and over all the power of the enemy: and nothing shall by any means hurt you. Notwithstanding in this rejoice not, that the spirits are subject unto you; but rather rejoice, because your names are written in heaven.

—St. Luke 10:19,20

A *Sacred Name* is the tone-name one was given upon entering this eternity system and by which he is known and called in the Heaven or Higher Worlds. In each eternity system, one has a different Sacred Name. In rare instances, a Sacred Name may be revealed to the disciple by the Teacher. Jesus gave to Peter his Sacred Name and He gave to Paul his Sacred Name.

When a Teacher is spiritually authorized to disclose Sacred Names and Grace Names to certain disciples, this is called the *Power of Sacred Nomenclature*. When one uses his Sacred Name in the earth, he aligns himself with the Sacred Beings of the Higher Worlds; he also has earned the power to travel in the night, and to freely go in and out of the sacred precincts of Heaven.

A *Grace Name* is a name one has used in a former life when he accomplished great works of grace; this name enables him to revive the grace-power of his soul's medallion. A Grace Name has a combining of vowel tones that makes him more penetrable to his Guardian Angel and Recording Angel so that he might function in an unceasing stream of grace. Parents may have the grace to give their children Grace Names at birth; however, it is more often the case that a disciple gains his Grace Name and Sacred Name due to his alignment with the Higher Worlds and also with his own spiritual works of former lives. A worthy person, or one close to sainthood, may be born with a Grace Name and, during some illumination or initiation, he may become aware of his Sacred Name. In such an initiation, one is united with the diamond medallion of the Higher Self.

In special catalyst alignment with one's spiritual Teacher, one may receive his Grace Name through the Teacher. The Grace Name is never received out of timing. The soul knows when one is ready to use the sacred vowels within the Grace Name and the sentient fire associated with the consonants in the Grace Name. In a Grace Name, the vowels are spiritual conduits; the consonants are stigmata points through which one sometimes undergoes persecution from worldly persons.

If one is wrongly named by his parents, he may undergo maladjustment, conflicts. The custom of a child bearing the first and last names of his father may invoke a double portion of karma upon the child. However, if the parent is highly evolved and the child is highly evolved, the child will inherit a blessing or a mantle of protection through the use of his father's name. If a child of grace is named after the name of a Saint, this is holy grace.

The Sacred Name correlates to the Higher Self and to worthy works. The Grace Name correlates to the soul and good works. The ego-karmic name correlates to the debts made by the ego or individual from life to life. The ancestral-karmic name correlates to the dweller aspect of the Family-Atom. The ancestral-karmic sire name is the name one inherits from his parents. The vibrational tone of the ancestral karma is bound up in the name one is given at birth.

When there is heavy dweller action in the Family-Atom, ancestral karma is predominant in the name given to one by his parents. The ego-karmic name is one which enables the individual or ego to work out his karma or the debts of past lives. When there is a sacred Family-Atom, a person receives his Sacred Name, as in the case of Jesus.

> *But while he thought on these things, behold, the angel of the Lord appeared unto him in a dream, saying, Joseph, thou son of David, fear not to take unto thee Mary thy wife: for that which is conceived in her is of the Holy Ghost. And she shall bring forth a son, and thou shalt call his name Jesus.*
> —St. Matthew 1:19,20

Jesus, while in earth, was in the Absolute Constant. He now lives in the Absolute Constant which functions in the Archetypal, Higher Unconscious Realms.

The *Name* of Jesus is a co-atom polarizing Name for the Higher Self. When one becomes co-atom to Jesus, he enters into the Jesus *Name* cyclic timing.

When one uses the mantra: "Jesus. Jesus. Jesus.", he becomes aware that his prayers, his materialistic petitions and demands in the Name of Jesus do not always coordinate in every instance with the Jesus cyclic blessings and healings—for one's material-petitioned demands very often are unlawful or are unsuitable for one's true need and call of the soul.

Every name has its vibrational cyclic law. When one receives his Grace Name and sometimes his Sacred Name, he enters into higher frequencies and vibrational cycles. This will produce different life-styles, different self-estimation and self-desires.

The Sacred Name does not come out of a race history or a nation history or a blood history. A Sacred Name comes directly from the God-sent Sound retained from one's own direct star or former eternity system from whence he comes. The Sacred Name dwells in the Constant, retaining its direct-star supremacy as a sojourner for God.

When Moses struck the rock, water came. When one uses his Sacred Name through the hierarchy nature, the Will of God is manifested. Sacred Name contains holy electricities superior to name-calling on psychic-matter levels. The Constant vibrating the Sacred Name activates hierarchy-nature power within the Will of God.

The ego resounds: "Me. Me. Me." The soul resounds: "I am. I am. I am."

The Sacred Name sounds what its bearer is. If one is Truth as a Constant, it is sounding: "Truth. Truth. Truth." Or if one is in the Constant resurrection and exorcism, it is sounding: "Resurrect. Resurrect. Resurrect." The name the Constant resounds—and the virtue it represents—is one's own mantra.

There are two stages in the life of an initiate in which he is chosen and called by name. The first is through the Grace Name; and the most-high state of being chosen is when he is called by his Sacred Name.

The Sacred Name contains and expresses one's Constant. It is rare to receive one's Sacred Name. Adepts of the past, having used spiritual powers with integrity, ethic and honor receive their Sacred Names from one who has Sacred-Name recognition and power.

The Grace Name stems from the Sacred-Name Tone in the Constant; it sounds within the soul's pulsation point. Soul-power works directly through the Grace Name, using the grace-actions of former lives through which one divulges the spiritual knowledge to the world. Grace Name enables one to identify the nomenclature functioning in all name-calling in the world.

The power of Naming is given by grace directly from our Father which art in heaven. The Adam humanity was given the power of Naming in the beginning of this eternity system. In the original Hebrew, the name Adam means *mankind;* it also means *red,* as having blood.

> *Whatsoever Adam called every living creature, that was the name thereof. And Adam gave names to all cattle, and to the fowl of the air, and to every beast of the field.*
> *—Genesis 2:19,20*

The Sacred Name is the primordial identity name. This name dwells in the Great Unconscious of the Archetypal and Archetonal vibrations encased in the Constant.

The Great Archetypes and Archetones in the upper reaches of the Third Heaven have a level of sound which contains the Name-of-God Mantra. The Name-of-God Mantra as the Constant over all life is an Archetypal vibrational tone sounding into the Constant of all consciousness beings in the earth. To receive a Grace Name is to connect oneself with his Constant and His own Sacred-Name sound in the Great Unconscious or the Third Heaven.

To use a Grace Name or a Sacred Name, and to have others use it, is the same as the use of a mantra.

A Grace Name is a divine blessing to one who receives it,

enabling him to use his accumulated grace from past good works in former lives. The moment one receives his Grace Name, the vowels in the name determine how the consonants are sounded in physical works.

The consonants in a name are the wheelbarrows. The vowels in a name are the treasures in the wheelbarrows. Through the vowels, one masters his karma and expresses his grace. The vowels are the destiny; the consonants are the fate.

A Grace Name attracts to one Grace. A Sacred Name attracts to one Powers and Gifts. One who acts within the vibration of his Sacred Name is fully immersed in his Constant. In this vibration, God's Guidance and Healing are infallible.

All Grace Names are Soul Names. All Sacred Names are the Names resounding in the Constant. All names given at birth are karmic names, with the exception of an advanced-soul birth recognition between parents and child where a Grace Name is given. Grace in the family name is passed on to the Grace Name; one preserves his grace.

When one rejects his sire name and his name called karmically at birth, he often attracts to him a *nickname*. If he should use this until the day he dies, he has failed to move toward the receiving of his Grace Name.

Many in the world hate their names. And many who love their names through the side of their ego-pride, are fixed into Undersoul levels of karma.

Those who make their names infamous through atrocious crimes and exploitation sound a subhuman tone-sound for the satanic. The name of Judas is an infamous name which has become entitized through the world's despisal.

Children hating their names do so because they are intuitively impressionable to an inharmonious sound which they seek to throw off and reject. Thus, in playing with so-called invisible playmates, they name and call their companions by names they are at home with in their own tone-natures.

An animal in the Family-Atom environment named by the family portrays a tone-sound existing in the Family Atom.

In the beginning, when God gave man the power of Naming, man gave titles first to the species, as a dog is a dog or a bird is a bird, etc. As man progressed through Tribal-Genesis into Family-Genesis, he began to name the creatures he took into his domicile by heroic names. In the Self-Genesis time of the present, man names his dog, as a rule, by a certain insight into his own karmas. He may name his animal with a ridiculous name, something suitable to the decreasing of his own ego-pride.

The Grace Name is especially affected through the lunar flow of cycles. To name a house having a lunar-tone emphasis is to commune with certain laws governing family assemblies and gatherings which are expressed as festivals and gala occasions.

Where a Sacred-Name person is present in a Family-Atom, this attracts resistance by karmic-named members of the family.

The Yantra Initiation

The Lord's voice crieth into the city, and the man of wisdom shall see thy name: hear ye the rod, and who hath appointed it.

—Micah 6:9

When one receives his Grace Name, he is initiated first in smaller degrees and, later, in greater degrees into the

Yantra system of the Archetypal Logos. This is called the *Yantra Initiation,* which provides the evangelistical Esse or Holy Spirit Gift of articulating what is experienced in the five higher transcendental stations.

In receiving a Grace Name, through soul-pulsation acceleration one begins to receive the holy staminas or steadfastness in faith. The grace flow through the soul's pulsation sweeps aside the veils in karmic encasements or ignorance or blindness as to God. All five transcendental stations are in some degree opened at once. When the Holy Hum in the soul's pulsation sounds through the Grace Name, one is once more united with his Eternal God-Spirit nature.

To receive a Grace Name and accept it in a trivial manner, discarding what it entails, is to suffer blindly the corrective modus operandi working upon the Undersoul.

It is important, on receiving a Grace Name, that one detach it from any form of ego-specialization. If he has the grace to understand and to know what is meant by receiving a Grace Name, the buds of reverence in his heart will soften the harsh side of his intellect. With the receiving of a Grace Name, the beginning of a spiritualized intellect is manifested.

In the Yantra state, one must unite with the human race through the heroic side of names; the Saints' side of names; the inheritance of myths as allegorical names; and within his dream states must learn the code-names received in dreams which seek to lead him to his Sacred Name dwelling in the Constant.

WOMB NAME

At the moment of conception, the name-tone of one to be born is resounded into the world. The child-to-be in the womb knows its grace-connections and its own tone-sound or name sounding in the soul's pulsation point. If there is grace for the parents, they will be led by Omnipresence to a person who will Pass to them a *Womb Name* for their child-to-be.

It has been proved by science that the sense of hearing through vibration is active in the embryo or babe-to-be.

In the first three months, the bio-energies of the ancestors sound the combined ancestral tone into the forming embryo. In the first stages of the embryo, the child-to-be is more directly connected with the tone-sound of the ancestry. This vibration assures that the gene-inheritance will repeat itself through the babe.

The first direct contact with the soul comes when the babe moves in the womb. This leap or movement thereafter opens the interior consciousness of the forming babe to soul-memory power. During the remainder of its stay in the womb, the forming babe will have access to both the ancestral tone and the soul-tone.

If there is grace and faith in God within the parents who have conceived the babe-to-be, they are led to the one who can bless the quickening of the babe in the very beginning of pregnancy. A person having Sacred-Nomenclature powers, giving to the parents a Womb Name, is a blessing sent of God.

In the present time, there are certain areas of psychology which seek to hypnotically induce recall of womb experience. This is a bewildering experience to those who do not understand the laws of reincarnation.

Parents who understand the laws of karma and reincarnation, and are willing to accept what is behind the wall of unknowing as to previous-life existences, move through the birth-experience with normalcy and balance.

In this latter part of the Kali-Yuga darkened time, those who reject their children—whether by abortion or by birth itself—are self-destruct in their own life-force and destruct in the life-chain of gene regeneration. Every woman who willingly or ignorantly aborts a child has rejected a soul-presence in her life. At some time, the woman who aborts her babe is compelled through karmic law to give birth to the same soul she would have borne. This may not occur until a coming life when restitution is more equitable.

If husband and wife look upon birth as sacred, they intuitively recognize and know their child from the very beginning of conception. To call their child by a Womb Name is to assure the interior listening of the child in the womb that he is welcomed and loved and wanted. The practice of the Womb Name through love assures the child that he is loved and desired.

Womb Cradle Song

Instruction: Expectant parents may speak or sing together the following mantram for the babe-to-be whenever they desire. If they sing, their singing should be in free logos expression. It should have cradle-like tones, a hammock-like nuance, with laughter and tenderness intertwined.

Little babe, child and man to be, you are loved; little babe, in your cradle womb, growing in our love for you. Our love warms, feeds and comforts you, little babe in the womb of love.

Note: the word "man" in the above mantram pertains to mankind.

Womb Mantram Visualization

Speak the Womb Name in using the following mantrams. Speak the Mantram for the Month at any time of the day or night when one feels a longing to make union with one's child in the womb. The mantram also can be used with meditation, thus sharing with your child as a soul-presence in your meditation.

The following mantrams may be spoken by expectant fathers and mothers.

1st Month

Soul of my child, I am with you. With my love I open my heart to your coming. Be at home with me. Accept my love. We will grow anew and renew our growing.

2nd Month

You are growing, child of my seed and of my soul. I rejoice in the miracle of your first breath. We will share life in the grace of reunion, as we walk the way of this life, this earth.

3rd Month

In the quiet place, the part of me that is in your growing gives to you, my child, welcome; you are loved. As you grow, I grow.

4th Month

All of my strength of soul I give to you, child of my seed. All of my grace I share with you. Be not afraid, O soul child to be. I am waiting to see your eyes remembering me.

5th Month

> Child of my seed and of my soul, the grace of my soul is watching with you. This journey you now take toward me is a journey of coming timed to my love. Welcome; blessings for us all who await your first cry.

6th Month

> Child of my seed and of my soul, in the days of old when we have walked, our love has remembered. Our love has sounded. I make a heart-home for your coming. I make a braceway. The good walk of the past shall give joy to our service for God. Hala!

7th Month

> Because you are near to your first cry, your first breath, I remind you that you are loved with a special love.

8th Month

> Inside of your heart, my child, is the shared flame of our hearts. As *three* we flow and grow with love toward the birth to come. As you were sure you wanted us, we are true to you and sure in our combine of love.

9th Month

> I will see your face and know that you are mine as a gift to love, to know, once more in the play and ploy of the joy. Behold, child of mine, the light of our love.

The Five Stations of the Constant of God in Man

- The Higher and True Self
- The Constant duplicating the Constant of God.
- Buddhi in the Indestructible Atom.
- The Soul's Pulsation.
- The Mouth of God in the Medulla Oblongata.

To reach the Constant to heal through the hierarchy nature, one begins with meditation in the heart. He moves beyond the intellect, beyond analysis, beyond ego-interpretation.

In hierarchy healing, one begins at the heart chakra where he unites with the Love of God.

One lifts the love he has experienced through the Love of God, to the Christ-Consciousness Center between eyebrows, which is *Light*.

The soul's pulsation accelerates the Light.

Next, he automatically opens the Mouth-of-God Center.

Following this, the Buddhi Center in the middle of the forehead opens.

He next becomes aware of his own Constant, where he is in perfect eternal equilibrium with the Constant of God.

He then unites with the Higher Self. The Higher Self contains the Eternal Sustaining Atom, which assures him of Eternal Life.

Balanced meditation assures that one will be flexible, relaxed and receptive within the five transcendental stations or chakras beyond the seven chakras controlling the natural life of existence in earth.

To use a mantra in meditation opens one to the Great-Mantra Name-of-God residing in one's own Constant. The refinements and sensitivities gained through touching one's own Constant give him the freeing through his own hierarchy-nature healing powers.

NAME-CALLING HEALING

And when he thus had spoken, he cried with a loud voice, Lazarus, come forth.
—St. John 11:43

All the good works one has done are recorded in the Great Unconscious. When these have reached a certain state, one inherits this virtue as a Grace Name. The Grace Name sounds as an Archetonal sound of the virtue.

A Grace Name is given or Passed by one having the Gift of Holy Nomenclature. One receives and hears his Grace Name as a blessing through which he is called to serve God.

In the Coinciding-Principle nature of man, the name is a vibrant communicating asset in the spiritual and physical life.

In visitation powers, the name vibration of the one traveling in his invisible body as a healer of sickness and conditions gives testimony that the healer is there, present.

In the hierarchy-nature healing powers through the calling of the Grace Name or Sacred Name, there is a holy healing technique in the use of the Constant.

Jesus, on raising Lazarus from the dead—using the

Constant of Lazarus—called his name, saying: "Lazarus, arise." On healing Jairus' daughter, Jesus called her name: "Tabitha, awake." So does the hierarchy-nature healer use the Grace Name or Sacred Name in calling up health of life for the one sick or suffering.

I. The most effective healing through the hierarchy-nature power within the Constant is to call the one to be healed by his Grace Name or Sacred Name:

> While sounding the name of the one to be healed, take all of the heart's love in its essence and Esse nature as visualized through the will. Lift it to the light between the eyebrows and to the middle of the forehead, being aware of the Constant, which is centered over the Divine Thalamus situated directly above the medulla oblongata.
>
> Move the visualization to the lens center of the Indestructible Atom in the center of the forehead.
>
> Call the Sacred Name or Grace Name of the person to be healed and say:
>
> > _____ (Sacred or Grace Name), beloved, you are imaged of God.
> >
> > _____ (Name) is never sick.
> >
> > _____ (Name) is a perfected creation willed of God to be peaceful, happy, pure, beautiful, successful.
> >
> > _____ (Name) cannot fail.
> >
> > _____ (Name) cannot be sick.
> >
> > _____ (Name) is well.

If the Grace Name is not known to the one visualizing, he should say: "Your name is written in heaven. I speak to your Grace Name."

II. The hierarchy healer, in calling the Sacred or Grace Name of the person to be healed, should visualize the perfection, the innocence, the health, the well-being of the person. He should see through hierarchy-nature visualization the one whom he would heal at the same time he calls out the name. With a holy firmness, knowing the healing will happen, he should visualize the calling of the name and say:

_____ (Sacred or Grace Name), the Perfection of God in you is not sick.

The Perfection of God in _____ (Name) is health, is innocence, is purity, is peace, is love, is joy.

_____ (Name), healing is perfection in you.

III. Hierarchy healing may be done for oneself; he may call his own Sacred Name or Grace Name. He begins by arranging his heart. He then takes his thought power through the will upward to contact the different hierarchy-nature stations. These are:

1. The Heart.
2. Between the eyebrows.
3. The Soul's Pulsation in the crown of the head.
4. The Higher Self.
5. The Constant.
6. The Calling of the Grace Name.
7. The Indestructible Atom Lens.

Next, he speaks the following words, using his own Sacred Name or Grace Name:

TiSeila* is not sick.
TiSeila cannot be sick.
TiSeila is perfected in the sight of God.

*The author's Sacred Name.

The health matrix within the Constant of *TiSeila* is a whole, glowing, warm, vital and beautiful, perfected body.

The perfected *TiSeila* matrix knows not sickness, pain or suffering.

TiSeila is well, harmonious, pure and true.

HEALING FOR THE ETHERIC, PHYSICAL, EMOTIONAL AND MENTAL BODY

The matrix for the physical body is in the lower etheric body.

The matrix for the self which responds to the calling of the Grace Name is in the higher etheric body.

Psychic-matter nature works in the matrix within the lower etheric body. The psychic-matter matrix is obedient to the perfected matrix in the higher etheric body.

When the psychic-matter matrix is disconnected from the commands of health sent forth from the higher matrix in the higher etheric body, all of the energies of the lesser matrix in the etheric body directing the health in the physical body are disorganized. These energies become antagonistic to each other. The result is sickness, discomfort, accidents, disease—chronic and acute.

Through visualization in the hierarchy-nature healing and the calling of the Grace Name, one brings these energies into order within the Will of God. A perfect healing is manifested.

The Sacred Name and the Grace Name are both in the Constant. When one calls the Grace Name through the hierarchy-nature healing visualization processes, he firms up and activates the perfected matrix in the higher etheric body. The higher-etheric-body matrix takes control of the psychic-matter matrix in the lower etheric body. A perfect healing is manifested through hierarchy-nature power in the Will of God.

To call the Grace Name or Sacred Name is to produce in the psychic-matter matrix an obedient response as to the cause and the solution. The lower psychic-matter nature operating in the Undersoul, using the subconscious receptivity, projects into the outer consciousness the healing as perfection, peace, happiness, purity, success, etc.

It is important that one having the grace within the vibrational laws of tone learn to transenergize totally the lower vibrations being experienced in ill health.

The Sacred Names of all souls are sounded at midnight every night. This is the holy roll-call sent forth by the Constant of God, making each person responsible for his earth experience, identifying him with his true nature as a son of God.

Every Saturday at 11:00 A.M. all who are to die, and all who have recently died, respond to the sounding of their name-call in heaven. All who are ready to die subconsciously respond to the coming experience of dying. At this time, they receive what is known as *apprehension grace* which alerts them to the coming experience of death. This may be experienced in dreams, or it may be experienced in a subconscious preparation in their physical affairs for the impending time of death. As an expectant mother apprehends the birth time of her child by a supercleansing of her house, as a bird prepares its nest for its coming young, so do soul-alerts flow into the mind of the one to die.

The true Teacher-and-chela experience begins even before each enters the world through birth. From the beginning of the Teacher's awareness of his calling as a Teacher, he is resounding in his own hierarchy nature the names of those who are to extend his work and purpose of coming. Thus, the chela or disciple knows his Teacher and trusts him. He *knows* his Teacher is God-sent, for he has longed to hear his name spoken on the lips 'of his Teacher from life to life.

To find this holy Teacher is to be in a state of Grace and to be anointed by the name-calling in a Grace Name or in a Sacred Name. Conjoined names between Teacher and chela, filled with the vibrancies of spirituality, lift the world and change life as existence in the earth.

Hallowed be Thy Name.
—St. Matthew 6:9

TENTH-DAY-AFTER-THE-NEW-MOON FAST

The Tenth Day is the Creditable Day.

On the tenth day of the increasing Moon, there is a unique function of gravity, which gives to man certain levitational powers of the etheric body, and especially of the emotions and mind. This raising power on the tenth day of the increase of the Moon enables one to rise beyond obstacles in the emotions, and move beyond his fears and timidities. It is also a day in which revelation in certain portions of the mind endows one with interdimensional aspects in thinking and in thought. This is more likely to begin to be present after the third month's fast.

Union must be made between motion and movement. Motion is that which is set up by and through the rotation of the planets. Movement is that which responds to the Sun. The solar energies produce synchronization and mastery over the Coinciding Principle.

The Tenth-Day-After-the-New-Moon Fast initiates one into levitation powers, where the etheric, out-of-the-body experience or mind-extending visitation travel becomes a reality.

The Tenth-Day-After-the-New-Moon Fast is called *Levitation Day*. It is the day when motion and movement become one within the solar plexus and the medulla oblongata. It can also be called a Day of Resurrection, for the consciousness rises to an overlook in dimension.

The tenth day after each New Moon is a vital day of union with the Initiatory Presences. On this day one should be aware and alert as to telepathies; he should make his meditation a time of lucid and receptive telepathies. In waking and in sleep, one may experience a very special downpouring of Intelligence and Guidance. The tenth day after the New Moon is a Day of Holy Affirming.

The tenth day after the New Moon is a *Lazarus Cycle,* the calling forth from the tomb to new life.

In fasting one has access to energies which formerly were spent in appetite, in eating, and in digesting, assimilating and excreting. The energy obtained in a fast, when used with conscious awareness of what the fasting is for and what it does, enlarges the propensities of the emotions and mind.

Fasting is essentially renunciation and is used in greater initiations not so much for denial of the body but for mastery over the habit patterns which seek to be sovereign of the body. Fasting develops its own habit rhythms. In certain initiatory cycles, fasting stirs up the body's instinctual craving nature, such as, desire for sex, food or drugs used in the past. The habit system of the body, when fasting is irreverent or solely for health progression, can produce a jaded reaction in the subconscious mind, thus giving little revitalization for the body and little expansion for the soul.

The physical body and the emotional body are designed to desire always more. This is an especial function of the greed related to the third chakra. In the tenth day after the increase of the Moon fast, one rearranges the desire patterns.

The first Tenth-Day Fast very often creates in one inward irritations. These etheric irritants set up a war against the imposition of fasting. Pleasure habit-patterns within one's nature are severely tested.

In the tenth day after the New Moon, one enters into the spontaneity realm, which is not habit-binding. One opens the Coinciding Principle and moves out of the labyrinths of emotional bondage to the senses.

All fasts suggested in the initiatory practices are necessary to keep one in alignment with the interflow between the inner and the outer nature. One should never extend his fast beyond the suggested time of one day without consulting a physician.

The initiate must be made aware that he is constantly seeking a third activity within his own nature. By any form of extremism, he will injure rather than reap the good. His hierarchy nature cannot live in the world of extremism or appearances unless he makes room for the inner nature.

All other fasting rhythms which have preceded the fast of the tenth day after the New Moon are so much gold or diamonds to be called forth in this levitation time of fasting. At the time of the tenth day after the New Moon, a certain state of gravity functions to loosen the boulders of the earth; this also affects the initiate as to negative fixities in his desire nature. Each negative fixity is as a great boulder that receives a signal to be loosened and to roll away.

On this tenth-day fast, the fixed patterns in all other

states of fasting also release their good, and one literally frees the Path, whereby the Path and the Power of God in him become one.

One should look upon the tenth day after the New Moon fasting as the coming forth from a limbo of unknowing regarding his nature, for it is the law that one cannot utilize his hierarchy nature until he knows his own nature.

To fast on the tenth day after the New Moon is to work with Time and Space; to experience this brings an awareness of enlargement and freedom. The Divine Omnipresence on this day says to the initiate: *"Behold, I am the Omnipresence. I am come forth, that ye may live in abundance, and break free from enclosures of habits. I am Free Spirit. When thou art free, I am the Living God in thee."*

Man in his primal and lesser-genesis nature is locked into mental and emotional fixities. It is the Moon that says to the babe in the cradle: "Forget now what has been. Live for your race, for your ego. Forget that you have lived many lives." On the tenth day, this is laid open to him who would make himself aware of past lives, of spiritual powers. From the time of the tenth day after the New Moon, gravity-freedom is experienced into the Full Moon. The Full Moon experience is a Yin and Yang experience, acting as a will-power point of achievement for the one who regularly practices the fasting on the tenth day after the New Moon. Thus, he who observes this tenth day fasting has an experience in the following Full Moon that others not so observant do not experience.

The tenth day after the New Moon is the crossing point between Yin and Yang. Yang, as will, becomes predominant in the spiraling Sushumna electrical fire within the spine of the initiate; he becomes a power Aaron's rod with full budding for God.

The two hemispheres of the brain are united in the tenth

day after the New Moon. The bud, the flower of the greater lotuses or the upper chakras seek to levitate into full bloom. One walks physically lighter with less gravity pulling the body down to old age, chronic sickness and impossible situations in karma. He can be said to be Mercury-heeled or fleet of foot in all he seeks to do in the physical world.

There is a very special *Sun* work on the tenth day after the New Moon, which enables the mental planets—Mercury and Saturn—to come closer to the initiate. These planets are the two mental planets affecting man's solar nature and his mind-building propensities. Mercury and Saturn are especially free as energy powerhouses in the mind of man on this day of fasting.

Mercury and Saturn in one's chart indicate what sort of levitation work will be done on these days, and also will reveal to the initiate where his own astronomical home is in his chart. One's astronomical home in his chart is where his sextiles are indicated. If these sextiles are harmoniously arranged with Saturn and Mercury, he will have unusual initiatory powers of exploring during sleep on this fasting day. Saturn releases Teacher-revealing powers to free those who feel snuffed-out mentally.

THE FAST OF THE CREEDLESS WORD
Tenth Day after the New Moon

The Anointing oil should be placed in the center of the forehead. The Anointing is *three times* (not seven as for other days of fasting). Each Anointing of the forehead should be the sign of the Cross.

This Fast readjusts the minerals in the body, and brings a freedom of forces in the etheric body that takes one beyond the negative habit-patterns, especially of the mind and body influences affecting health. The observance is like a hand pushing one over a hill so that he can gain a third strength, a third vitality, to make him equal to the task. It is an equal-to-the-task covenant.

The following mantrams, spoken while placing the oil in the middle of the forehead, can be said aloud; one mantram for each fast.

Speak: The Spirit of God in this oil
is anointing and healing
my holy aperture where dwells
the Creedless Word.
May I be free
in and out of the body,
that the Soundless Sound,
the Great Archetone,
will speak into my ear,
my mind, my eye.
My words and actions
shall be interflowing
with all creedless religions;
healing the improbables;
overcoming the anxieties;
reading the Scrolls of the Holy Word.
I will speak their testimonies
through the Soundless Sound
made flesh.
Amen. Amen. Amen.

*

Speak while pouring the oil:

There is no barrier in consciousness save my consciousness makes it so. I pray for this day of levitation-powers of the mind, of the soul, to heal the improbables and the impossibles.

This mantram should be spoken aloud as one touches the center of his forehead, making the † cross three times.

> I accept this anointing in the Name of Christ Jesus
> who resurrected Himself on the third day
> and who ascended into the spiritual worlds,
> where in heaven He has prepared a place for me.
> I pray on this day of fasting
> that I shall receive the levitation-powers
> over evil thoughts and emotions,
> over evil actions and obstacles.
> I pray that I shall know a free mind flow
> in the Great Unconscious or Purusha,
> whereby my consciousness shall be
> a whole and perfect instrument
> as a healing vessel for God.
> Amen.

*

Pouring of oil: Speak aloud with resonance and reverence:

> I pour this oil for the tenth day,
> that I may make wider my consciousness in the Realm of Light.
> May my service to God be offered up in thought,
> in emotions, in body and in energies.
> May the Increase of God lead me to Enlightenment.
> Amen.

Anoint the forehead three times with the forefinger of the right hand, making the vertical and horizontal lines of a Cross.

> I take this Holy Cross of Enlightenment
> and join the true crusade

of the Immortals.
Immortal wisdom
shall bless
my coming and going.
Amen.

*

Speak the following words while pouring the oil:

Blessed God, Thine Omnipresence in all, I pour this oil as a vehicle for dedication. I accept this oil on this tenth day of the New Moon, receiving it in the spirit of atonement, renunciation. I receive it in the spirit of praise, thankfulness and gratitude. I receive it that all negative articles and particles may be removed, all heavy ponderances may be removed, standing between me and Thy ministry in the Light.

Anoint the center of the forehead with oil, with the forefinger of the right hand. Anoint three times, each time making the vertical and horizontal lines of the Cross †.

O Lord, make me Thine apostle. Through Thy Holy Word, remove the stone from the tomb, that the Lord Jesus may come forth and fulfill His mission in the hearts of all. Amen.

*

Pour oil and speak:

On this tenth day after the New Moon, I pour this oil as a holy vehicle for anointing.

Anoint forehead and speak:

I pray to the Father to lift all obstacles,

that I may be moved beyond the karmas which
restrict me from serving God.
I pray that the Lord Jesus shall be with me in this tide,
this cycle of energy,
and that I may move with it,
for I would move beyond the vibrations
of the sins I have committed,
of errors, of mistakes, and of foolishness.
I pray that I shall enter into the Kingdom through
a consciousness lifting on this powerful day.
I dedicate and consecrate this day to God as a
fasting day,
in the Name of the Father, the Son and the Holy
Spirit.
Amen.

*

Pour oil and speak:

I pour this oil, knowing it to be a gift of the Spirit through the Will of God.

Place the symbol of the Cross on the middle of the forehead three times while speaking the following words:

I ask for this day sanctification,
that I may arise and ascend beyond negations,
beyond the harboring of ill against any one
or any soul in the earth.
"Father, forgive them; for they know not what
they do."
And I give those the love of my soul,
and pray for patience in all hearts and minds.
Father, lead me in Thy Holy Guidance

over the Holy Mountain, that I may enter into
   the valley
of Thy Peace, and know Thee.
Father, give unto me a whole spirit in the
   Name of Thy Son.
May my anointing become an unending Anointing.
Amen.

14

CONTACTING THE THIRD MUSIC

In duality, God has a decrease and an increase; but in the Third Music, He is Timeless and Spaceless, ever in total union with His Creation.

A decrease of God is man's opportunity to see himself as a projection of God. The increase of God is the ever-flowing versatility of the Infinite, organizing, resounding, perfecting.

The Effulgent Tides of the Holy Spirit or Esse

The spiritual tides overflowing into the physical world or plane are more effulgent and obtainable by the spiritual seeker during the fulcrum hour of 11 P.M. to 12 Midnight; during the superconsious hour and the absorption of the rising-of-the-Sun energies from 2:30 A.M. to Sunrise; and during the memory-of-the-sleep initiatory processes falling into the conscious or objective mind, thus contributing to guidance for the day from Sunrise to 10 A.M.

The most yin and receptive time to heal the impossibles for the weak and the young, for the afflicted and the helpless, for the animal kingdom, and for the most vital aspect of energy for the etheric body through the Divine-Mother effulgence is at 11 A.M. to 12 Noon.

The least psychic time of the day and the most profound soul-magnetism and union with heavenly resources, inclusive of prayer power and direct union with the etheric body of Jesus and the etheric bodies of those one would heal, and the most powerful meditation time of the day in which one is free from the lower siddhi psychic powers is 3:30 in the afternoon through Sundown until 9:00 P.M. From 9 P.M. until 11 P.M. is the most powerful time to receive and to offer instructions regarding the Masters and the Dharma.

The fulcrum hour is the time when good and evil at 12 midnight are homogenized by Omnipresence, the Angels and their Divine Companions who work with the initiatory process of the earth. At 12 midnight, the heel of good is pressed upon the neck of evil so that man may sleep and be rejuvenated, and believe in his own good, self-worth, and power to master the forces of evil through his own divine nature.

GOD-REALIZED PROMPTINGS

*The hour glass of my time
flows in the Eternal.*

*In the Eternal I Know,
I live, I am.*

Never be discouraged by the size of your task as a channel for God. In your own soul there is infinite power to meet all the terms of life offered to you.

Do not let the word *spiritualization* frighten you. The life of the Spirit is natural to you. It is your nature. In this nature — the hierarchy side of you — is the power to rise beyond immorality and to see in the overlook the true design for all.

God as the Spirit of Love has made us all beautiful, true and good. To be this, we seek to Know, and to act upon our Knowing.

Your Most High Soul is an energized vehicle of constant love, centering your reality as a child of love in God. Learn through the three stages of meditation to absorb this love, and you will experience God as Love in His Life, His Light, His Will.

The third stage of meditation is called in Sanskrit *Samadhi*. Christ Samadhi gives to you the understanding for a whole eternity. Thereafter you are living in the divine nature, or hierarchy nature equal to the gods or deities.

Call upon Great Souls of your own soul and higher-mind wavelengths to mediate for you. Learn that the spiritual walk is not alone.

Learn to relax and to recharge your body within the restoring vita which is available at all times to heal and to bless.

1. Lie down on the floor at least once a day; learn to drop your bones, becoming fleshless, just a floating self of Light in God.
2. Let the *vita* flow from the soles of your feet to the crown of your head slowly up to the center point of your head where the soul's pulsation beats. Stay at this soul's pulsation point until warmth completely fills your skull and head.
3. Let the Light come down softly to your feet, spreading out into life and the world.
4. Repeat three times. Each relaxing time should be approximately three minutes.

*

Take hold of your life. Use your right to choose. Make a leap into Self-, Soul- and God-Realization!

Choose this day whom you will serve—Judas in you, or John the Beloved in you.

Judas, divided in heart and mind chose death for himself and for Jesus. John the Beloved chose to serve his Lord into longevity years.

All of the world and in the world are experiencing Initiation into Self-Genesis. Only through a constant heart and mind fixed on God and His Son can we of this world gain the victory over the two selves in all of us.

Meditation brings us to the third in our nature, which is the hierarchy nature, the Niscient self.

> *I draw aside the veil of nescience in me,*
> *and see within the clear Niscient light.*
> *Esse. Esse. Esse. I am free, Niscient.*

Begin now to understand *Will* and *Willing* in a very special way. This is called: To make a *Sankalpa*, which means Resolution.

1. Visualize your most impersonalized desire. Breathe up; *hold* and see or image your desire. Know it is going to happen.
2. Breathe out; let the flow of acceptance of all changes to come flow with the breath, touching all of the emotions, the body functions.
3. Feel it as joy.
4. Know that the Resolution will not harm anyone.
5. Send Ahimsa-love to all; no exception, enemies too.
6. See everything as the Plan in action.
7. Get up and move about. Keep busy.

*

Free in the Esse, I am free in Redemption Grace. I am free.

Child of God, use the OM to be Knowing or to be Niscient upon the soundwaves or currents of the Love of God.

Keep the Constant of God alive in your hierarchy nature by sounding a *mental OM* into the frontal lens in the center of the forehead.

See, vision, visualize *OM* going forth to God as sent from and returning to this *Lens center point,* whereby your testimony of God will be realistic, true and powerful, to teach and spread the Holy *Vibration or Word of God!*

Do this at quiet intervals or at interim times when there is relaxation. *Desire it. Returns* are magnificent!

In God we are. OM!

It is good for the disciple on the Archetypal Path to know of his *Constant.*

God is the Constant, and you as His child and eventually His son have also a Constant. This is your direct relation to God.

All of your devoted loyalties and thoughts within come directly from your Constant.

To be firm in faith and successful in your physical life and also in spiritual practice reveals to you that God is All. The Constant in your Higher Self acts also as the Guiding Principle due to the Constant.

Feel the cool certainty of your Constant when you meditate.

> *The Increase of God is leading me.*
> *My Constant reveals, God Is.*

Use your White Light, which is by nature the product of the Constant in you.

Think of the White Light at the end of the spine; bring it up to the back of the head where the *Divine Thalamus* is centered. This is directly above the medulla oblongata.

Let the Light rest on the Thalamus approximately ten seconds.

Flow it back down gently to the end of the spine.

Do this six times. Through this, the Constant will be revealed.

At the end of the exercise, speak the mantram: *"The Risen Christ in me is free."*

When men read the *signs,* they see and hear the Inner coming to birth. In the present, the signs are: poverty, hunger, separation, godlessness. These now prepare the way for prospering in the spirit, in the soul nature, in the intimacy, in the thirsts for God.

All seers surface in these times; all prophets are heard.

The Continuum Sacrament taken each day opens the Inner, giving answers to the signs, to the mortal cry made immortal.

Practice without ceasing the Marking-and-Tracing activities, that you may take hold of the hard unknowing with the true informing Esse, and therefore be always Constant in the Coinciding Principle.

> *I abide in the Constant, in the One.*
> *I image and live in the Absolute Constant,*
> *God in me.*

Three Energy-Matrixes

There are three energy-matrixes through which man maintains life in the physical body, life in the lesser etheric body, life in the emotional body, life in the mental body. These matrixes survive death in some degree and are everlasting, actual, energy skeletal-like frameworks for life in earth and in spirit.

An energy-matrix never dies. In the case of physical

death, the energy is merely transposed to the plane where consciousness is active.

In the state of physical death, the lowest matrix retains its mold even though the physical body and the lesser etheric body undergo the dissolution process of death. The lower matrix remains as a potential framework in its energy processes for earth experience when one comes to birth in the earth. Thus, one reproduces his likeness again and again in coming to the world due to the indestructible and undying activity of the supporting matrix for a particular body.

The lower or duality matrix extends from the feet to the horizontal line just above the pelvic center. The psychic-matter nature controlling the biological forces ends at the pelvic line.

The middle or center matrix functions horizontally from the pelvic to above the diaphragm just below the heart. The center matrix is the field for the desire and emotional nature; the psychological and metaphysical level of consciousness; the lesser mind.

The highest or supreme matrix energy-frame exists from the heart to the Higher-Self point of light above the head. The supreme matrix supports the soul, higher mind and spirit. All of these function in the Higher-Unconscious Realm.

When the three matrixes are sealed away from each other, there is sickness of the mind and the body. If one of these matrixes is more active than the others, the other matrixes are phased out in their energy-processes. One is then fanatical and obsessed. When the three energy-matrixes coordinate with one another, perfection is manifested in all bodies.

When one who has died is seen by one living in the earth, it is the matrix-energy atomic framework one sees.

This appears to the one seeing as stencil-like lines of light, energy and scintillating movement.

The three matrixes make it possible for the everlasting body to be present in the perishable body of earth existence. Everything having a form is supported by this matrix system.

The seed has its matrix which commands shaping, forming and growing of the seed.

Each organ of the body has its own energy-matrix. Positive health is assured when the matrix of the organs correlates in symmetry with the form-matrix supporting the organs. Thus, in surgery, when an organ of the body is removed, the form-matrix and the matrix of the organ are retained. Even though the physical organ is removed, the energy-processes of the organ remain as vital containment for the physical body or for whatever body is sick.

The three matrixes presently work to add another matrix. The Undersoul and the soul work in this period of man's evolvement that a fourth matrix will be added; another brain function will become active. The three brain functions of the present time will be extended into a higher-mind function destined for man in this world, that he may enter into a fifth dimensional consciousness as a God-Realized center for creation.

The middle matrix supports the psychological, the metaphysical and some portions of the psychic-matter nature whereby one uses supersensible powers through Self-Realization. The ego and the Undersoul have a unique task. Presently, the organizing consciousness of man has its most intensive play of thought and inspiration fixed upon psychological premise and metaphysical play of the lower mind.

Through extension of the senses in the second or intermediary matrix, all in the earth are seeking to expand their thought worlds and their energizing processes of consciousness into a spiritualized intellect.

The present ways of learning in this earth, dependent upon conceptual testing through the senses, are in a state of revolution. What men have called "the psychic" in the past will become the commonplace. Through observation, through Marking and Tracing, the Initiate begins to observe himself and his way of thinking, and thus opens other dimensions of understanding.

The total play of the second matrix relies upon the desire or emotional nature. Intense suffering presently is occurring in the abdominal areas of man; this includes the adrenals, the kidneys, the intestines, the spleen, the liver, the pancreas. These are the organs which are undergoing matrix extension.

Nutrition will play a most important part in man, coming to birth to his spiritual nature through the third-matrix functioning. All areas of the third matrix begin in the sacred atom in the heart, moving upward through the thymus-gland system, the thyroid system, the pituitary system, and the pineal system.

The third-matrix energies support the heart, the speech, the breath, the sight, the hearing, the thought of the higher mind; the Constant, the hierarchy nature, the Higher Self.

Presently, the third matrix-mold provides the supporting framework for the higher etheric body. All of these energy-fields of consciousness from the heart upward are held together by what is called *The Third Eye*, which is the outpouring center for the pulsation point or heartbeat of the soul.

When one understands the three matrixes, he will no longer fear death. He will recognize that that which retains him in God is supported securely by the Godly processes which function in his eternal nature. His eternal nature extends into all of the processes of life. There is no death. What men call death is change. There is no dead energy or ending of energy processes. Energy processes exist in what men call density or physical as well as soul and mental.

When one dies, his consciousness, which is the offshoot of his Constant, merely moves into a different atmosphere of energies supporting his state of consciousness. He is, however, never absent from the three energy-matrixes supporting his physical, etheric, emotional and mental bodies.

Consciousness is selective. The Constant keeps alive the selectivity processes in consciousness.

The present era of energy will give to all men new perception and perspective as to *who* they are, *why* they are, and *where* they are going.

The three energy-matrix fields will be proved by science. As men come to know more and more the laws of magnetism and electricity, and especially of the atomic and molecular systems, they will gain a new factualized approach to the unseen Kingdom of God.

The energy-play in each matrix has a central and controlling *Constant* yantra form.

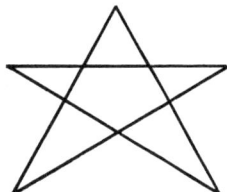

The high or supreme matrix molding line pattern is in the shape of a five-pointed star. This resides in the Constant.

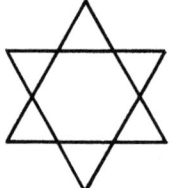 The middle-matrix pattern is the six-pointed star.

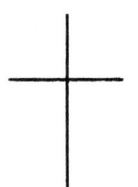 The lower matrix pattern is the cross.

In every mandala, these symbols surface as: ⊕ ✡ ⛤

The cross correlates to the number 4; the six-pointed star, to the chakra called the six-petaled lotus; the five-pointed star, to the higher mind and the ideal mind-state of consciousness.

Hierarchy works with the chromosomes. The planets, the Moon and the Angels work with the genes. The Sun is the energy used by the Hierarchy to stabilize the chromosomes and balance them.

The lowest matrix is connected with the Moon. The middle matrix is connected with the Sun. The highest matrix is connected with the True Self. The spiritualized person cultivates and develops the third matrix extension through the mind.

The involuntary nature of man is a gift from God. The involuntary system is directly connected with the Law of Increase in God.

The third matrix determines how the self evolves. There can be no reality of self until one relates himself to the spiritual through and of and by himself.

Until the coming of Christ through Jesus, man lived totally within the involuntary system. With the Passion of Jesus, and the opening of the Indestructible Atom, man began to create himself. Consequently, all sins of mankind caused by offense against the chromosome system and the gene system must be transversed or mastered by the infinite processes of unfoldment through the self.

THE LIVING BODY COMMAND MANTRAM

The power to heal begins with the Lesser Etheric Body of the initiate. His Lesser Etheric Body determines how much power he may channel to the world. If the Lesser Etheric Body is an unruly body, one lives in a world of forces rather than greater creation. Therefore, it is necessary that the healer seek to live within harmony to the laws of Nature, and to understand himself so that he may qualify his desires to blend with the greater intent of God for man. If he would serve, he should build a body for such serving.

The Lesser Etheric Body is a transparent-like body of fine ether. It is shaped identical to the physical body, and interpenetrates and saturates every cell of man's physical body. When the Lesser Etheric Body is in a healthy state, it extends three inches outside every part of the physical body. Its structure is of twelve vortice-flames which move clockwise when in harmony and contraclockwise when depleted or devitalized. The vortice-flames in the Lesser Etheric Body move in circular, rhythmic motion. Thus, when a person is negative, he is constantly throwing off from this body his own agitation and discord—and the contraclockwise action in the Lesser Etheric Body invites and attracts outer discord by this same circular, weaving, rhythmic motion. When healthy, the Lesser Etheric Body is the body of life-giving, life-sustaining, and living vitality. In this, the Lesser Etheric Body may be said to be the *Living Body*.

The Lesser Etheric Body has its immunities and insulations built through the gamma-red rays of the Sun. The gamma-red energies around the field of the Lesser Etheric Body repel disease and immunize the physical form from outside contagion. When the gamma-red on the outer boundary of the Lesser Etheric Body circulates normally without agitation, it acts as a protection; but if there is force from within as of the emotions and thought, the gamma-red field of the Lesser Etheric Body will invite negations into the person's life and will also send outwardly into the world—with a powerful catapulting action—forceful desires and thoughts colored by selfish discernings. Therefore, unless a person is loving, this gamma-red action will make him seem repelling to others. Rather than the power of insulation, it becomes the power of isolation.

The Lesser Etheric Body or Living Body is the representative of a microscopic form-image centered within the seed-atom of the heart. In the second Great Interval during the creation of this earth or eternity, this form-image was sealed into the seed-atom by the Father, the Hierarchy, and activated by the great Saturn Archangels. This work by the Father determined the type of form that would be suitable for man's expression in a gravity world. Because of this form-image of MAN, man will always be man in earth, and he will be enabled to experience the many and varied expressions of the ego through countless lives, each life being uniquely individual.

The microscopic form-image within the seed-atom of the heart is as the lens of a camera. Its representative, the Lesser Etheric Body, has the capacity to mirror all things affecting it day by day and year by year. Thus, each thing man sees, feels, thinks upon, and acts upon is registered, photographically, by the lenslike action of the form-image within the heart. These recordings of grace or negation are activated, in right timing, to man's outer experience — determining the trend of karma in the present life and the trend of karma as well as the appearance, the attitudes and the talents of the personality in the next life or some future life.

The Lesser Etheric Body does not survive death. However, the microscopic form-image residing in the seed-atom of the heart survives death. The form-image must rebuild a new Lesser Etheric Body for each new physical-life experience of the ego in earth. In this, the actions, motives or values of the former life or lives are imprinted by the form-image upon the Lesser Etheric Body, thereby determining the type of Lesser Etheric Body one may use as an instrument for the ego's experience in earth.

The microscopic form-image may build a healthy Lesser Etheric Body if the former-life physical, emotional and mental action has been of pure intent and motive. The form-image may build a malformed Lesser Etheric Body due to abuse of will in former lives. This may be reflected in the physical experience of the ego by any condition restraining the physical, emotional or mental will.

The form-image may build a weakened vehicle of low vitality if in former lives there has been an overuse of tension, haste or impatience, or excess of habits. Untimely causes of death, such as suicide or death by war, will produce in the next life a disorganized Lesser Etheric Body. The microscopic form-image may build a body saturated with fear due to a just previous death experience, or may be fortified with courage due to former-life attitudes in the latter years.

From the time of birth to the seventh year of life, the

Lesser Etheric Body grows rapidly, in a balloon-like manner, until it reaches adult size. Hence, the extreme vitality found in children.

Every seven years, until the seventieth year of a person's life, the microscopic form-image sends forth a new life impulse through the Lesser Etheric Body. This is known as an *etheric cycle*. In each new cycle, the Lesser Etheric Body receives certain compulsions from the just previous life and other lives, which are to be included into this life's action.

The healer should recognize that all defects of the physical body and all weaknesses apparent in physical discomforts are but the outer reflections of the Lesser Etheric Body. All deformities at birth, lack of vitality, imbalanced organs, maladjustment of emotion and thought, and all tendencies to negation habits, emotional and mental, are reflections of imbalanced actions in former lives and are caused by the profaning of the microscopic form-image.

The physical body *imprints* all physical habits and actions, good or bad, into the Lesser Etheric Body. The emotional body *mirrors* all emotional actions, feelings and desires, good or bad, into the Lesser Etheric Body. The mental body *etches* into the Lesser Etheric Body every level of thought. The Higher Etheric Body *inscribes* into the Lesser Etheric Body, through atom action and the greater degrees of light, the intelligible truths of the spiritual worlds, for the Higher Etheric Body is the representative and perfect reflector of the Higher Self.

God made it possible for man to come into this earth or eternity with the image of what the soul *had been* in other eternities. This eternal-image is the Higher Self. The Higher Self is animated by a consciousness gathered in other eternities and also by its unceasing alignment with the archetypal and spiritual worlds. The Higher Self awaits to instruct and to channel the greater wisdom of the real and true to man. It is timeless in its patience, in that it works with the eternals. Even though man may resist, deep in his heart he is always aware that he should blend with his Higher Self.

It is the Will of God that one become more than that which he entered with in this eternity. It is destiny that he produce out of his actions in earth a creation as only the experience in this earth can make possible.

With each pure prototypal experience in earth, man records as grace his works of good into the Diamond Medallion around his Higher Self. Thus, the good fulfilled by him in this eternity shall merge, inevitably and ultimately, into the Higher Self. Through repeated lives or reincarnations he will bring forth the greater atoms in all of his bodies so that he may eventually be at one with his Higher Self.

The Higher Self is centered within the Eternal Sustaining Atom located directly over the head. If the initiate will place his arms upright over his head and touch his fingertips, he will locate the exact distance of the Higher Self over the body.

The Lesser Etheric Body of man pertains to the physical world and works through movement, sound and color. The Higher Etheric Body pertains to the spiritual worlds and works through tone and light. The Higher Etheric Body is a perfected body; all other bodies (physical, emotional, mental) are in a state of evolving. The Higher Etheric Body, having twelve perfected atoms, is able to function in the highest degree of ether and is not subjected to negation or death. It is the body for higher perception in night-flight or dreams. As the Higher Etheric

Body is closer to the spiritual worlds than any of man's bodies, it is the body reflecting the spiritual action of the higher worlds.

The Higher Etheric Body can approach the earth and be in close proximity to the Lesser Etheric Body because of the ultra-violet rays of the physical Sun. Its proximity to the spiritual worlds is sustained by the greater prism of the Light of the Christ. The twelve atoms of the Higher Etheric Body, working with the ultra-violet rays of the Sun and the prism of the Christ-Light, enable the Higher Etheric Body to be a perfect body for the Healing Presence to be channelled to man.

The Lesser Etheric Body has twelve energy vortice-flames of whirlpool-like action. These cuplike vortice-flames intelligently respond to, and become the resting places for, the twelve over-dwelling atoms of the Higher Etheric Body. When the Higher Etheric Body atoms move toward the vortice-flames in the Lesser Etheric Body, the vortice-flames, through the proximity and blending of the spiritual atoms, may sometimes give off a warmth which may be experienced by the disciple in meditation.

When there is perfect alignment between the Higher Etheric Body and the Lesser Etheric Body, the Higher Etheric Body atoms transubstantiate the vortice-flames' action into total light; thus, Illumination on the gravity level is made possible for the initiate. When the vortice-flames are out of alignment with the Higher Etheric Body atoms, the result is discord in the Lesser Etheric Body, and one becomes exposed to the more turbulent fiery forces of Nature, to the negations of the astral world, and to the negative thought telepathies in the world.

As the Higher Etheric Body is the shepherd body for spiritual action of man, the Lesser Etheric Body is the shepherd body at night, for it protects the physical body and assists in the restorative functions while man sleeps. Sleeplessness at night is caused by a *jammed atom*. Due to a person's over-concentration creating tension, the Lesser Etheric Body's vortice-flames and the Higher Etheric Body's pinnacle atoms become set or fixed, preventing the Higher Etheric Body from releasing itself as the body for night-flight.

1. *Total alignment.* Only the Lord Jesus had a continuity of perfect alignment between His Lesser Etheric Body, Higher Etheric Body and Higher Self. The dedicated initiate, through rhythmic spiritual practices, seeks to achieve this alignment.

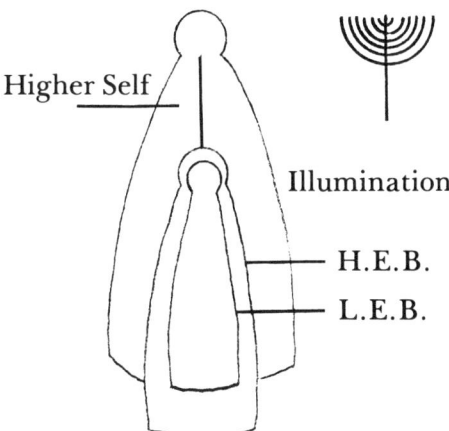

2. *Two-thirds alignment.* A person who has two-thirds alignment to his Higher Etheric Body is enabled to sustain alignment with spiritual impulses for extended periods. Through his Mental Triad Atoms' action, he has spiritual inspiration and telepathic alignment with the higher worlds. He expresses reverence, selfless serving, dedication, and spiritual gifts.

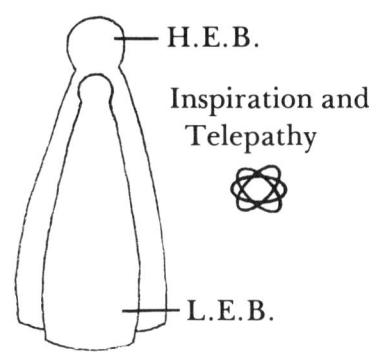

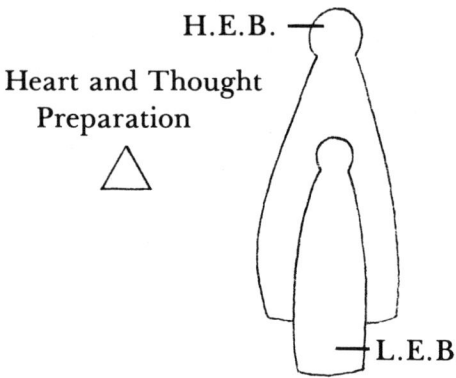

Heart and Thought Preparation

3. *One-half alignment.* The person in this level of evolvement receives spiritual impulses from the Higher Etheric Body's pinnacle atoms onto his brain. He aligns himself with talents from former lives, and expresses the mystical, metaphysical, or esoteric. He works to overcome egotistical conflict and precocious individualism. (Armageddon of the senses.)

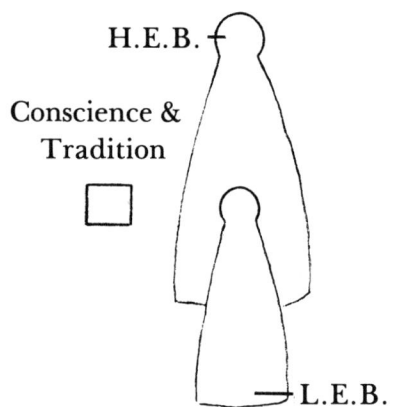

Conscience & Tradition

4. The average person has approximately one-third alignment with his Higher Etheric Body. Such a person receives spiritual impulses onto his brain through the help of the Higher Etheric Body. This is expressed by him on the level of religion and conscience. He works to master the Ten Commandments and fulfill Tribal-Genesis and Family-Genesis action.

L.E.B. – Lesser Etheric Body
H.E.B. – Higher Etheric Body

LIVING BODY COMMAND MANTRAM

O Living Body, let the Healing Presence in.
O Living Body, let the perfect work of thy true Image begin.
O Living Body, tranquilize and make serene my senses.
O Living Body, renew my cells, my veins, my nerves.
O Living Body, restore my arteries, my glands.
O Living Body, revitalize and activate my organs.
O Living Body, heal my bones.
O Living Body, let the mighty currents within my brain direct my muscles into perfect coordination, suppleness and grace.

O Living Body, let the Healing Presence in—
And become thou the perfect servant or server in Healing Peace.
Quicken the Spirit's fire within my heart's flame.
Cleanse out and remove all soilings of lust, passion and unrest.
Be thou quickened, O Living Body, that I may live in Grace, in Love, in Light.

The Living Body is the Lesser Etheric Body. The Lesser Etheric Body moulds after any pattern of command. It is a body of 100% servitude in that it will respond to anything that is asked of it. It will respond to commands from the higher will or the lesser will. It can be either a perfect body or an imperfect body.

When God created the earth, He used four Forces or Fiats. When man uses a command, he uses direct Fiat action. The Living Body Command Mantram is a Mantram for self-command. It is possible for the initiate through commands to the Lesser Etheric or Living Body to change its currents, to bring it into order, and to make it into a good servant, keeping it in obedient alignment with the perfected Higher Etheric Body and, therefore, become at one with the Healing Presence.

The Living Body Command Mantram is as necessary to the initiate as any daily practice. To become a joyful, responsible, peace-giving and loving channel, one should use this Command Mantram twice daily, preferably mid-morning and mid-afternoon, and experience the joyousness and aliveness in its freeing action. If these times are inconvenient, one may choose whatever times are convenient for him. However, this Command Mantram should not be used as part of his regular meditation and contemplation rhythms, as it pertains to another rhythm and would interfere with that seeking to be accomplished in meditation and contemplation. The Command Mantram should not be used more than twice a day, otherwise it becomes repetitious and therefore ineffective.

Through separative karmas, the Lesser Etheric Body has followed for many years an old orbit of obeying wrong commands or self-indulgent habit imprints, which interfere with a spiritual life. Thus, it is important to continue in the daily use of this Command Mantram and, in time, the Lesser Etheric Body will respond to the higher commands. The Living Body Command Mantram will organize the body functions, stabilize the emotional action, clarify the mental attributes, and spiritualize the vital creativity in the thought process.

It is necessary that the initiate find harmony in all qualities of his nature so that he may heal others. To become a dedicated healer, a complete emptying out of all interfering obstacles is necessary. To retain karmic soilings, anxieties or tensions in any degree is to be an imperfect instrument as a healer. When one is concerned more with his personal affairs rather than selfless surrender toward the healing of others, he fails in his dedication to heal.

The Living Body Command Mantram is for self-healing, and works in purifying and re-chemicalizing action. The initiate should use it prayerfully, reverently, and with absolute faith.

There are thirteen archetypal statements in the Living Body Command Mantram. The healer should relate himself to each statement with a firm inner knowing that the Lesser Etheric Body is actively responding to each word said. Therefore, he should have an expectancy of immediate response, and speak each word slowly, purposefully directed toward an instantaneous activity. Between each line there should be a pause so as to record the resolving action of each powerful spoken command to the Lesser Etheric or Living Body.

The Living Body Command Mantram should be spoken aloud; the Lesser Etheric Body will not respond if this Command Mantram is only casually read or thought upon. It is also recommended that one refrain from using any other wordings than that given in the Command Mantram, as he will change the rhythmic intent and interfere with the response.

The joy of life comes from an obedient Lesser Etheric Body. The Living Body Command Mantram is designed to give help to one who would serve as healer.

If one fulfills the daily rhythms of speaking the Living Body Command Mantram with full sincerity and dedicated and reverent application, it will aid him to open the Third Music, which will cleanse out soilings of magnetism and protect him from absorbing the karmas from others in his environment and taking on the soiled magnetisms in sicknesses or persons near by. He will become a sustaining point of light in filigree action through Mediation.

For Contemplation while Speaking:

O Living Body, let the Healing Presence in. The initiate will come to know when he has made alignment with the Healing Presence.

O Living Body, let the perfect work of thy true Image begin. He will be aware of the work of the microscopic form-image in the seed-atom of the heart.

O Living Body, tranquilize and make serene my senses. The subduing of the senses will be felt and recorded. In this, a reverence for the use of one's senses—seeing, tasting, smelling, hearing, touching—will gradually be manifested and the four Fiats influencing the soul will be given wider range of action.

O Living Body, renew my cells, my veins, my nerves. The initiate may experience the cells responding like colorful rainbow sparks.

O Living Body, restore my arteries, my glands. The initiate may express a new vigor. The human level of joy is determined in the physiological construction of man by healthiness of the glands. If it were not for healthy glands, man would be saturnine or somber. In speaking this line, one may, at times, be aware of the pancreas in its restoring action of energy; of his kidneys, as a station of power.

O Living Body, revitalize and activate my organs. The initiate may be aware of the heart and its tremendous importance. He may have in this time a sweet love rapport with his heart organ. He may also feel the love of God, the love of life, the love of peoples in the world. He may be aware of the intelligence in his organs, of the liver's willing function, of the spleen's patient conforming action with the blood and vitality. He may feel a happy coordinating action, a living aliveness in these organs. His body may hum as one harmonious whole.

O Living Body, heal my bones. On speaking this line, the initiate may, at first, be aware of a resistance, as his words shall move against the power of the vertical energies within the bones built out of the ages of cartilege formation. As the wind would bend a tree and not break it, so may he feel his bones supporting him, framing him, and yet sustaining him as a structure perfected out of the ages, a structure fitted to command the gravity forces.

O Living Body, let the mighty currents within my brain direct my muscles into perfect coordination, suppleness and grace. The initiate may become aware of the great and ingenious working of the brain cells. He may see his muscles as mighty rivers of fluidic movement in his body through which his will moves. He shall then know that haste is negation, and that dedication to action with reverence is henceforth his plan, his way.

While one is speaking the words in the Living Body Command Mantram, he may be aware that he has taken his body for granted and has little revered it. However, upon his concluding this Mantram, he man feel a sacred reverence for his body; he shall be closer to his Maker, the Father; and he shall be closer to his Creator, God—the Eternal One.

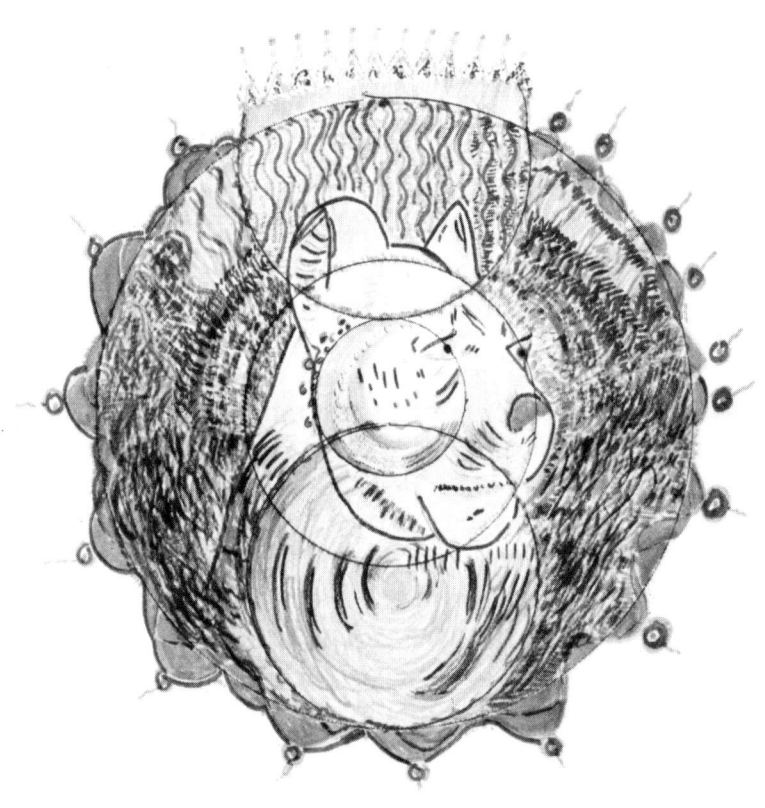

A BIRTHDAY MANDALA:
THE CROWN AND THE LION
BY ANN REE COLTON

15

MASTERY THROUGH THE MANDALA

> The Mandala symbol is not only a means of expressing, it works an effect. It reacts upon its maker.
> —Dr. Carl Jung
> From *The Secret of the Golden Flower*

Mandala, in Sanskrit, means *sacred circle.* God uses the circle continually in His Creation. The Earth, Sun, Moon, planets and stars are circles. One can look into the mirror and see two of the most beautiful circles ever created—the eyes. Nature's circles or *mandalas* are everywhere.

The *circle* symbolizes the physical Sun, the individual, the soul, protection, the Eternal. The *circle with a dot or Bindu in the center* symbolizes the Eternal Self, the Christ within, the Invisible Sun, the Celestial Angels' helps, Archangel protection.

When one draws a mandala in the spirit of devotion, giving himself wholly to God, miracles come into his life—changing and transforming.

When one makes a mandala or does anything with the idea of getting something for self, this becomes magic. Magic has its limitation and leads one into a dead-end.

The magical arts were developed by fallen initiates who ceased to have the power to consummate miracles.

To make magic, one makes union with elemental forces. To produce miracles, one makes union with the Angels, Jesus and our Heavenly Father.

The mandala can be interpreted through what is happening in the Undersoul function; what is happening in the outer consciousness; what is happening in the Constant. The mandala is interpreting what the Bindu is saying; interpreting the thunderbolts; interpreting the Dharmic flow or the teaching in the mandala; interpreting the perfected potential. The mandala is opening the energy-fields of the soul's medallion; releasing one's self from the records of karma; opening the Undersoul; uniting with the Coinciding Principle; freeing the nadis energy-flows; speeding up dream cognizance through the creation of an early-morning mandala.

One may make a dedication or a novena to create a number of mandalas in a successive number of days. Through the creating of a mandala, one extends his senses and opens the Yantra myth-flows and archetypal symbols.

The mandala is not an art form; it is a meditation form. The making of a mandala is a meditative practice. In mandala design and coloring, one draws upon the Higher Unconscious for creation, for peace. There can be no peace for the outer conscious mind until one comes to terms with his subconscious mind and Higher Unconscious.

The process of making a mandala stills the emotions and the thoughts, and enables the conscious mind, the subconscious mind and the Higher Unconscious to be as one, thus clearing the field of karma.

A mandala is the product of the soul's medallion. To create a perfect mandala. one must be at one with his soul's pulsation.

A mandala portraying the Sun enables its creator to open the Third Eye within, setting up a process of light in the mind over-directed by the soul. In ancient times, the Sun was thought to be the Eye of God. Men worshipped the light proceeding from the Eye of God.

A seed-mantra spoken and contemplated before making a mandala gives steadiness and control of the mind; it also opens creativity, and union with the soul.

One begins the making of a mandala knowing it to be a form of meditation. He draws a circle, and within the center he places a dot, which represents the Bindu-point or seed outpicturing the soul's pulsation.

The mandala is a kaleidoscopic process of forms, patterns and energies flowing out of the pulsation point of the soul. All persons are in an unceasing state of creating these mandala or geometrical forms from the soul's pulsation.

In a low vibration, one creates solid masses of colors which are very often in opposition to each other as energy masses. These are projections of restless thought forms and unidentified thinking. In souls sensitive to their intuitional powers, the mandala processes unceasingly project themselves into yantric patterns and designs of symmetrical beauty.

The balance of soul-light is kept equalized through the organized processes of color and pattern falling within the nimbus range of the soul's medallion. When one makes a mandala, he projects this moving, scintillating, identifying color and geometrical pattern onto the paper upon which he draws, paints, or objectifies.

Color in a mandala unites one with the great prism of colors beyond the natural prism of colors or primal colors. One produces colors directly sensitized by the soul's pulsation. The soul-colors pour down into the palate or the roof of the mouth where the Archetypal Cord or Audible Hum of the Sound Current may be experienced. The finer soul-colors are etherically saturated with primordial light.

From color, one intuits beyond ordinary intuition. In his making of a mandala, insight and sight become one. Thus, one who centers himself in a state of mandala-making will experience in time a supra-normal meditation which gives to him an insight into things to come—that is, places his life in his own prophetic future.

The imaging process of the hierarchy nature comes forth when one makes a mandala as a regular spiritual practice. Making a mandala twice a week unites one with the Coinciding Principle and with the Informing Principle of Buddhi.

Colors chosen to make or form a mandala must be soul-choice colors. Therefore, one should not intellectually or artfully portray what he thinks the colors should be in the mandala. He should draw upon the Bindu center as the directing intelligence in selecting and inspiring the colors used in a mandala. In time, the continued practice in the use of the mandala as a meditation expansion will produce flawless patterns, beautiful balances, intelligible insight as to what is being said in the mandala.

One does not need to be an artist. To make a mandala is not an art session.

The colors in one's soul-prism are seeking to come out of him. The freeing process in a mandala produces steadiness of mind, calmness of emotions. In time, a perfected mandala becomes a soul-disc or seed mantra for the use of contemplation and meditation.

The mandala belongs to the maker of the mandala. No one else should concentrate, contemplate or meditate upon it. It is one's own soul-design containing the vibration of his Higher Self.

All mandalas are circular. As one progresses in meditation, the design of the mandala varies through stages of evolvement and progression in the spiritual life.

The technique in the creating of a mandala and its use in meditation is a soul-building and spilling-out process, uniting the three aspects of consciousness: consciousness, subconsciousness and higher unconsciousness.

If one's first efforts seem crude, he should not be discouraged. Every line and color is significant. As time advances, he will produce a mandala belonging solely to himself. When one finally achieves this, he can use his mandala as a meditation, contemplative disc.

The advanced techniques of Marking and Tracing seek to make one into a spiritual scientist with direct knowledge through his own experience. Every step given in spiritual training leans in the direction of one's liberation and union with God.

The mandala exercise unites one with the Yantra myth symbolic kingdom and the Archetypal-Image kingdom. Through mandala realization, a Yantra symbol opens up like an expanding telescope, wider and wider.

All Yantra symbols maintain virtues and assure their continuity. Beyond the Yantras is articulation. Mandala is a part of Yantra training.

All experiences in life are progressive. Progression in the outer life can be interpreted literally and satisfactorily through seasons and cycles and the units of Time.

Physical life is initiatory through which one masters the play of consciousness through association. The inner life as an experience in Time far exceeds the outer-life existence cycles. One who steps into the inner life must be prepared for the quickened processes of Initiation through exposure to forces and energies.

The articulation given to man by God to understand and know these energy-processes of the inward life is through symbols.

When one enters the base-of-the-skull Yantra Kingdom where the master images are absorbed, he becomes familiar with the Yantra system; a symbol or a series of symbols are enacted out in the play of consciousness as dramas, as myths, and as transcendental.

The medulla oblongata is the station for the Yantra. It is called the Rudra station or John-the-Baptist station.

Yantra knowledge is more than insight, more than intuition. Yantra speaks as power of the symbol itself in the nature of one adapted through Yantra-knowing.

Yantra-knowing is used by the Esse or Holy Spirit to create power-situations. This appears first in the Initiate as a form of evangelism, prophecy.

In the mandala, one becomes an Initiate of the Yantra. The Esse as spiritual power provides him with transcendent powers of speech and of communication, or gives to him a God-tongue which will not be killed, stilled or denied.

The mandala belongs only to that one making the mandala. It can be the property of none other; it can neither be bought nor sold. The mandala is not an art project; it is a soul practice; it is a key to a liberated conscience, mind and soul.

He who makes a mandala develops a shining face of virtue which comes from an honest Marking-and-Tracing avidity in the desire to know and to gain self-knowledge, and thus unite with the Self.

Every mandala experience is a freeing of the tensions in the Undersoul. It is inevitable that one who practices the making of mandalas will come to the day when he must face through self-honesty that which is speaking through his soul and Undersoul. Through this comes an accumulative Initiation wherein one avoids seeking to compromise or to shunt aside what has been revealed.

Mastery Through the Mandala

All spiritual practices concern the mastery of mind and soul energies. These energies inevitably must be channelled.

The speaking of the mantra, the mantram and the prayer vocalize what is experienced in the mandala. The mandala geometrizes that which is awaiting to come forth into life, to be recognized, to be *utilized*.

The mandala should never be used as the only way to make alignment. It is one way or means of calming and stilling the vibratory hum of karma intruding upon one's thoughts before meditation.

To create a true mandala geometrically fashioned from the energy flow of one's own soul medallion will unite one with his True Self, wherein rests his true desire.

The mind of Christ in each soul is not a subjective mind. The making of the mandala enables one to move beyond the subjective mind into the supernal mentality where God as Spirit reigns.

The mandala, being from one's own soul, is never to be given away, nor should it be used by any other person in any form. It is to be kept as a sacred portion of one's own true self, a reverent vehicle of light, illumination and peace.

One cannot create a mandala with the intellect, nor can he draw one to use for himself as a copy of someone else's mandala. A mandala is not an artistic form; it is a divine formula objectified into a design for the soul's overflow. All perfected mandala designs are the soul's overflow from the higher side of quelle or the Higher Unconscious.

Until one makes of his consciousness a pure vehicle for God, he will see in "a glass darkly" or through the horizontal serpent astral vision. He will hear voices unintelligible, unspeakable.

364   THE THIRD MUSIC

INTERPRETATIONS

Betrothal Mandala created by man and woman devotees during the month previous to their marriage.

The four-petaled mandala indicates harmony between souls. The theme of the mandala relates to reincarnation-association in which in other existences they have shared a covenant as devotees of God.

The theme-colors, gold and blue, indicate spiritual and soul clarity. This may be titled a *Mandala of Remembrance.*

MASTERY THROUGH THE MANDALA

Revelation of Numbers. This mandala is a kabalistic mandala revealing this person to be a 4-8 energy-dispenser.

The 8 suns portraying the crowned Christ at the uttermost top of the mandala reveal two of the faces looking toward the crowned Christ, and 5 of the faces looking downward toward the Earth indicate 2 soul-powers seeking to function through the 5 senses.

The projected numbers over the 4-petaled Lotus show the present state of consciousness of this disciple. The numbers pictured slightly to the right of the mandala indicate this one's need to make practical her emotions.

The number 1 obscured by the 2 indicates a strong aggressive will self-disguised as inoffensiveness.

The number 5 capturing the center of the mandala indicates the desire for attention in the physical and a need for centering in the spiritual.

The number 7 slightly above the 5 indicates the mandala-maker feels that she is under disciplines to laws and rules.

The number 3 below the line of the Ego-Gate indicates the need to learn the balancing power of association with persons.

The colors' emphasis being gold and blue shows soul-purity.

On the whole, the mandala speaks of struggle to obtain her rightful use of soul-powers; conflict from the lesser mind.

In this mandala, the number 6 is weak and difficult to discern, which indicates that sex or sexual attitudes are the basic point of struggle or stigmata.

This soul came into this life feeling oppressed by the masculine or yang force. The conflict is the need to balance the yin and yang polarities in the fifth chakra or the throat center where speech as Truth concerning self and all persons is necessary.

The soul-purity indicated on the soul-side of the mandala shows mastery over these emotions and victory through initiation.

Soul-Pregnancy: The Birth of the Unicorn and the Rose. The lateral lines in this mandala indicate Truth-climbing and perception. The circular lines show the molding and sculpting aspect of the mandala-maker.

The goal in this pregnancy is to give birth to the rose of Saint Francis. The unicorn, which is the progeny of this pregnancy, reveals the opening of the Third Eye through the Fourth Light Stream under Saint Francis.

The Bindu or the Seed. This mandala portrays knowledge of the Bindu or the Seed. It indicates soul-harmony as related to the Supreme One. It also indicates that this one is united with the life-chain of all growing and living things; the need for space, for creation.

The mandala, created in monotone colors of bronze and white, with a slight peach inference, shows the scale for the learning of this one is cosmic, etheric; is both microscopic and macroscopic.

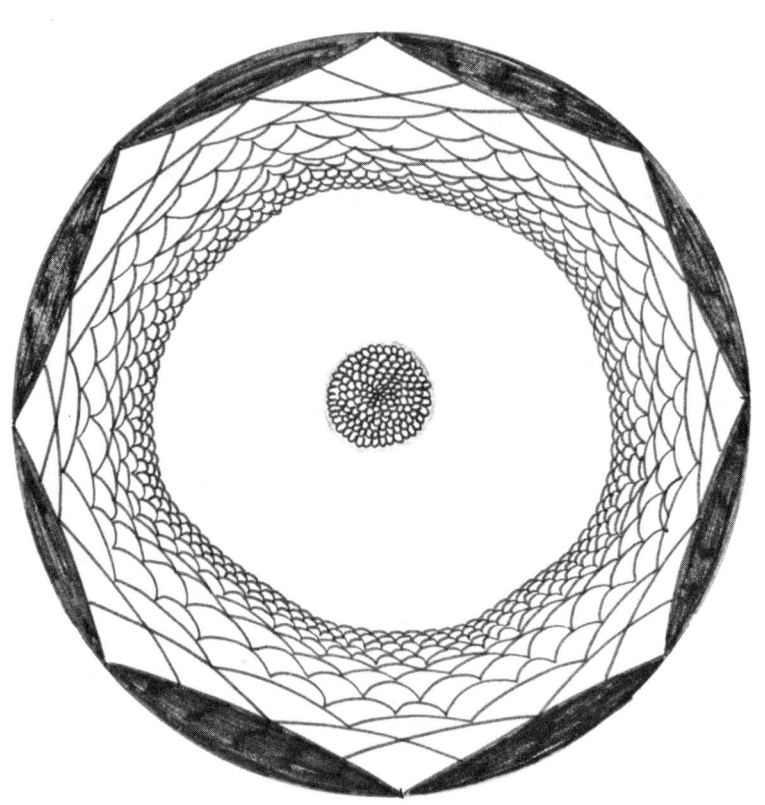

A Doodle Mandala. All casual markings in semi-contemplative times in ink, color or pencil are important.

This mandala, titled *The Sushumna Thread and the Serpent,* reveals that this person has opened the gate between the eyebrow center and is yet to raise the two kundalini currents of Ida and Pingala to equal Sushumna's thread.

Looking to the right of the mandala as the base of the skull, following the serpent's line to the meridian ascent which would be approximately the 11th house in a horoscope chart, one sees the serpent with ten diamond inverted points.

The wavy lines at the bottom of the mandala indicate the thought and mind waves, of which there are six, showing this person to be a healer.

The central Sushumna flower reveals him to be a will initiate. He is working presently to command the yin and yang, or Ida and Pingala breath flow and coordinate it with his soul-flow. Initiates with his experience are taught repeatedly through patience, contemplation, devotion to be introspective on the level of the soul, that they may produce the Christ-Consciousness through this gate between the eyebrows.

The serpent's head being pointed upward to the God-Gate of the mandala shows that he is aiming for God-Realization.

All doodles or careless making of lines reveal something of one's desires and especially of the soul's desire to be heard, to be witness.

In making a mandala, one should be always attentive to how many forms there are and what the forms are saying. For example, in this mandala, at the Soul-Gate five cups are shown, which tell the doodler that his five senses are full of soul-knowledge.

It is often the case in a doodled mandala that one receives more significant illustrations of the soul and its hungers; it especially affects that very second or moment in one's life. In the law of Godly mathematics there are no accidents. One should listen to what the soul is saying in what one does subconsciously, consciously and unconsciously. By this, he will know himself.

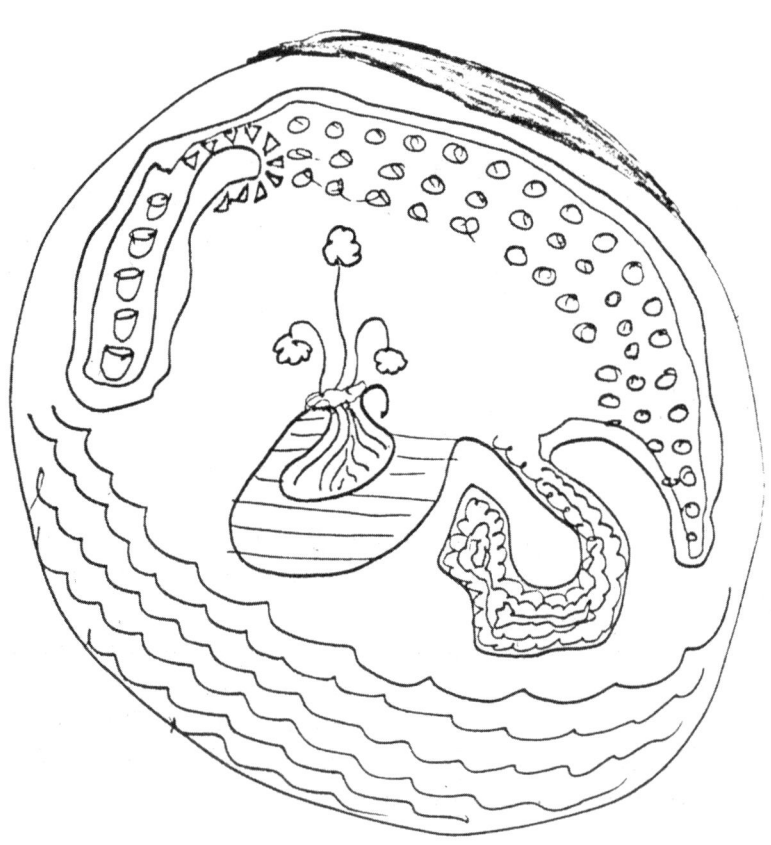

The Crucible of Healing. The pyramid point at the base of the mandala with its center of emerald green speaks of a healer.

The pyramid point forming the circle of the Lotus etched in violet and blue shows integrity in the Hippocrates' scale of healing.

The flames at the meridian or uttermost point of the healing-crucible mandala show this one to be a Saturn initiate.

The dark blue flames indicate a Truth-person who must be at one with his conscience.

The Soul-Gate of this mandala testifies to the utilization of past-life knowledge.

The right side of this mandala with its jagged lines or sharp lines indicates willing sacrifice for the sake of mastery.

The tear drops falling from the sword of surgery making the cross from Soul to Ego Gates indicate suffering from the past has produced sensitivity of healing.

The Flame and the Music. This mandala speaks of the Flame and the Music. The Flame leaning more to the left, forming a Saint Andrew's Cross, shows this disciple to be off-center and out of coordination of soul-forces.

Shaded portions of the Mandala at the Soul-Gate and the Ego-Gate indicate lack of self-confidence at the time of the mandala's making.

Gold, green and red, making up the flame, indicate soul healing power. Madonna blue in one portion of the Saint Andrew's Cross indicates a yin sympathetic absorbing nature.

The Saint Andrew's Cross yet to be centered is laid out for the initiate as his point of initiation to master moods of depression regarding his own worth. Such a mandala reveals to the maker that humility is his Path.

Bright crimson, blues and greens overshadow the depressive points — which show victory to come.

Mastery Through the Mandala 373

The Malta Cross and the Four Gates to Mandala Power.
The Lotus theme and the Cross in this mandala indicate the Christ initiate. The highest point of the mandala with the Cross head downward indicates this disciple to be a protege of Saint Peter.

The four heart butterflies reveal this person to be expressing the Fourth Light Stream under the direction of Saint Francis.

The color emphasis being sultry dark green indicates mastery over depression.

Touches of the color peach reveal etheric knowledge and abstract capabilities.

The inner Maltese Cross being dark red or the color of dried blood shows sacrifice as the key to Intentional Suffering as the Way.

THE FOUR MANDALA-GATES

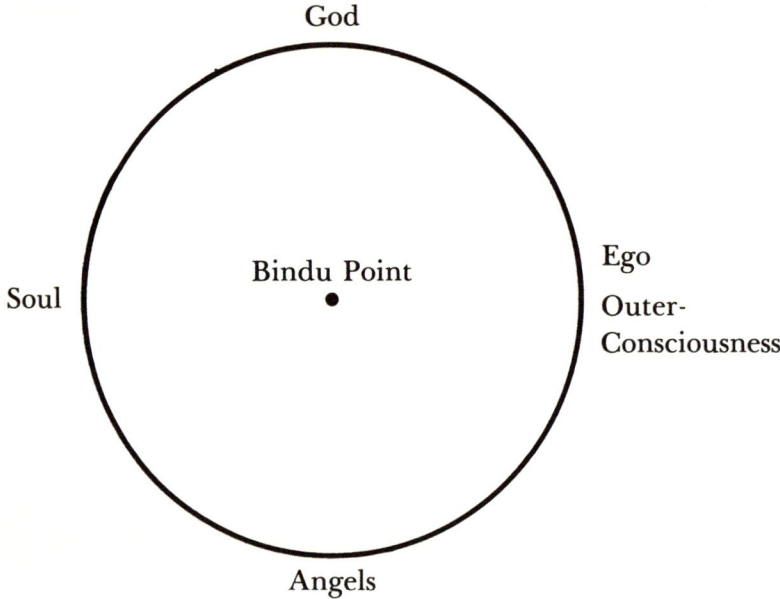

The Southern Gate is the Angelic Gate. The Left Gate is the Soul-Gate. The Topmost Gate is the God-Gate or Eternal Gate. The Right Gate is the Ego Outer-Consciousness Gate. The center is the Bindu Point, the entry to the Supreme Self.

How to make a mandala:
Use any size paper desired.
Put a plate down on the paper and draw a circle.
Use pencil, colored pencils, crayons, pastels, pen and ink or paints.
Before beginning your mandala, have a few seconds of silent contemplation. Ask God to speak through your Unconscious. Give thanks. Do not seek to draw or reproduce any vision you have had. Let the mandala be the canvas for your soul, and let the Esse-flow of the Holy Spirit flow into your hands, into your heart.

Put a dot (Bindu point) in the exact center.
Place the palette of colors before you and choose the colors to which you are drawn.
Start the flow of color from the Bindu point.
Let the Inner from your Unconscious come forth. Place on the paper the colors and designs according to your mood.
Do not intellectualize your mandala. Be careful to retain a feeling of receptivity. Let your soul speak to you in color so that you may unite with your soul's medallion and grace. The continued practice of the mandala results in mind-strength, soul-poise, and overflowing of spiritual gifts.

Everything in the mandala practice is learning the force and soul fields of the self, the mind and the emotions.

Persons are either electric, magnetic or dynamic. A person to be whole is dynamic, which is a balanced combination of the magnetic and the electric. The first three mandalas reveal the electric and magnetic balance.

A person who is over-critical draws a mandala showing too much electrical. In order to draw upon the holy magnetisms of charity, he should meditate upon the Heart Center, using a seed-mantra symbol of a flower in the heart.

When colors of muddy orange and brown are over-emphasized in a mandala, one should meditate upon the Heart Center each day. He should activate some form of sacrifice or selfless service without thought of gain.

If the colors in one's mandalas are too pale or vague, he should contemplate a holy countenance, such as the face of Jesus or Mary. He should reinforce his contemplation by speaking mantrams or mantras. Persons using pale colors should energize their life-forces by vigorous exercise through the use of the arms and hands. Yoga, walking or Esse movements are recommended. They should also master some form of bookkeeping, budgeting, or science of numbers. These provide practical organization of the soul-faculties.

The *electric* force in a mandala is identified by sharp, lightning-like jagged lines. The *magnetic* is portrayed by circles, spheres, ovals, tear-drops. The *dynamic* is expressed when the sharp lines and the circles are equally balanced.

The converted triangle signifies the dynamic. The inverted triangle signifies negation, depression; also expresses yin nature, timidity.

Dynamic is Androgynous. Magnetic is Feminine or yin. Electric is Masculine or yang.

1, 3, 5, 7 Initiatory and action (Electric).
3, 6, 9   Reverence and spirituality (Dynamic)
2, 4, 6, 8 Harmony (Magnetic)

The numbers in a mandala representing the masculine are 1, 3, 5, 7, and 9. The numbers in a mandala representing the feminine or yin are 2, 4, 6, 8.

The number of petals of a lotus appearing in a mandala determine whether the mandala is yin or yang.

Lotus: 2-petal – Duality.
3-petal – Yin and Yang Marriage.
4-petal – Karma.
5-petal – Speech.
6-petal – Creating.
7-petal – Initiation.
8-petal – Devachan mastery.
9-petal – Law.
10-petal – Hierarchy.

Yin Colors: Pink, red, orange, brown, purple.
Yang Colors: Yellow, blue, green, black, navy.
Yin: Oval, round, spherical.

Yang: Square, electrical, force fields, arrows, zig-zag lines.
Serpent: Yin-Yang. Kundalini.
All pastel colors are yin.
All strong colors are yang.
Faces are Prototypal Initiation.
Flowers: Grace.
Moon: Yin.
Sun: Yang.

The most frequent symbols appearing in a mandala are the cross, the pyramid, the triangle, the circle and the square, the lotus, and the serpent.

Angular lines which appear to be electrical represent electricities of the mind. The square represents karma, encasement, enclosure. The circle represents spherical oneness. However, without the Bindu controlling-point, a mandala is vacuous, with no meaning.

To consciously interpret what happens when one makes a mandala, he should visualize himself as rising over his body, looking down into the crown of his head. He should see the two hemispheres of the brain and also the frontal lobe of the skull and the brain stem in the back of the head as geometrical forming stations of consciousness of the transcendental.

Looking into his nostrils, left and right, he should see the Ida or yin polarity of breath in the left nostril. In the right or Pingala side of the head, he should see the breath as yang. He then should look to the top of the bridge of his nose and see these two flows crossing, one flowing the right side of the nostril's breath into the left side of the brain, which expresses the materialistic side of man. He should then see the left side or yin flow of breath flowing into the right hemisphere of the brain, which expresses the spiritual, the ultra-phenomenal, the transcendental.

Now seeing yin has become yang, and yang has become

yin, he sees the two hemispheres of the brain becoming one or androgynous. This is the true state of mind phenomena in the mandala, that one neutralizes the yin and yang into the oneness of God-Knowing, and thereby gathers both transcendental knowledge and unitive knowledge as related to the earth.

The total skull or head of man is a mandala. The head is the realm where self-knowledge is known and God-knowledge can be experienced. The mandala enables man to project the geometrical Yantra language of the soul onto the plain white paper. The soul-language flowing from the Bindu in the central point of the mandala explains one's self and desires.

The outer rim of the mandala is especially significant. The color, pattern and form one draws or makes on a mandala on the outer rim determine how he is breaking free from Undersoul density and ego-tension. This is called the *Thunderbolt* area of the mandala, which means blasting free of the disorganized tensions in mind and emotions. In loosening the tensions in the Thunderbolt area, one becomes spiritually daring, openly speaking as a channel for God.

If one desires to attain the greatest results from making a mandala, he should set up a mandala environment or atmosphere where twice a week his palette of colors and his rounded sphere drawn upon pure white paper will release and free that which is speaking through the soul's pulsation. In this, he will open the Imaging process in his own nature. He will unite with dream cognizance, the Coinciding Principle, Buddhi, the Informing Principle. In time, he will come to be in command of his own knowledge of Marking-and-Tracing processes.

Every mandala should be dated and initialed.

Mandala Contemplation

When your first mandala is perfected, place it on a small easel or stand it in front of your eye-level vision, approximately three to five feet away. If possible, hold the eyes without blinking or watering, and think of your deep desire to know God. Keep no other thoughts in mind. Look into the Bindu point. Use only once a day; begin with two minutes for each session, never more than ten minutes. Use until next mandala is expressed. Be alert in the days ahead, seeing the Marking and Tracing extended to respond to the higher supernal directives which come from reflecting upon God, the One.

Concentration upon one's own mandala for a short period each day, beginning with a two-minute period graduating up to a ten-minute period over a time of five months—adding two minutes each month—aligns one with his own soul's record of the past and also with the auric tone sounding from the True Self.

In the practice of the mandala, one melds the two hemispheres of the brain together so that the yin-yang flow of mind polarities in the outer consciousness are equalized; thus, one is open to superconsciousness in even the commonplace events of the physical life.

Every day one should observe all spiritual rhythmic practices and reap the joyful rewards of a centered life.

A mandala is the outpicturing of one's own soul-nature and soul-tone. A mandala should be centered as a flawless geometric design in the center of a canvas or paper with all parts equally balanced.

The mind is strengthened by creating a mandala. In mandala realization the mind is under control of the Higher Unconscious rather than the lower subconscious aspect of quelle.

To avoid wrong use of the mandala in concentration practice, one should never use a mandala as a personal problem-solver, a psychic vehicle to prove, or for psychic inquiry. The mandala is to be used by the Initiate as a contemplation receptor or to still the unruly forces of the lesser will and mind. *The mandala does reveal.*

The first mandala when fully formed provides the first progressive step to Self-Realization. Total dependency upon the mandala, however, will be controlled by the divine laws of equilibrium of the soul. If one steps over the ethic in the use of the mandala, he will cease to find it a fluidic means of revelation. If used with reverence, receptivity and as a dedication vehicle to *live out or functionalize* the stream-flow of higher thoughts resulting from regular contemplation and meditation, one should use the first mandala until another mandala appears in the natural order of etheric practice.

A mandala is a coordinator for cognition.

MANDALAS BY ANN REE COLTON

MEDIATIVE HEALING

THE CORNUCOPIA

THE MYSTIC ROSE

FLOWERS OF GRACE

Mastery Through the Mandala

CHASTITY

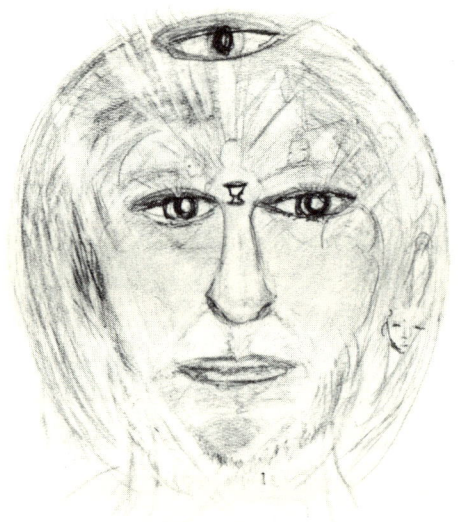

THE CHRIST WITHIN

16

THE THIRD MUSIC

My Mission as a Passing

I am not just a body.
I am a soul with a mission.
He who leads me toward my goals of the heart
    and soul comes as a Saviour
    with a crown of salvation.

My Jesus, a gift to me from God,
    is my Saviour.
Through Him, I will not falter.
I will fulfill within the skills of God.

From the Passion of Jesus, I have received my
    Passing.
From my Passing Point of mission,
    I mark and trace
    the trails of my being
    and the trials of my becoming.

Every diseased portion of the anatomy or the body of my conscience is being removed by the surgical appliances of the Holy Angels. One by one, each diseased part, or faulty part, is being clipped, cut, cauterized, that my conscience may become a foolproof, vital, verifying instrument.

For the perfect Word and Will of God to dwell in my conscience, I must be clean and whole. My well-being depends upon my conscience. If my conscience contains one tinge of the unholy, the whole of God cannot live in my conscience.

If my tongue be faulty against the tuning-fork of my conscience, I shall lose the power of speaking true. Therefore, I must erase, eradicate, all portions of partial-truth speaking.

My conscience must be as open as a plain having no trees, where the Sun of enlightenment and illumination shines upon each object between me and the horizon of Truth. Every object or every non-virtue having become a full and dimensional virtue will cast no shadow upon the plain, revealing the states of my conscience.

My conscience is a holy vehicle, a God-Voice speaking to me directly of the perfect and right thing to do, to say, to hear, to articulate. God is the Voice in my conscience. I no longer walk with non-hearing in the old gardens of confusion and misconception.

In my Constant I am conceived as a seed of God vibrating with rightness. My heritage and my potential are the Image of God dwelling in me as my Constant, pressing forth with the Increase of God.

I must strike out to strive for the whole calling in Christ. In this, a whole conscience will provide the way through which holiness as God will speak through me, in me and of me.

A perfect conscience will provide for me the perfect way, the perfect embodiment, the perfect knowing, that I may be with the Angels a shining light at home in the perfected spectrum as seen in the Imaging Power of God in me.

I have been washed in the synchronization process of many prototypal and ego forms. I have been challenged in the synthesis-making processes of becoming.

I am in a pure conscience never separated from my Constant where the Image of God wills me to do His perfect work, that His perfect Holy Word may reach those who crave to expand the soul-vibrancies of the Eternal through the conscience. Through my hierarchy nature, I throw off the negated images which have been impressed upon me by manipulating, distorted conscience and self-conceived ideas from the many.

The ear of my conscience will hear Truth, and glory in it. The mind of my conscience will know instantly a right and true thing. The heart of my conscience shall cease not in its rhythm of joy-linking with my Constant.

My conscience verifying God as Truth, as Reality, as Eternal Creation, ever in the state of Perfect Creation, shall beat rhythmically with the Tone of God sounding the life, for more life; light, for more light; love, for more love.

My conscience never sleeps. It is in a perpetual and eternal state of soul-vigilance. It is never absent from the measuring plumb-line of angelic assistance. My conscience shall move mountains, make worlds, heal diseases, extend God-knowing, provide transfusions, energies.

Everything in my life existing on human-plane knowing depends upon my conscience and my Constant. Every revealing aspect in my conscience is a gradated state of entering into the holy waters of revelation and informing through my Buddhi-lens of knowing.

My conscience cannot die. My Constant will never die.

That which makes memory comes from the union between my conscience and my Constant.

I have stepped into the electrified velocities of the holy waters. I have been immersed in trillions of baptisms provided by my conscience and my Constant. I am seeking to be washed clean and made whole under the tutelage of my conscience working with my Constant. I am in a holy state of holy joy immersed in the electrified waters of the cleansing vibrancies.

My conscience is a sharing vehicle. It cannot thrive in singular atmospheres of the ego, of the possessing. It is my very precious gift. It is indeed God's portion of Himself in me.

My conscience must be always under the commands of my Constant. God Himself lives in my Constant. The God-one I am to be as the Ultimate of my Constant and of God in me has been determined.

I must learn the difference between choice of the ego in me and the Will of God as destined in me. I must know through Marking and Tracing, the why of the rod, which comes against choice made by ego in me. I must be willing to work for the seed of the Eternal processed, and wait for the holy harvest of fulfillment.

My true Angel given to me from the beginning cannot live near my conscience when linked to ego and ego choice alone. It is the nature of the Angel assigned to each soul that he must stand and draw his polarity-energies from the light of the conscience over whom he watches, mediates, cherishes.

There are so many bliss-ways to be happy, but none of these comes until my conscience has reached a throttled state of throbbing rightness.

There is not a second or a moment of the day when I

am absent from conscience and my Constant. These are my teachers. And that which is God as the One in me dwells within these teaching states as given to all and to me.

The conscience is a memory-vehicle for the ego; but when it works with the Constant, it is a memory-vehicle for the Eternals.

There is an earth-memory, an ego-memory. There is a soul-memory. The greatest memory of all is the Eternal Memory, whereby God speaks through the Constant into the conscience, and man becomes the *chosen* of God. He walks the Path of the Eternal while remembering the Music playing in the intricate steps as notes and tones and sounds for the Third Music of God in the Constant.

Through the conscience, one weighs and judges omissions and also rightness for the ego's dance or walk in the earth. Through the Constant, the Greater Music is heard when linked to the conscience. The far-off music of the Constant is near and clear as a summoning bell tone calling the conscience to make the temple whole; to make the Architect or the Self a precise and perfect creator; to make the ego a perfect builder linked with the Creator in the Constant.

The pull of the polarities must be mastered. The Space between the conscience and the Constant must come together to become as one.

God as Will, God as Life, God as Light, God as Love in the Constant reveals the perfect hierarchy son-of-God to be. The wandering star must come home to the core of the Constant of God, whereby all worlds, all life-energies, all creating-processes work, that Creation may be ever in a state of perfect balance.

That which is normal to God is continuity in Creation.

That which is normal to man is continuity in birthing and dying. And that which provides the Third Music is God in the Constant.

The Third Music uniting dissonance with harmony breaks open, freeing the total harmonics between dying and living.

In the Third Music, one moves beyond division, duality, separateness, struggle.

That which lives in the Constant dies never. That which lives in the ego dies, but that which is the essence in the ego dies not, for the essence is the God-stuff by which the Eternal and the eternity are made one.

Revere Timing as you would revere the keeping of the flame to bake the perpetual Bread of God for the Altar. Revere Space as providing that vision and that perfected state of the Omnipresent in the future.

When the Constant has become perfectly balanced with the conscience, Time and Space are transubstantiated, and that which man calls soul-record of the Eternals is free to speak. And that which man calls the Higher Self, diamond-like and scintillating within the power of making forms, is elevated beyond partiality, beyond misconception. Then only can man be sattvic. Then only can the rajasic cease in its fiery asserting. Then only can tamas awake. For when the sattvic has come, conscience and the Constant are married, and Space has become the community flowing and interflowing in beginnings and endings. Beyond this, one is immersed as a hierarch or son of God in the energy processes of creation, of building, of knowing, of being.

The clearer the conscience, the closer the Third Music. The more active the Constant, nearer is the state of seeing God as the Spirit in all Creation.

A soaring soul is free in the Third Music, sealed into the Constant by the Constant of God. Where the Third

Music abides, one lives in the Coinciding Principle. Where the Third Music sounds, there is the performance, a celebration between the conscience and the Constant.

Like Job, I have not turned loose of my Constant.

The Covenant

Gather my saints together unto me; those that have made a covenant with me by sacrifice.
—Psalm 50:5

This very eternity system is a system of Intentional Suffering. We came into it with a covenant for Intentional Suffering. Eveything gained in this Earth is gained through suffering.

We entered this Earth to develop a certain kind of consciousness. As an eternity body, we are an offering to the Christ, through which He unites us with God.

There is no freedom of mind until one realizes that *Reciprocal Maintenance* supports all worlds and universes. Man creates through taking on the weight of Creation as willing creators with God.

There is no creation without renunciation. Jesus came to remind us that our covenant is to learn through pain, denial, want and frustration. His life example of Intentional Suffering provides us with the Way.

When Intentional Suffering is accepted as a way of life, joy and creation begin. One steps beyond the Maya penalties for unknowing into the glorious transcendental knowing. He is energized by acceptance of Intentional Suffering, producing the third vital or third vitality where the Third Music is operative in the life of all sentient and conscious beings. The more accepting of Intentional Suffering as the right Way and the Life and the Truth, the more one stands free of his suffering.

Those who bear the greater electrical velocities of Intentional Suffering are healers and anointers. Through them the Passing of the Kingdom is passed down to those who are yet to know the face of suffering as to its meaning.

The things one does to make other persons happy express a portion of Intentional Suffering. When one goes out of his way to make others happy at his own inconvenience, he is in the state of Intentional Suffering. When one undergoes prolonged servitude to a cause, sacrificing his ego and personalized desires, he is also in a state of Intentional Suffering, whereby the third vital as grace will bless him.

I cannot remember when I have not suffered in this life. When I was making wrong choice, I suffered. From this came Intentional Suffering and knowing of rightfulness, of truth. When I went out of the way to assume burdens of the weakness of those near me, I was in the state of Intentional Suffering. My personal unit of measure was in harmony to Reciprocal Maintenance when I assumed willingly unavoidable burdens placed upon me.

When I nursed my child, sick and weak, I shared the suffering of my child and experienced Intentional Suffering. When my child was healed through prayer and supplication and mediation, I was in the midst of grace, which is the natural result and response in Intentional Suffering.

When I took on the financial burdens of those who had lost their way in moral ethic as to debts, I experienced Intentional Suffering, and thereby opened the vital grace of prospering. This is what Jesus meant when He said: *". . . and him that taketh away thy cloke forbid not to take thy coat also." (St. Luke 6:29)*

In Reciprocal Maintenance, nothing is my possession; I may by grace have leased it or borrowed from my accumulation of grace. If I understand that possessions which I call "mine" belong to the Universal Reciprocal-Maintenance account, I then shall be bestowed with all forms of prospering under the Law of Reciprocal Maintenance, where I shall lack nothing.

In this moment and time, I am a lessee with stewardship ethic. Nothing I possess or any object which contains my name shall be a burden. Free from greed in my own nature through Intentional Suffering, my giving shall be unending, sharing the riches of Universal Maintenance.

Every thing I possess will have its own sense of direction, going where it will serve the best and support the true. Therefore, I shall not know theft or become the victim of covetousness, but things which are objectively necessary to my functioning will flow in and out of my life within units of measure as to my timing and need.

I shall not be done out of any inheritance because no man owes me, as a person, anything. God alone decides who shall will or give or share with me their stewardship prospering and grace.

In Intentional Suffering there are no laws manipulating my will which can touch me. Being filled with the virtue of the Maintenance of Suffering, I, having suffered all, am beyond that which seeks to force alien suffering upon me.

In Intentional Suffering, I am not notional or impulsive. Walking the sharp edge of Truth, that which I Am does not suffer. That which is seeking to think itself to be the I Am knows suffering because it does not know.

When Intentional Suffering is acceptable and functioning, the first impoverishment one puts away is unknowing. He becomes willing to learn, willing to take the leap into Buddhi, where the Informing Principle will make him aware that he is a Nisciene, a Knower.

In Reciprocal Maintenance, I can draw on the strength of those who sustain and support what I am as a unit of measure for God. I can draw on Nature, on the generosity of those who know Intentional Suffering and understand Reciprocal Maintenance. I can draw on the Saints and the Angels — all to succor me in my times of need to fortify what I am in service to God, as it is to their first vital interest as also to mine, that that which is true may be maintained as Truth, and that which is right may be maintained as Right. This is the Law upholding the Prophets and the Saints. Their virtues reinforce mine, and foresee my reinforcement for those who also knowingly activate the Kingdom of Reciprocal Maintenance.

When one sins, it does not only affect one's own need for restitution, but sinning sets up an unholy contagion, whereby all associated with one add their sins to his. As birds migrate in clusters, so must sinners return to Reciprocal Maintenance and seek to make restitution as a form of Intentional Suffering.

One person erasing sin in his own nature immunizes thousands of those who would turn to God. So is a bracework made against the seas of negation.

There are holy infections and unholy infections. He who carries the Light must enlighten. And he who carries the dark must die to that which makes him dark — which is sin.

Men are presently in the latter days of a darkened era. Now coming forth to be rajasic, they must face and trace through Marking and Tracing their errors. They must be willing to be totally helpless and surrendered to the Light, for sin is so filled with self-justification that it is ever seeking to falsify its right to sin.

One must enter into the cool silence of Niscience or Knowing that he is limitless, infinite, eternal. By this comparison, a sinner sees how small he really is in his self-importance.

Inasmuch as sin is limited, it is also perishable. So, when sin dies to sinning, where is the sin?

Only the belief that one is happy in sinning sustains a life of sinning. The greatest lie told by Maya is that man is in the earth for total self-pleasure at the cost of anything or anyone. This is the first sin: to believe in privilege, superiority.

It is a lie to believe in separateness and to foster a life built upon separation. There is no separation and there is no death; of that which is divine in us, there is union.

Holy Poverty is the most substantial stewardship existing in the world, for it is part of Intentioanl Suffering taken on through a desireless, selfless nature.

Impoverishment may be experienced in rich and prosperous households by one who makes himself involatile through greed and laziness and parasitism. Impoverishment on the level of karma has been caused by one's unwillingness to work. His karma has decided his poverty, for he has detached himself from his own vital volatile creativity in times past, and thus his hunger comes from his refusal to participate as a steward in the energized processes within the life-force.

The spiritual life requires that one travel light, unencumbered by possessions that possess him. To serve God on the Path, one must be enlightened as to right possessions.

An honest laborer is worthy of his hire. What he gives with his heart is worth more than what he gives with his body. If both heart and body are given, this is a steward crowned in prospering.

> *In the center of Substance, I am.*
> *In the center of God's Gift of Life, I am.*

*In the center of God's Prospering in me,
I am His gift to give, to share.*

The Yoke

Come unto me, all ye that labour and are heavy laden, and I will give you rest. Take my yoke upon you, and learn of me; for I am meek and lowly in heart: and ye shall find rest unto your souls. For my yoke is easy, and my burden is light.
—St. Matthew 11:28-30

In this period of intense astrolocity psychism, men have lost the key to the meaning of suffering. The greatest illumination received during initiation is that one discloses to himself the cause of his suffering.

Any one who enters the Path with the intention of healing others and teaching others enters into Intentional Suffering.

At this time, the initiate is offered the opportunity to take upon himself Intentional Suffering. Through Intentional Suffering, hierarchy nature and Self-Genesis nature act as one. One frees himself from suffering through taking on the sufferings of the world. By this and through this, one becomes a transenergizing healer.

The meaning of the Crucifixion of Jesus is laid open to him at this time. And he truly comes to know and experience the *yoke* of Jesus. His labors become light within the Light. His Ahimsa heart nature bleeds for those who bleed. By this, afflictions are accounted as glory.

The planet Earth and the Saints work within the sacrificial enfoldment of birth. The Earth is groaning in its growing. The sound of this growth can be heard with the extended ear given through suffering. On the terms of Universal Creation, all things born with unknowing must struggle to enter into the mastery of self-awareness, whereby consciousness is born.

Intentional Suffering is an empathy far deeper than sympathy. It is an empathy carrying both divine responsibility and detachment.

The whole Universe is controlled by Reciprocal Maintenance, and it is natural for the strong to have a greater responsibility than the weak. However, each must carry his own weight in the Universal Morality. One being placed at the point of Intentional Suffering is but partially effective if he is unaware of the part he plays in the maintenance of Universal Harmony.

It was not human assumption in Jesus when He took upon Himself the sufferings of an eternity system. His point of Intentional Suffering produces for mankind *polarization,* whereby one may make restitution for his personalized weaknesses and for his resistance toward moral responsibility in life of the earth.

One should be patient in his learning of Intentional Suffering. Intentional Suffering has been with us since we started out in this eternity system, called *Earth.* Intentional Suffering does not take over one's life in a single lifetime as in the case of Jesus. It is a natural encounter with pain through the sound-tone current of the Earth. Every life has some degree of pain. God gave man pain so that he may experience its opposite, joy. God works to give men mastery over pain through Jesus. Pain is the mid-wife to bring consciousness of a higher order. Pain creates new states of mind.

I move beyond the vibration of fear
in the peace of Knowing in Christ.

Salvation

> *Therefore I endure all things for the elect's sakes, that they may also obtain the salvation which is in Christ Jesus with eternal glory.*
> —*2 Timothy 2:10*

The Saints have become Saints because of their Intentional-Suffering martyrdoms. In the Law of Reciprocal Maintenance, they work with those who have taken upon themselves Intentional Suffering for the salvation of others.

The word *salvation* means to salvage, or to bring up from the impossible. To transenergize evil-carelessness is to pass salvation to others, salvaging their good that it may be used for those whose morality has been weakened by exposure to evil.

To call on the Saints is to be *salvaged* and to stand in the passageway of Salvation. To loosely use the word "salvation" by saying that one has been "saved" is to remain as a wolf in sheep's clothing. The word "saved" in its saintly and spiritual sense means to have received salvation through the emissary works of the Saints.

He who believes himself to be saved and continues with evil companions, giving amoral acceptance to immoral acts, is not saved, neither has he known salvation. Such of these are spewed out and are in no degree to be considered saved or salvaged from evil works.

To walk another mile for Jesus develops saintliness. However, to ignore evil and to fail to follow the precepts of self-restitution and helps for the restitution of others is to remain in a neutral field, which is to be neither for good nor for evil. He who indulgently looks upon vice or deviation from the laws of purification dwells in the gray shadows of unenlightenment.

God is *Light*. In His Light there is neither variableness nor darkness.

Some are born to this world to contest evil. If they use this virtue with complacency, they become evil and eventually evil motivators of others.

There are two things in which we are bound together: we are bound together in our sins; and we are bound together in our souls. We are all morally responsible for each other's sins. In the Lord's Prayer it says: "Forgive us our trespasses, as we forgive those who trespass against us." We have to pray for the majority because the majority is involved in sin.

We pray as being with the majority in sinning. There are sins in our nature which are a mystery which we do not understand as being a part of the associated morality principle.

The worth of the human race is no greater than its accumulated sin-body, and no more reliable than the human-race conscience.

So Christ was once offered to bear the sins of many; and unto them that look for him shall he appear the second time without sin unto salvation.
—*Hebrews 9:28*

HOLY REMISSION

Then opened he their understanding, that they might understand the scriptures, And said unto them, Thus it is written, and thus it behoved Christ to suffer, and to rise from the dead the third day: And that repentance and remission of sins should be preached in his name among all nations, beginning at Jerusalem. And ye are witnesses of these things.
—*St. Luke 24:45–48*

Those having Holy Remission Powers coming from sanctification do the impossible in the midst of Intentional Suffering. Such sanctified ones can stop instantly the bacterial progress in sickness, making non-infectious the diseases considered terminal and fatal.

The Silver Cord and the Archetypal Cord of sanctified ones have a vibrancy elevation intensity beyond the vibrations of disease. In their own states of dying, they undergo prolonged releasement from earth through death. In this period and time, their sanctified jurisdiction to heal and to teach is powerful.

Ailing ones in the earth touched by the aura of Saints in the state of dying receive dispassionate, non-intrusive healing energy-processes. Their recuperations, healings and responses are retained. An enlargement of these Holy-Remission effluvias comes through the refined spiritual processes as life transfusions, strength-supporting and vital encouragements.

Out of the very electricities of Intentional Suffering is Creation.

The Path of Intentional Suffering

Though he were a Son, yet learned he obedience by the things which he suffered; And being made perfect, he became the author of eternal salvation unto all them that obey him.
—Hebrews 5:8–9

The Path of Jesus is the Path of Intentional Suffering. Jesus, in taking on the suffering of the world, labors unceasingly. Through Intentional Suffering on the Cross, He mediated for all in the world. Jesus was the Scapegoat for the souls of all men.

You are not ready for Intentional Suffering until you are ready to take the Cross. There is nothing more dynamic than sacrifice.

The Path is very serious; it must not be played with.

Every time I take on suffering, I am releasing people from their Undersouls so that they can come into Enlightenment. When this occurs between me and one or a cluster of students, it is not that they are seeking to do this to me; it is that I am as their accepted Teacher undergoing Intentional Suffering.

In the heart pain I suffer, each time I am close to death; that those for whom I suffer must die to their sins. In this Intentional Suffering which I take upon myself, I undergo labor pains through my heart, that those who turn to me with the weight of their suffering may be healed.

I am taking on the group suffering. I am making it easier for them to enter into their practices and to simplify and glorify their lives.

I am a scapegoat for the healing of others. I make restitution for their sins which also include my own sins in this life and other lives.

Jesus in the core of my heart gives the freedom to make restitution for my sins and the sins of others. To call on His Name is to be instantly in His Presence, which resides in the core of my heart. When I place my weakness in Him and the weaknesses of those I would heal, I receive the instant twinkling-of-an eye healing for the cause in the sin which caused the sickness.

The whole New Testament is Intentional Suffering and the victory over suffering and death. To me, that is my religion.

I have taken on Intentional Suffering to discover new and expanded gifts of healing.

Take, my brethren, the prophets, who have spoken in the name of the Lord, for an example of suffering affliction, and of patience.

—*James 5:10*

There is persecution within reasonable limits, teaching one. Persecution *beyond* reasonable limits produces Intentional Suffering on the persecuted, whereby he becomes one with the Christ on the Cross.

Intentional Suffering by masses of people in one nation is used to arouse mercy in a yang nation knowing not the use of mercy.

Men have to learn how to use their mercy by the utilizing of their gifts, for gifts without mercy are but talents dwelling on the psychological level of man. Gifts with mercy stem from the Christ through the door of Jesus, the Saviour of the world.

The right Path, the straight Path, is the Path of Intentional Suffering. Spiritual life is a life of participation. Service to God is in its most perfect setting when one has reached the time of Intentional Suffering, accepting it as the yoke Passed to him by Jesus.

All who enter the Path through the door of metaphysics reach the time when they must understand what is asked of them: Intentional Suffering. For there is no other way to proceed in the Spiritual Path until one assumes his share of the burdens of the world. By this, he finds his point of Light and accepts his soul-station as a sentinel for God.

All in the earth who are sleeping to their conscience are seeking to live in the Pleasure Principle.

Persons entering the ego-metaphysical door seek to follow the Pleasure Principle. They gain the world and lose touch with their souls.

Many today expressing the prospering side of the Pleasure Principle have forsaken the Name *Jesus* on the Altar and in the marketplace. The choice of the Old Testament's use on the Altar is predominantly used in the church so that men may be aware of the laws of karma which relate themselves to the Family-Genesis level of conscience. Also, the Old Testament, emphasizing tribal laws rather than the Sattvic laws of the inner-part natures, is being spoken on the Altar to those who have failed to move with the interflow of the Christ through Jesus.

The Gospels are a guiding principle for the Intentional-Suffering Path. The life of Jesus in every degree laid down the Blueprint for the Intentional-Suffering Path.

The Book of Revelation, which promises the spiritual ultimates for man and mankind, leads the one who has accepted the Intentional-Suffering Path disciplines into the true Initiation of Deathlessness and Everlasting Life. The church defined in the Book of Revelation, karmically laden with latent emotions and desires, indicates that more than individual man is being researched through Hierarchy Law. The church must come to salvation and return to the true mystical body for the Holy Spirit, where Christ may resound His Logos and the Spirit may say to the churches: *"He that hath an ear, let him hear what the Spirit saith unto the churches." (Revelation 3:22).*

Who is hearing the seed when it is hurting, when it is crying? Who is hearing? Who is hurting? Who is hearing the suffering when it is suffering? Who is crying?

The Crown of Thorns and the Householder

Then Pilate therefore took Jesus, and scourged him. And the soldiers platted a crown of thorns, and put it on his head, and they put on him a purple robe.
—St. John 19:1–2

Jesus works as co-atom through those who take upon themselves Intentional Suffering. As householders in His Household, we walk with Him the Path of Intentional Suffering.

The disciple on the Path of Intentional Suffering must contend with the World Undersoul.

Every person who is agnostic and cynical concerning Jesus contributes to the thrust of the thorns on the Crown of Jesus. The agnostic is superciliously insensitive to compassion, mercy. His ego-environment is limited to self-supremacy. He sees the one who must transubstantiate the rust in the nail holes into glory as stupid.

The agnostic cannot live in the Household of Jesus. He cannot know the code-key to the Passion containing the Passing, nor can he know the transenergizing of the bitter poison, of the taking of the Cup. Agnosticism is an agony path.

It is important that we face ourselves; this is one part of Intentional Suffering. The energy that comes from facing oneself and being honest flows out as compassion for all others who make mistakes.

When a mother has many problems with her children, this is Intentional Suffering. Or if a man works to earn money for his family in a work that does not satisfy his vocational desires, this is Intentional Suffering. When a person takes on the care of a person to comfort him in his latter years, this is Intentional Suffering.

He who walks the Path of Intentional Suffering must open the stigmata points of the nail holes through his own suffering. To clear the rust from the nail holes invites the crowning of the thorns, where mental pain as a fire frees the buds of knowing in the Crown of Knowing.

He who wears the Crown of Thorns as a householder in the Household of Jesus has made the bitter, sweet; has made the rust into living waters; has made the Crown of Thorns into Illumination.

Then said he unto them, Therefore every scribe which is instructed unto the kingdom of heaven is like unto a man that is an householder, which bringeth forth out of his treasure things new and old.
—*St. Matthew 13:52*

RECIPROCAL MAINTENANCE AND INTENTIONAL SUFFERING

Those who have the Passing have been through Intentional Suffering—and they have the Third Music.

Intentional Suffering moves into non-suffering where suffering directly below the achievement of Intentional Suffering exists in another dimensional state of consciousness. Pain experienced in the sub-octave planes of ego-suffering is suffering singularized to one's personal experience and learning.

Pain is the sculptor of consciousness. Pain one suffers in the acceptable Intentional Suffering exists on the wavelengths of compassion for all suffering.

Profound compassion attained through direct Intentional Suffering anesthetizes pain, placing it upon the wavelengths of dimensional understanding in all relationships. In this, healing techniques come forth as special anointings of grace. Vibrations of pain in one who intentionally suffers are obliterated through willingness to experience pain as the alchemizer to produce a greater chemistry in life-substances of the soul.

Sickness is a vibration of dissonance. Through sickness, one experiences alien, opposing energy masses uncoordinated to emotions and thought. The discordant vibrations of pain occur when the three energized matrixes upholding the skeletal structure of the bodies are out of alignment with one another. Contemplation, meditation, the speaking of mantras, uniting with Buddhi — the Informing Principle — all assist in bringing the three matrix molds into harmony with one another.

Emotions and thoughts alien to one's own essential purity produce discordant stridency in the three matrix bodies. This in turn affects the etheric-matrix molds sustaining each organ of the body. In sickness, one of three organs at a time may be discordant to one another, producing disruption of cellular union and harmony.

The movement of Esse, the creating of a mandala, the state of meditation, the speaking of a mantra, prayer — these spiritual postures are levitation energy-processes enabling one to move into the state of pure and original health as designed in God's intent for man.

In sickness, one must realize that the organ or the portion of the body sick indicates what emotion is out of alignment. Marking and Tracing will enable one to track down and identify what emotion is creating the intensified energy collectivity.

The physical body is a perishable body. The lesser etheric body is also perishable. All other bodies are permanent bodies. The permanent bodies of man live after physical death. The three energy matrixes supporting these bodies also live after death.

The physical body is a Time-machine limited to units of measure, of expression as related to karma. Physical-body life is a leap into the mastery of earth atomic energies and of molecular dispensation.

Each earth experience is limited in time. Therefore, death comes to the physical body and the lesser etheric body.

Life after death is a life of refinement of energies operating at etheric levels. Men are learning that mind, thinking and consciousness are energy states. After-death experience provides the expansion of these energy states on levels of refinement and sensitivity.

All after-death experiences are preparation to return through reincarnation to an earth-body experience where a mastery of Nature forces, inclusive of atomic forces, is experienced.

In the life of Intentional Suffering, one accepts the fact that he is on a sojourn in the physical world which is overdirected by his soul-nature. Intentional Suffering has neither a back door nor a front door to consciousness. Life and death are one in the ever-flowing river of consciousness.

After-death consciousness is not obliteration to what one has experienced as consciousness in the physical life. After-death consciousness is an experience of consciousness dimensional-perception limited only by one's energy capacity as to units of measure in going in and going out in the physical into the spiritual.

It is the plan of God for all in the earth to be given a time-limit period to live in the physical world. In each life, one extends his range of learning. What he takes with him at death determines what he will bring with him to earth-existence in coming lives.

Presently, the knowledge of the Marking-and-Tracing system as the way to free the stagnating energies within the Undersoul is the opening to greater vistas in dimensional consciousness after death and also in life. One can only come to full knowledge of Intentional Suffering through the Marking-and-Tracing techniques used in the cleansing of the Undersoul. This is true salvation or salvaging of the old energies transenergized into the new.

Reciprocal Maintenance, when applied through cosmic

interrelationships, produces a new canvas for the master artist, which is the Soul. Reciprocal Maintenance and Intentional Suffering are self-realized as two conjoined and inevitable processes whereby man becomes more than man; he becomes a son of God, or as Jesus said: *"I said, Ye are gods." (St. John 10:34)*

If men are sons of God, they are deities-in-the-making. What is a deity? He is one who, through extended states of consciousness, sees all galaxies, all starry bodies, all eternity systems as one within the one directing Deity over all.

If man is imaged in the likeness of God, he must realize this likeness and fulfill it by earth visitation. By heavenly resuscitation, he eternally sojourns in whatever state of consciousness Time and Space allow him.

Men are now coming to master *light,* not light as of the Sun, but light as of God. This light knows neither Time nor Space.

Intentional Suffering assumes a responsibility through grace: a grace-knowing, a grace-awareness of one's own sacred responsibility. Life centered in God; immune to fears related to death, disease, to failure—the Intentional Sufferer carries a cargo which must be left at each station.

There are no self-delivered persons in this world. Deliverance comes from unison with the Laws of God. The Intentional Sufferer is *in* the Law. He is therefore the anointer, the healer, the teacher.

Jesus, the most Profound of all Intentional Sufferers, has laid down the way for the Path. It is His Path we must follow. His Ethic we must give heed to. His Abounding Grace of love we must cling to. We must draw upon our own souls' maintenance which resides within His Soul-Maintenance.

The Coinciding Principle works automatically with

Reciprocal Maintenance. The Coinciding Principle supports Intentional Suffering by providing the soul acoustical language animating all living souls.

The Great Organizing Principle and Reciprocal Maintenance work as one within the Law and the Will of God. The Coinciding Principle is the voice for these, whereby one is instructed within the Buddhi or Informing Principle.

The inner voices of guidance, the expanding flowers of intuition, budding and growing—all are experienced within the Coinciding Principle which is the language of Reciprocal Maintenance.

He who abides in Jesus abides in God. The language of God is heard throughout the Earth and in Heaven as one Language spoken by the soul-tongue within the Coinciding Principle.

If one would live within his own Constant, drawing upon his Intentional-Suffering Grace, he will do these things as Jesus admonished him. He will rise up as did the first Apostles to follow Jesus.

On the Cross, Jesus set the rhythm for Intentional Suffering. In the Garden of Gethsemane, by acceptance of the Will of God, He entered into the World Intentional Suffering, and thereby opened to mankind as a whole a way to rise to its divine nature as being one with God.

Whatever burden is placed upon you, accept it. Look upon it as an opportunity to experience the Reciprocal-Maintenance reinforcements of enlightenment, knowledge, and spiritual power.

That which is disenchantment in you as fantasy, cleanse away with the broom of Marking and Tracing.

Your truth, your morality, your ethic, all depend upon your realization that you are a unit of measure reinforced by uncountable resources of love, of healing, of manifestation.

Let all of your dreams be in wakeful cognizance of knowing God as the One.

Let all of your waking hours be moments and seconds of awareness of God and your oneness with Him as Spirit Eternal.

Your freedom comes when you use your creation; also, when you learn the law of noninterference with the Plan and Will of God. Your self-respect begins when you cease intruding upon the will of others.

Fantasy in you desires to manipulate, to impose, and to shift your burdens. Self-responsibility begins with the first breath in the state of Maya life. Self-control begins when one recognizes the value of his own will to make choice, decisions; and especially when he becomes aware of the scales in the balance of karmas. When this occurs, one knows the rightness of God and the Justice within the Law of God.

Humility is Intentional-Suffering Grace-nature. Generosity, forgiveness, all of these express one's true and eternal nature. A magnified soul is a magnanimous identity, displaying the treasures of God which are unending in creation.

> *Beyond the tears, you have to hear*
> *the beat of the Music in the suffering.*
> *You have to hear the Music beyond the tears.*
> *The beat of the Music is in the heart, in*
> *the soul, where the symphony*
> *swells and sounds and roars.*
> *You have to hear the Music beyond the bird.*
> *You have to hear the Music in the water, in*
> * the wind.*
> *The Music has a beat; it has a tempo sweet.*
> *You have to hear the Music, the Music, the Music.*

The Third Music

You have to hear the Music in the feet.
You have to hear the Music in the morn, in the
  night, in the sleep.
You have to feel the Music in the dance.
You have to hear the Music in the tremors
  of your fears.
You have to hear the Music in the bleating
of the sheep, in the wings of the butterfly.
You have to hear the Music in the morning's
breaking of the bread.
You have to hear the Music in the discords of
  the hates.
You have to hear the Music in the burdens
  heavy, strong.
In the dance, in the dance, you have to hear
  the Music. It is there.

INDEX

A

abortion 10, 313
Acting Principle 215
Adam 308
Adepts 307
Admonishing Principle 253
adultery 46
after-death shell 241
afterlife 33
Agape 19, 24, 34, 35, 67, 136, 157, 183, 217, 222
Age of Light 6
Agni 94
agnostic 10, 187, 228, 406
Ahimsa 171, 184, 196, 198, 200-202, 222, 398
akash 26, 212, 282
alcohol 55-57, 238, 244
altar 100-103
amorality 237, 238
ancestors 30, 31, 46, 50, 62, 124, 136, 137, 184, 222, 299, 306, 312
Ancestral Rosary 299-302
Angels 12, 38, 57, 61, 68, 93, 101, 120, 121, 135, 154, 158, 164, 194, 209, 214, 230, 231, 254, 289, 292, 301, 302, 306, 333, 342, 358, 374, 387, 389, 390, 396
   Celestial 357
   Kingdom 237
   Guardian 28, 68, 184, 248, 305
   Luminosity 68
   Niscience 68
   Pure Desire 68
   Recording 68, 93, 184, 193, 256, 305
   Seraphim 214
   Species 164, 243, 257
   Warring 5
Ancient of Days 93, 168, 248
androgynous 50, 51, 216, 376, 378
anger 42, 43, 118, 258
animal(s) 164, 207, 231, 243, 244, 256, 257, 310, 332
anointing 69, 196, 209, 210, 331, 394, 410
Antakarana 22, 23, 72, 156
anti-matter 197
Apostles 69, 411
Archangel(s) 69, 100, 357
   Luciferic 92, 170, 244, 287
   Saturn 344
Archetone(s) 101, 278, 280, 281, 287, 308, 327
   Sound 152, 308, 317
Archetypal 129, 139, 154, 162, 175, 176, 185, 186, 199, 200, 204, 205, 207,

216, 227, 243, 245, 277, 281, 283, 290, 308
Consciousness 126
Cord 86, 360, 402
Day 39, 43
Hum 294
Ideas 94, 164
Image(s) 293, 361
Kingdom 200, 201
Knowing 142-145
Light 85, 200, 202, 204
Logos 311
Path 220, 336
Power, Laws of 202
Presence 200
Realm 202, 281, 306
Samadhi 144
Symbols 358
System 202, 205, 217
Wisdom 171
Worlds 226, 347
Archetype(s) 184, 199, 275, 276, 280, 281, 291
  Destroying 48, 92, 185, 202, 204, 206, 274
  Greater 69, 95, 106, 152, 199, 202-204, 206, 308
  Moving 97, 200-206, 287
Aries 164
Asana man 303, 304
ascension 65, 69
  of Jesus 242, 251
astral 11, 15, 22, 26, 35, 42, 46, 54, 88, 109, 111, 125, 128, 133, 138, 158, 161, 167, 168, 183, 197, 201, 227, 292, 295, 363, 398
astral world 5, 45, 55, 244, 348
atheist 10, 187
Atma 141, 145, 299
atmosphere(s) 10, 18, 26, 35, 39, 111, 134, 154, 159,

166, 196, 209, 274, 280, 282, 341, 378, 390
Atom(s) 3, 9, 11, 21, 73, 88, 102, 107, 131, 132, 161, 166, 197, 206, 211, 213, 230, 237, 238, 247, 265, 282, 292, 293, 346-350, 408, 409
  Emotional 51, 52, 96
  Eternal 131, 132, 184, 185, 283
  Eternal Sustaining 86, 132, 271, 276, 316, 347
  Family 203, 217, 241-243, 301, 302, 306, 310
  Heart 131
  Indestructible 131, 195-197, 227, 271, 272, 288, 316, 318, 319, 343
  Mental 51, 52, 247
  Sacred 340
  Seed 344, 345
  Spiritual 185
attitude(s) 31, 55, 59, 134, 264, 290, 345, 365
Audible Hum 281, 360
aura 48, 106, 107, 152
Avatars 47

B

Baptism 97, 98, 100
beauty 6, 11, 267, 359
Bhakti 42, 96-101, 103, 104, 157, 166, 222
Bible 249
Bindu Center 58, 59, 296, 357-360, 368, 374-379
birth 4, 7, 8, 10, 12, 30, 31, 35, 37, 46, 47, 51, 80, 123, 127, 129, 131, 136-138, 143-145, 183, 190, 201, 203, 220, 225, 292, 299,

302, 305, 309, 312, 313,
  321, 345, 346, 392, 398
Bioform   137
Biotron   139, 140
Bi-polarity Laws   154
bliss   16, 17, 20, 46, 63, 75,
  78, 87, 96, 149, 189, 227,
  281, 390
blood   24, 25, 154, 203, 210,
  211, 215, 216, 248, 278,
  302, 307, 308, 355
Bodhisattva   15, 73, 247
bones   355
brain   8, 9, 90, 136, 157, 181,
  190, 191, 279, 284, 293,
  296, 325, 339, 350, 351,
  355, 377-379
Bread of the Sacrament   210-
  213, 215, 217-219, 392
breath   8, 21, 59, 296, 314,
  340, 377, 412
Buddha   188, 189
Buddhi   42, 62, 72, 77, 86,
  90, 124, 131-133, 141,
  143, 154, 156, 165, 171,
  181, 205, 206, 213, 271,
  272, 279, 281, 285, 288,
  294, 316, 360, 378, 389,
  395, 408, 411
butterfly   291-293, 373, 413

C

Cancer (sign)   53
Causal System   217
cell(s)   24, 52, 62, 191, 193-
  195, 216, 248, 293, 355,
  408
  Omniscient   90
Chakra(s)   14, 15, 44, 54, 55,
  94, 131, 248, 281, 283,
  287, 292, 317, 342
  Fifth   365

First   236, 237
Fourth   55, 221, 237, 246,
  281, 316
Second   54, 202, 237
Sixth   94
Third   55, 237, 324
upper   326
character   31, 56
charity   117, 222
chastity   77, 132
Cherubim   93, 117, 190, 240
child(ren)   139, 172, 174, 211,
  233, 255, 302, 305, 307,
  311-315, 321, 346, 406
Christ   12, 13, 15, 31, 45, 46,
  50, 73, 77, 110, 129, 137,
  140, 142, 162, 167, 186,
  187, 197, 199, 201-203,
  210-212, 215-218, 226-
  230, 252, 261, 262, 271,
  274, 284-287, 289, 294,
  296, 299, 316, 337, 343,
  348, 357, 365, 369, 393,
  399, 401, 404, 405
  Initiate   373
  Mind   163, 170, 216, 247,
    283, 284, 293, 363
  Name of   291
  Samadhi   334
Christmas   212
chromosomes   342, 343
co-atom   66, 164, 204, 228,
  230, 306, 406
Coinciding Principle   18, 83,
  141, 149-163, 167, 170,
  173, 176, 177, 180, 181,
  206, 266, 317, 322, 324,
  337, 358, 360, 378, 393,
  410, 411
Collective Unconscious   199,
  200
color(s)   98, 359, 360, 364,
  365, 368, 371-378

coming lives 251, 256, 345, 409
Command Mantram, Living Body 343-355
Commandments 40, 41, 225, 234-238, 266
 Ten 46, 235-238, 350
compassion 15, 228, 256, 266, 406, 407
confession 159, 239, 256, 261
conscience 5, 22, 25-27, 30, 41, 45, 47, 49, 52, 72, 77, 79, 84, 95, 109, 114, 133, 137, 140, 149, 157, 168, 169, 177, 178, 184, 187, 190, 204, 220-222, 232-235, 237, 239, 240-242, 244, 246-248, 251, 254-260, 263, 279, 350, 362, 371, 387-392, 401, 404, 405
Constant 4, 139, 152, 160, 176, 180, 181, 185, 186, 188, 189, 271-274, 276, 303, 306-309, 311, 316-321, 336, 337, 340, 341, 358, 388-393, 411
 of God 74, 151, 186, 336, 391
Constellations 167, 303
Continuum Sacrament 208-231, 337
contrition 208, 209, 226, 241, 248, 249, 256, 262, 264
Correcting Principle 179, 194, 252, 253
Cosmos 3-9, 13, 14, 26, 129, 169, 170, 192, 219, 223, 229, 281, 304
 Disciples 167, 175, 203
 Genesis 203
courage 157, 158, 190
covetousness 194

creed 102
Cross 211, 228, 230, 296, 326, 373, 402-404, 411
Crown of Jesus 406
Crown of Thorns 228, 229, 406, 407
Crucifixion 77, 251, 398
cycle(s) 3, 4, 7, 8, 14, 45, 48, 51, 57-59, 62, 127, 140, 157, 172, 174, 178, 185, 188, 197, 200, 203, 204, 206, 212, 285, 288, 306, 307, 310, 330, 361
 Etheric 346
 Initiatory 323
 Law of 190
 Lazarus 323
 Lunar 59, 91
 Prodigal-Son 201
 Reincarnation 282

D

dancing 71, 128, 413
Darshan 153, 214
death 4, 6, 8, 45, 47, 80, 88, 91, 123, 127, 130, 131, 141, 143, 144, 161, 186, 195, 198, 225, 226, 228, 231, 241, 245, 248, 263, 264, 292, 296, 299, 309, 321, 335, 337, 338, 340, 341, 345, 392, 402, 403, 408-410
demonic 54-57, 59, 61, 158
depression 53, 54, 59, 185
Dervish 68, 71
desire(s) 26, 42, 43, 46, 48, 57, 62, 68, 101, 123, 324, 363, 378, 394
Destiny 285, 347
Destroying Archetype(s) 48, 185, 202, 204, 206, 274

INDEX 419

Destroying Principle 245
detachment 140, 399
Devachan 46, 155, 158, 159, 227, 244, 376
Devas 69, 107, 154, 231
devotion 246, 257, 285, 357
Dharma 153, 166, 167, 216, 233, 250-253, 303, 333, 358
Diamond Medallion 347
diary 113, 153
dimensional consciousness 197, 201, 284, 285, 339, 407
disciples 69, 89
disease(s) 28, 39, 158, 183, 184, 190, 191, 194-196, 228, 233, 248, 258, 320, 344, 389, 402, 410
Divine Companions 172, 173, 226, 264, 333
Divine Eye 170
Divine Harmonics 6, 7
divine matrix 185, 186
Divine Mother 133, 213, 228, 297, 333
  Rosary 297-299
Divine Thalamus 271, 318, 336, 337
dream(s) 23, 26, 53, 67, 76, 83, 95, 96, 178, 180, 181, 191, 212, 213, 221, 222, 234, 249, 264, 295, 306, 311, 321, 347, 358, 378, 412
  Diary 83, 91, 95, 178
drugs 55-61, 237, 244, 323
Dwapara-Yuga 283

E

earthbound dead 244
Easter 212
ecstacy 24, 55, 75, 120, 229

Eden(ic) 76, 79, 168
egotistical shell 22, 23, 36, 63, 129, 225, 241, 289
Elect 167, 168, 204
electricities 166, 169, 375-377, 402
  black 40
  holy 12, 307
  psychic 257
  red 145
  self-aggressive 41
  white 169
elements 53, 106
Elohim 33
emotional body 7, 49, 57, 96-98, 125, 134, 180, 181, 217, 225, 227, 324, 337, 341, 346
enclosure power 241, 325
Enlightenment 15, 58, 142, 144, 150, 170, 198, 212, 267, 274, 296, 328, 388, 403, 411
enthusiasm 85, 185, 215
Epiphany 210
equanimity 293
Equinoxes 91
Esse 9, 13-24, 26, 31-36, 40-46, 48, 52, 54, 61-84, 93-122, 126, 131, 135, 139, 141, 143, 145, 152, 153, 156-170, 174, 181, 186, 198, 215, 218, 242, 274, 275, 278, 291, 296, 297, 311, 318, 332, 335, 337, 362, 374, 376, 407
  different kinds 105
  Apology 117, 118
  Group 117, 119-121
  Heal Another 115-117
  Prospering 113
  Scriptural 118, 119
  Self-healing 112, 113

Single 112
Sitting 114, 115
Unburden Undersoul 113
for World Peace 115–117
Eternal Atom 131, 132, 184, 185, 283
Eternal Life 20, 316
Eternal Self 4
Eternal Sustaining Atom 68, 132, 271, 276, 316, 347
ether 65, 72, 73
etheric body 7, 22, 49, 52, 57, 70, 79, 82, 96, 107, 133, 134, 185, 191, 212, 217, 227, 235, 322, 326, 333, 341
  Higher 185, 320, 340, 346, 349, 350
  Lesser 123, 190, 320, 337, 338, 343–353, 408
  Matrix 320
Ethic 9, 55, 153, 157, 174, 222, 232, 250, 253, 254, 290, 297, 308, 380, 394, 411
  Jesus 238
Eucharist 101, 210, 218
Everlasting life 12, 101, 229, 405
Evil(s) 15, 17, 30, 32, 40, 44, 45, 48, 54, 56, 84, 93, 125, 140, 157, 159, 220, 222, 233, 240, 244, 247, 249, 255–257, 259, 260, 262–264, 328, 333, 400, 401
Exorcism 40, 54, 56, 61, 229, 250, 251, 262, 307
Eye of God 265, 359

F

Face of God 21, 134
faith 16, 22, 23, 41, 43, 44, 98, 135, 156, 159, 173, 183, 186, 192, 216, 221, 222, 230, 231, 234, 291, 312, 336, 353
family(ies) 241, 242, 298, 300, 302, 310
Family-Atom 203, 217, 241–243, 301, 302, 306, 310
Family-Genesis (also Human-Genesis) 203, 242, 243, 310, 350, 405
fantasy 28, 29, 32, 39, 42, 46, 55, 56, 130, 134, 158, 172, 179, 190, 227, 244, 252, 256, 289, 411, 412
fasting 226, 322–331
  10th-Day-after-New-Moon 322–331
Father 66, 95, 127, 140, 141, 163, 172, 173, 186–188, 196, 198, 226, 235, 247, 253, 271, 284, 297, 308, 329, 344, 355, 358
fear 157–159, 183, 190
Feminine Principle 213, 298
Fiats 351, 354
fiery trial 133
fifth-dimensional consciousness 285
fluidic matrix 98, 99
forgiveness 100, 222, 249, 260, 262, 298, 299, 302, 412
former lives (see past lives)
Fourth Dimension 141, 217
  consciousness 141, 142, 197
Fourth Light Stream 367, 373
free choice 219–222, 259, 390, 412
freedom(s) 3, 7, 31, 42, 67, 70, 74, 110, 112, 116, 128, 134, 135, 180, 194, 325, 326, 393, 403, 412

INDEX 421

free will 206
Full Moon 58, 59, 325
future lives (see coming lives)

G

galaxy(ies) 90, 110, 138, 140, 145, 207, 237, 291, 410
  consciousness 129
Garden of Gethsemane 411
Gates (Mandala) 369, 371–374
generosity 412
gene(s) 30, 31, 139, 184, 190, 195, 200, 225, 299, 301, 302, 313, 342, 343
  inheritance 194, 301, 312
genergy 139, 140
Genesis 203, 233, 243, 256, 325
Gibran, Kahlil 228
giving 202, 260, 261
gland(s) 52, 128, 248, 255, 278, 296, 340, 351
Glory of God 267
God-Realization 11, 31, 72, 94, 110, 122, 142, 154, 169, 176, 178, 179, 188, 200, 210, 227, 286, 289, 294, 335, 339, 369
Golden Rule 266
good 17, 19, 30, 41, 49, 55, 108, 125, 135, 192, 196, 222, 244, 247, 257, 325, 333, 346, 347, 400
Grace Name(s) 304–311, 317–322
Grand Dimensional Scale 237
Grand Man 304
Grand Psyche 41, 133, 187, 239, 240, 279
gratitude 117, 192, 256, 257, 291, 295, 328

gravity 4, 7, 33, 36, 47, 59, 76, 78, 87, 88, 94, 107, 108, 123, 127, 131, 132, 138, 153, 154, 167, 196, 197, 204, 212, 265, 280, 281, 283, 285, 322, 324–326, 344, 348, 355
Great Exorcisor 140
Great Immortals 12, 167, 295
Great Interval, Second 344
Great Souls 334
Great Teachers 167
Great Unconscious 86, 106, 110, 111, 199–202, 221, 308, 317, 328
Greater Archetype(s) 95, 152, 199, 202–204, 206, 308
Guardian Angel(s) 28, 68, 184, 248, 305
guidance 13, 38, 83, 99, 100, 172, 174, 175, 178, 225, 257, 263, 264, 277, 293, 309, 323, 330, 332, 411
Guiding Principle 9, 10, 20, 34, 58, 173, 175, 177, 179, 277, 336, 405
guilt(s) 22, 24, 25, 48, 52, 70, 84, 102, 128, 133, 158, 159, 191, 240, 254, 259, 263, 274, 299
Gunas 41
Guru(s) 22, 167, 223, 265, 294

H

Hall of Learning 76
happiness 16, 38, 40, 46, 63, 67, 69, 87, 116, 128, 186, 191, 192, 218, 254, 255, 290, 291, 321, 390, 394
Harmonics, Divine 6, 7
hate 39, 40, 42, 43, 55, 96,

100, 117, 155, 192, 194, 288, 302, 309, 413
Heaven 21, 40, 61, 78, 119, 138, 150, 182, 183, 200, 229, 251, 295, 297, 304, 305, 321, 333, 411
   First 292
hell 182, 183
Hierarchs 33, 40, 127, 163, 164, 167, 168, 186, 188, 189, 235, 273, 299, 342, 344, 376, 405
higher etheric matrix 303, 304, 347-350, 352
higher mind 13, 14, 42-44, 46, 93, 136, 139, 141, 170, 189, 220, 275, 278, 281, 283, 339, 340, 342
Higher Self 13, 46, 49, 53, 63, 65, 72, 85-87, 102, 107, 122, 129-131, 150, 151, 154, 156, 163, 186, 242, 243, 271, 273-276, 278, 281, 282, 285-290, 305, 306, 316, 319, 336, 338, 340, 346, 347, 349, 360, 392
Higher Unconscious 9, 72, 86, 107, 112, 127, 133, 152, 156, 184, 185, 200-202, 204, 212, 218, 221, 226, 279, 281-283, 285, 306, 338, 358, 361, 363, 379
holiness 17, 40
Holy Ghost 13, 103, 227, 247-249
Holy of Holies 217
Holy Poverty 397
Holy Remission 401, 402
honesty 44, 94, 158, 159, 194, 233, 240, 259, 362, 397, 406
hope 83, 135, 260
hormonal system 140

householder(s) 76, 217, 229, 406, 407
humility 37, 67, 77, 134, 135, 185, 290, 372, 412
humor 78, 94, 177, 190, 254

I

illumination(s) 6, 26, 29, 37, 71, 82, 83, 94, 140, 196, 229, 249, 295, 305, 348, 349, 363, 388, 398, 407
Image 15, 34, 185, 186, 191, 195, 196, 198, 199, 235, 236, 297, 304, 344-346, 351, 354, 378, 389
   of God 32, 33, 195, 196, 207, 273, 389
Increase of God 114, 187, 190, 212, 301, 302, 328, 336, 342, 388
Incubation 289
Indestructible Atom 131, 195-197, 227, 271, 272, 288, 316, 318, 319, 343
India 53, 97
Informing Principle 72, 90, 107, 124, 141, 165, 177, 206, 272, 294, 360, 378, 395, 408, 411
inheritance(s) 31, 184, 188, 195, 311, 317
   ancestral 30, 137, 184
   gene 194, 301, 312
   grace 137
   Undersoul 30
Initiate(s) 63, 127, 130, 136, 155, 171, 174, 178, 205, 221, 222, 228, 289, 295, 307, 324-326, 340, 343, 347, 349, 352, 354, 355, 358, 369, 372, 380, 398
   Christ 373
   Western 294

INDEX

initiation(s) 13, 252, 253, 281–283, 285, 289, 305, 323, 335, 361, 362, 366, 372, 376, 377, 405
  abyss 256
  spiritual 23, 162, 166, 184, 202, 398
initiatory cycles 323
Initiatory Presences 323
inspiration 349
instincts 45
integrity 56, 177, 255, 308
Intelligence of God 160, 170, 216
Intentional Suffering 183, 184, 228, 229, 393–412
  Path of 229, 264, 302, 373, 402–406
intuition 177, 178, 219, 313, 360, 362, 411, 412

J

Jade Gate 272
Japa 294
jealousy 39, 40, 194, 302
Jesus 28, 29, 45, 47, 61, 63, 65, 66, 69, 76, 79, 81, 90, 100, 103, 118, 119, 129, 134, 140, 159, 163–167, 172, 187–189, 197, 202–204, 208, 210, 211, 213, 215–218, 220, 223–225, 228, 230, 231, 235, 236, 239, 240, 242, 247, 250, 265, 266, 272, 274, 284, 287, 294, 296–298, 304, 306, 317, 318, 328, 330, 333, 343, 349, 358, 375, 387, 393, 399, 400, 402–406, 410, 411
  Ethic 238
  Name of 69, 197, 211, 226, 306, 328, 330, 403, 405
Job 186, 393
John the Baptist 362
John the Beloved 69, 203, 335
Joseph 168
Journal 113, 178
joy 34, 40, 45, 46, 63, 67, 69, 70, 74, 85, 87, 111, 116, 121, 128, 149–151, 169, 185, 186, 192, 254, 266, 291, 297, 315, 319, 352–354, 379, 389, 393
Judas 251, 262, 309, 335
Jung, Dr. Carl 357
justice 40

K

Kali-Yuga 15, 22, 25, 35, 43, 44, 48, 51, 73, 74, 103, 137, 168, 200, 201, 232, 313
Karma, Law(s) of 201, 204, 206, 223, 232, 250, 251, 254, 255, 265, 306, 312, 313, 405
  Yoga 76
Kingdom(s) 81, 96, 110, 175, 183, 341
Klosha Veils 80, 133, 217
Kundalini 14, 68, 75, 116, 246, 292, 369, 377

L

Lao-Tzu 166
Last Supper 69
Law(s) 29, 40, 72, 92, 101, 145, 168, 169, 176, 202, 219, 223–225, 234, 243, 245, 248, 307, 376, 396, 410
  Bi-Polarity 154
  of Cosmos 223

Divine 84
Eternal Cyclic 88
of God 204, 219, 256, 264, 277, 302, 410-412
inward 44
of Karma (see Karma, Laws of)
of order 267
of Polarity 137
of Providence 9
of Reciprocal Maintenance 395, 400
of Reincarnation 312
Supernatural 88
Timing 153, 184
of Tone 321
Laying-on-of-Hands 210, 216
Lazarus 317, 318
 Cycle 323
learning 236, 409
Leo 261
Levitation 326, 327, 408
 Day 293, 323
 Powers 322, 328
Life Fiat 126
Life Principle 172, 213, 253
Living-Body Command Mantram 343-355
Living Teacher 66, 68, 159, 162, 166, 172, 173, 179, 201
Logos 136, 228, 272, 313, 405
 Archetypal 311
Lord's Prayer 267, 401
Lord's Supper 251
love 34, 35, 39, 40, 42, 58, 97-100, 103, 111, 117, 118, 125, 134-136, 150, 157, 159, 164, 171, 184, 191-193, 195, 216, 218, 222, 232, 237, 243, 244, 258, 260, 262, 266, 275, 276, 290, 291, 294, 301, 309, 313-316, 318, 319, 334, 354, 389, 391, 410, 411
lower mind 278, 279, 281, 339
loyalty 336
Lucifer(ic) 92, 170, 244, 287
lunar 45, 53, 138, 157, 204, 310
 cycles 91
 fast 212

M

magnetism(s) 333, 353, 354, 375, 376
 holy 128, 162
 soul 333
Maha Guru 295
Maha-matra 82
making 198
mandala(s) 19, 88, 128, 136, 342, 356-386, 408
mantra(s) 12, 13, 17, 44, 45, 69, 70, 72, 74, 83, 88, 127, 136, 154, 185, 221, 285, 296, 306, 307, 317, 359, 360, 363, 375, 408
 Name of God 294, 298, 299, 308, 317
mantram(s) 18, 59, 76, 83, 106, 112, 119, 126, 139, 221, 290, 296, 302, 313, 363, 375
 Living-Body Command 343-355
 Tenth-Day-after-the-New-Moon Fast 326-331
 Womb 313
 for World Peace 120
Manu 168, 169
Marijuana 56
Marking and Tracing 59, 77, 91, 95, 114, 175-180, 205,

217, 226, 337, 340, 361,
  362, 378, 379, 387, 390,
  396, 408, 409, 411
marriage(s)   31, 55, 203
Mars   164
Mary   375
Mary Magdalene   69
Masters   135, 145, 167, 168,
  294, 295, 333
Mathematics of God   204
matrix(es)   337-342
Maya   11, 13, 18, 19, 30, 32-
  35, 78, 81, 85, 86, 103,
  105, 107, 125, 130, 132,
  137, 138, 141, 167, 168,
  172, 179, 183, 187, 189,
  190, 192, 197, 201, 217,
  218, 235, 255, 280, 282,
  288, 393, 397, 412
mediation   19, 79, 93, 173,
  207, 333-335
meditation   17, 20-23, 26, 33,
  36, 52, 53, 58, 59, 62, 63,
  72, 74, 81, 83, 88-91, 94,
  96, 103, 106, 116, 117,
  119, 127, 132, 133, 136,
  139, 173, 178, 209, 214,
  240, 259, 281, 285, 316,
  317, 323, 336, 348, 352,
  358-361, 363, 380, 408
memory(ies)   26, 30, 33, 42,
  43, 49, 59, 62, 83, 84, 124,
  181, 193, 194, 199, 200,
  216, 231, 240, 248, 249,
  263, 274, 283, 299, 301,
  312, 390, 391
 gene   30, 31
menstrual period   53
mental body   22, 49, 57, 217,
  227, 337, 341
Mercury   326
mercy   99, 228, 240, 256, 264,
  298, 404, 406

of God   20
metaphysics   163, 289, 290,
  338, 339, 350, 404
mind   67, 70, 72, 75, 77, 78,
  82, 83, 87, 90
 higher   13, 14, 42-44, 46,
  93, 136, 139, 141, 170,
  189, 220, 275, 278, 281,
  283, 339, 340, 342
 lower   14, 42, 43-46, 48,
  49, 56, 62, 79, 136, 180,
  181, 189, 198, 338, 339
 sheath(s)   274, 276, 284-287
Mind of Christ   363
Mind of God   204
miracle(s)   46, 66, 154, 183,
  288, 302, 314, 357, 358
molecular 3, 21, 65, 197, 293,
  408
money   91, 92, 265, 406
mood(s)   52-54, 193
Moon(s)   11, 54, 55, 59, 62,
  69, 87, 91, 93, 127, 212,
  322-331, 342, 357
Moon, Full   59, 91, 325
Moon, New   59, 91, 322-331
 tenth day after   293
 Tenth-Day-After-Fast   322-
  331
morality   9, 15, 27, 56, 60, 81,
  84, 198, 221, 222, 232,
  237, 242, 394, 399, 401,
  411
Moses   79, 168, 235, 236, 307
Most High Soul   17, 18, 23,
  32, 33, 35-37, 43, 47, 52,
  53, 62, 63, 72, 116, 122,
  123-131, 136, 166, 251,
  278, 286, 334
Mother Earth   218
Mother Nature   236
Mother Principle   228
Mother of the World   213

motive(s)   61, 156, 216, 219, 345
Mouth-of-God (Center)   58, 59, 154, 272, 316
movement   3-8, 12-14, 17-19, 21-24, 33-36, 41, 48, 52, 54, 62, 63, 65, 67-72, 74, 75, 78, 80-83, 87, 88, 93-95, 98-100, 104, 106, 107, 110, 111, 113, 116, 117, 120, 122, 126-128, 135, 136, 139, 143, 145, 289, 322, 323, 408
Moving Archetype(s)   97, 200-206, 287
muscular system   55
music(s)   5, 8, 9, 11, 19, 21, 26, 71, 83, 106, 111, 115, 121, 128, 278, 372, 391, 412, 413
   of God   101
mystic   227

N

nadis   293, 358
name, ancestral-karmic   306
   ego-karmic   306
Name-Calling Healing   317-320
Name of Christ   291, 328
   of the Father   330
   of Jesus   69, 197, 211, 226, 306, 328, 330, 403, 405
Name of God   128, 263
   mantra   293-296, 308, 317
Name(s), Grace   304-311, 317-322
Name(s), Sacred   304-308, 310, 311, 317-322
Name, Womb   311-315
Naming, power of   308, 310

Nature   27, 28, 46, 76, 89, 90, 107-109, 133, 140, 203, 205, 236, 287, 343, 348, 357, 396, 409
Nature of God   134, 277-279
Neptune   56
nervous system(s)   24, 52, 55, 56, 69, 140, 278, 296
nescience   12, 14, 31, 32, 42, 44, 45, 47, 143, 257, 287, 288, 335
New Moon   59, 91, 322-331
   New Moon Fast, 10th Day After   322-331
New Testament   403
nickname   309
night-flight   347-349
Night Ministry   53, 182, 264
Nirvana   265
Niscience   14, 15, 31-33, 35, 44, 47, 50, 68, 70, 73, 82, 84, 89, 95, 99, 129, 131, 140, 145, 153, 160, 161, 165, 169, 171, 179, 200, 205, 207, 209, 220, 263, 287, 288, 297, 335, 336, 396
Noah   168
Nomenclature, Sacred   305, 312, 317
numbers   376
nutrition   218, 340

O

obsession   169, 194, 198, 338
Old Testament   405
OM   8, 13, 45, 64, 294, 297-299, 336
Omniform   137, 138
Omnipotent   81

INDEX 427

Omnipresence 8, 9, 11, 12, 14, 16, 17, 19, 24, 29, 65, 70, 74, 81, 93, 94, 102, 106, 120, 136, 151, 162, 163, 175, 183, 187, 199, 204, 206, 207, 209, 214, 245, 246, 249, 254, 264, 266, 276, 284, 286, 294, 295, 297, 325, 328, 333, 392
Omniscience 73, 230, 246, 312
Omniscient Cell 90
Omnitrons 139, 140
Open(ing) 36, 152, 165, 198, 200, 226
Organizing Principle 411
organs 191, 339, 340, 351, 354, 355, 408

P

pain 42, 130, 133, 183, 184, 191, 194, 211, 229, 259, 278, 320, 393, 399, 403, 407, 408
Pass(ing) 22, 25, 36, 40, 64-69, 71, 100, 152, 153, 165, 174, 198, 200, 207, 226, 228, 230, 242, 255, 263, 281, 288, 296, 312, 317, 387, 394, 404, 406, 407
Passion of Jesus 103, 165, 216, 217, 228, 230, 296, 343, 387, 406
past lives 30, 31, 46, 54, 57, 62, 95, 124, 127, 130, 137, 154, 158, 184, 222, 242, 295, 305, 306, 308, 309, 312, 345, 346, 371, 403

Path of Virtue 230, 241, 245
Path of Intentional Suffering 229, 264, 302, 373, 402-406
patience 125, 234, 347
peace 34, 35, 40, 63, 75, 104, 185, 191, 192, 194, 196, 243, 254, 259, 291, 319, 321, 331, 352, 358, 363, 399
penance 226, 260, 261
Pentecost 242, 251
perversion 5, 244
Peter 164, 250, 251, 304, 373
philosophy 170
Pisces 53, 261
planets 11, 48, 54, 62, 69, 91, 97, 105, 110, 127, 138, 161, 204, 326, 342, 357
plasma 65, 72, 73
  Intelligible 65, 72
Pleasance 52, 71, 136
Pleasure-Principle 42, 45, 46, 63, 141, 180, 189, 252, 324, 397, 404, 405
Polaris 293
polarization 51, 57, 81, 107, 119, 173, 189, 202, 293, 306, 399
polarity(ies) 140, 151, 162, 189, 192, 198, 201, 292, 293, 365, 379, 390, 391
Power of God 65, 204, 207, 213, 238, 325, 389
Prakriti 133
Prana 18, 36, 59, 75
prayer(s) 17, 19, 22, 36, 44, 45, 58, 72, 79, 89, 91, 103, 106, 107, 121, 136, 162, 209, 214, 215, 218, 234, 241, 245, 246, 257-259,

281, 285, 297, 306, 334, 363, 394, 408
prejudice   170, 171
prescience   65
primordial   71, 74, 98
procrastination   53, 92, 184, 254
procreation   168
Prophet(s)   27, 29, 159, 200, 228, 337, 396
prophecy   154, 165, 200, 222, 234, 259, 360, 362
prospering   394, 395, 397, 398
Prototypes   163, 164, 187-189, 197, 204, 237, 247, 293, 298, 347, 377, 389
providence   9, 20
Psyche, Grand   41, 133, 187, 239, 240, 279
psychic(s)   10, 35, 40, 43, 46, 56-61, 68, 72, 84, 96, 99, 100, 103, 104, 111, 125, 128, 142, 155-159, 162, 185, 189, 244, 257, 275, 290, 333, 340, 380, 398
  brain   124
  matter matrix   303, 304, 320
  matter nature   103, 104, 280, 307, 320, 321, 338, 339
psychology   14, 140, 141, 163, 187, 190, 312, 338, 339, 404
punctuality   91
purgatory   225, 244
purification   60, 98, 127, 162, 253, 259, 281, 400
purity   18, 19, 35, 37, 61, 135, 136, 302, 319, 321, 366, 408
Purusha   13, 86, 106, 124, 130, 132-134, 152, 199, 204, 218, 227, 274, 328

Q

quickening   230, 248, 312, 361

R

radiance   303
rajas(ic)   41, 43, 48, 50, 51, 73, 75, 77, 89, 137, 138, 141, 145, 166, 201, 206, 233, 238, 242, 392, 396
Ramakrishna   228
realization   35, 209, 222
Realm of God   328
Reciprocal Maintenance   393-396, 399, 400, 409-411
Recording Angel(s)   68, 93, 184, 193, 256, 305
rectification   239, 240, 258, 261 (see also restitution)
redemption   184, 186, 216, 223-225, 229, 296, 335
reincarnation   7, 11, 27, 31, 33, 109, 129, 130, 151, 200, 201, 203, 205, 241, 244, 265, 347
  Laws of   265, 276, 312, 409
  Cycles   282
religion(s)   14, 23, 27, 73, 97, 100, 101, 119, 237, 298, 327, 350, 403
religiosity   11, 103, 201, 205
renunciation   263, 323, 393
repentance   224-226, 239, 242, 258-261
resolution   335
restitution   184, 185, 209, 224, 225, 239, 240, 247,

252, 258-266, 313, 396, 399, 400, 403
Resurrection 65, 69, 231, 263, 284, 307, 323
revelation(s) 13, 35, 79, 99, 139, 152, 161, 165, 172, 194, 200, 262, 263, 274, 296, 297, 322, 380
  Book of 405
reverence 349, 353, 355, 363, 376, 380
rhythm(s) 3, 4, 7, 8, 14, 21, 24, 25, 57, 58, 82, 142, 172, 178, 204, 206, 219, 323, 389, 411
Risen Dead 225
ritual(s) 24, 35, 50, 100, 214
Rudra 362
running 107, 108

S

Sabbath 91
Sacrament 69, 102
  Bread 210-213, 215, 217-219, 231
  Wine 210-213, 215-219, 231
Sacred Name(s) 304-308, 310, 311, 317-322
Sacred Nomenclature, Power of 305, 312, 317
sacrifice 371, 392, 394, 398, 403
Sage(s) 21, 22, 53, 160, 171, 177
Saint Andrew's Cross 372
Saint Francis of Assisi 261, 367, 373
Saints 12, 38, 61, 135, 154, 210, 229, 230, 237, 247, 273, 302, 305, 311, 393, 396, 398, 400, 402

salvation 400, 401, 405
Samadhi 334
samskara 36, 50, 79, 87, 92, 93, 159
sankalpa 91, 221
Satan(ic) 45, 56, 57, 60, 101, 159, 234, 238, 251, 262, 263, 283
sattva 41, 48, 73, 83, 137, 138, 166, 192-201, 227, 228, 243, 392, 405
Saturn 326
  Archangels 344
  Initiate 371
science 14, 27, 97, 101, 187, 201, 205, 206, 296, 301, 312
Scorpio 53, 261
Scriptures 84, 102
seasons 127
second death 225, 226
Seer(s) 12, 21, 22, 27, 48, 97, 135, 141, 159, 160, 200, 201, 227, 228, 292, 337
self-denial 134, 226, 246, 289
self-discipline 162
Self-Genesis 310, 335, 398
  Higher 188, 203, 242
  Lower 187, 188, 203, 242
Self-Genesis Age 25, 30, 31, 48-51, 108, 128, 129, 168, 220, 242
Self-Realization 14, 63, 154, 175, 178, 179, 289, 335, 339, 380
sense(s) 20, 22, 33, 45, 49, 62, 75, 76, 88, 97, 106, 124, 132, 138, 144, 188, 246, 247, 281, 284, 324, 339, 350, 354, 358, 365, 369
Seraphim 93, 213, 214
Sermon on the Mount 237

sex   5, 10, 46, 54, 128, 233,
   238, 244, 255, 257, 323,
   365
Shiva   7, 12, 118
sickness(es)   184–186, 192–
   196, 227, 228, 233, 242,
   258, 259, 275, 320, 326,
   338, 339, 403, 407, 408
Siddhi powers   155, 333
Silver Cord   402
sin(s)   15, 22, 25, 29, 46, 47,
   49, 51, 54, 102, 113, 118,
   136, 140, 168, 183, 208,
   209, 217, 218, 225, 234,
   249, 262, 263, 280, 299,
   301, 302, 343, 396, 397,
   401, 403
Sirius   167
sleep   212, 213, 220, 221, 264,
   265, 295, 323, 326, 349,
   413
smoking   56–58
solar plexus   131, 157, 237,
   323
Solstice(s)   91
soul   6, 70, 72, 75, 89, 97
Soul-Realization   176, 178,
   289, 335
soul's record   85, 86
sound(s)   20, 26, 36, 60, 75,
   109, 327
Sound Current   8, 307, 360,
   399
space   4, 84, 88, 93, 97, 137,
   140, 145, 154, 167, 169,
   181, 212, 246, 273, 284,
   325, 391, 392, 410
Species Angeles   164, 257
speech   21
Spirit of Truth   13, 15, 102,
   103, 118, 181, 198
spiritualized intellect   85,
   169–171, 203, 220, 222,
   282, 311, 340

star(s)   357
   constellation   167
   direct   303, 304, 307
   five-pointed   304, 341, 342
   fixed   303
   six-pointed   342
stewardship   76, 397
stigmata   226–229, 305, 365,
   406
study   178
subconscious   24–27, 32, 36,
   48–54, 62, 70, 72, 83–85,
   87, 131, 156, 157, 163,
   191, 200, 212, 221, 239,
   265, 279, 283, 285, 288,
   299, 321, 358, 361, 370,
   379
   collective   73, 109, 137
   world   34, 51
suffering(s)   32, 47, 63, 72,
   109, 130, 133, 168, 169,
   183, 189, 194–196, 202,
   220, 222, 225, 229, 248,
   249, 254, 259, 278, 318,
   320, 340, 371, 393, 394,
   398, 399, 402–408, 412
Sun   11, 62, 69, 87, 91, 93,
   210, 228, 322, 326, 342,
   344, 348, 357, 359
superconscious(ness)   32, 37,
   124, 126, 127, 132, 136,
   139, 156, 166, 379
symbiosis   82
symbols   81–83, 95, 139, 152,
   265, 358, 361, 362, 375,
   377
synchronization   151, 153,
   160, 162, 165, 245, 322,
   389

T

T'ai Chi   71, 107
talents   225, 345, 404

INDEX 431

Tamas(ic) 16, 41, 47, 48, 50, 72, 73, 89, 137, 138, 141, 187, 201, 206, 242, 262, 392
Tao 166
Tanmatra Powers 45
Teacher(s) 16, 22, 38, 56, 59-61, 66, 68, 83, 159, 162, 166, 172-174, 179, 201, 219, 223, 232, 239, 246, 249-253, 294, 295, 304, 305, 321, 322, 326, 391, 403, 410
Teacher(s), Great 99, 167
technology 89, 97
Telepathic Disciples 175
telepathy 54, 55, 159, 161, 287, 295, 323, 348, 349
television 92
Ten Commandments 46, 235-238, 350
Third Dimensional Consciousness 284
Third Eye 8, 14, 271, 340, 358, 367
Third Heaven 308
Third Music 8, 9, 103, 111, 115, 152, 189, 210, 280, 332, 353, 391-393, 407, 412, 413
Third Vitality 141, 327, 393, 394
Tides of the Holy Spirit 332, 333
Time 4, 7, 14, 32, 44, 56, 58, 84, 87-93, 107, 137, 140, 153, 154, 167, 169, 176, 181, 185, 188, 190, 203, 212, 219, 245, 246, 248, 265, 282, 284, 287, 325, 361, 392, 408-410
tithe 91
tobacco 238
Tone, Laws of 321

Tone of God 389
transenergization 15, 35, 46, 66, 76, 90, 107, 127, 135-141, 165, 168, 173-175, 184, 188, 191, 192, 208, 213, 217, 228, 229, 280, 282, 296, 301, 321, 398, 400, 406
Tribal-Genesis 203, 243, 310, 350
True Self 21, 33, 34, 37, 44, 45, 47, 75, 77-79, 113, 119, 125-127, 132-134, 143-145, 156, 165, 166, 169, 276, 280, 284, 285, 299, 342, 363, 379
truth 16, 18, 23, 27, 29, 35-37, 40, 42, 54, 67, 80, 89, 92, 137, 152, 169, 170, 174, 198, 213, 233, 246, 248, 258, 280, 307, 366, 367, 371, 388, 389, 393-396, 411
Twenty-third Psalm 226

U

unconscious 9, 72, 86, 107, 112, 124, 127, 133, 156, 200, 212, 218, 221, 226, 279, 281, 282, 283, 285, 306, 338, 358, 361, 363, 370, 374, 375, 379
  Great 86, 106, 110, 111, 200, 202, 221, 308, 317, 328
  Collective 152, 199, 200, 258
Undersoul 5, 16-18, 22-37, 40-63, 67-89, 94, 96, 99, 103, 106, 107, 109, 110, 120-133, 135, 136, 140, 142, 144, 145, 155, 166, 168, 172, 174, 177, 180,

191, 192, 194, 218, 226, 242, 254–257, 274, 278–289, 303, 304, 309, 311, 321, 339, 358, 362, 378, 403, 409
Collective 34, 42, 244
World 406
Unicorn 367
unitron 140
Unmanifest 199–201
Universal Mind 132
Universal Spirit 199
Universe(s) 132, 140, 160, 207, 232, 237, 290, 393, 399
Upa-Soul 22, 23, 25, 35–37, 67, 68, 71, 72, 74, 76, 78, 84–86, 123–129, 156, 166

V

vajra 178, 252, 253, 296
Verifying Principle 175
versatility(ies) 40, 277, 288, 290, 332
vice 400
vibratory hum 109, 154, 157, 363
Vibration of God 183
virtue(s) 30, 38, 55, 107, 139, 157, 201, 209, 210, 215–217, 224, 230, 235, 236, 239, 240, 241, 245, 250, 260, 261, 279, 285, 301, 302, 307, 317, 361, 362, 388, 396, 401
Volition 40, 41
Voltage of God 40–42, 301
Vow, Holy 221
vowels 305, 309

W

walking 21, 52, 105–109, 375
Water Sign Prototypes 53
Western 109, 110, 167, 294
Initiate 52
Will Fiat 126
wisdom(s) 23, 78, 83, 128, 135, 143, 145, 154, 170, 171, 177, 181, 214, 219, 221, 222, 279, 328, 347
Dream 221, 222
Womb Cradle Song 313–315
Womb Name 311–315
Womb Mantram Visualization 314, 315
Word 71, 182, 274
of God 119, 336
work(s) 19, 21, 36, 40, 52, 62, 106, 111, 128, 216, 221, 225, 226, 309, 397
World Soul 184
worship(s) 11, 19, 100–103, 136, 178, 187, 209, 210, 214, 215, 236, 245, 285

Y

yang 24, 48–52, 90, 325, 365, 369, 376, 377, 379, 404
yantra 60, 154, 190, 341, 358, 359, 361, 362, 378
dreams 180, 181
initiation 310, 311
yin 24, 49–52, 90, 174, 298, 325, 332, 365, 369, 372, 376–379
yoga 68, 71, 107, 375
karma 76
Yoke of Jesus 398, 399, 404

Z

zodiacal 163, 164, 188, 247, 299